CALIFORNIA INDIAN SHAMANISM

Ballena Press Anthropological Papers No. 39
Editor: Sylvia Brakke Vane

CALIFORNIA INDIAN SHAMANISM

Edited by
Lowell John Bean

A Ballena Press Publication

General Editors: Sylvia Brakke Vane
                   Lowell John Bean

Volume Directors: Karla Young
                  Pauline Sanchez

Ballena Press Anthropological Papers Editors:
                  Thomas C. Blackburn
                  Sylvia Brakke Vane
                  Lowell John Bean

Library of Congress Cataloging-in-Publication Data

California Indian Shamanism /edited by Lowell John Bean.
          p. cm. -- (Ballena Press Anthropological Papers : No. 39)
Includes Bibliographical references.
ISBN 0-87919-125-2: $33.00 (alk. paper)--
ISBN 0-87919-124-4 $27.50 (pbk.: alk. paper).
          1. Indians of North America--California--Religion and mythology. 2. Shamanism--California--History. 3. Indians of North America--California--Rites and ceremonies. I. Bean, Lowell John. II. Series.
E78.C15C294   1992
299'.7994--dc20   92-6167
                                        CIP

Printed in the United States of America

TABLE OF CONTENTS

List of Figures iii

Sources vii

Introduction
Lowell John Bean 1

The Shamanic Experience
Lowell John Bean and Sylvia Brakke Vane 7

Power and Its Applications in Native California
Lowell John Bean 21

California Religious Systems and Their
Transformations
Lowell John Bean and Sylvia Brakke Vane 33

California Indian Shamanism and Folk Curing
Lowell John Bean 53

Shamanistic Aspects of California Rock Art
Ken Hedges 67

The Shaman: Priest, Doctor, Scientist
Florence Shipek 89

Sierra Miwok Shamans, 1900-1990
Craig D. Bates 97

Yurok Doctors and the Concept of "Shamanism"
Thomas Buckley   117

Dancing on the Brink of the World: Deprivation
and the Ghost Dance Religion
E. Breck Parkman   163

Notes on the Wintu Shamanic Jargon
Alice Shepherd   185

Wintu Sacred Geography
Dorothea J Theodoratus and Frank LaPena   211

Ridge Walkers of Northwestern California:
Paths Toward Spiritual Balance
Jack Norton   227

Ajumawi Doctoring: Conflicts in NewAge/Traditional
Shamanism
Floyd Buckskin   237

References Cited   249

LIST OF FIGURES

Figure 1. Petroglyph, Lagomarsino, Nevada. Photo by Ken Hedges.

Figure 2. Patterned-body anthropomorph with projections from the head, Renegade Canyon, Coso Range, Inyo County, California. Photo by Ken Hedges.

Figure 3. Horned anthropomorph, the "Watcher of the Winter Sun," La Rumorosa, Baja California. Photo by Ken Hedges.

Figure 4. Crenelated fortification patterns in rock art: a) phosphene (Oster 1970:82), b) Tukano shamanic art (Reichel-Dolmatoff 1978: Plate IV), c) rock painting, Montevideo, Baja California (Hedges), d) petroglyph, South Mountain, Arizona (original oriented vertically; Hedges), e) petroglyph, Grapevine Canyon, Nevada (Hedges).

Figure 5. Basic Phosphene designs (Kellogg, Knoll, and Kügler 1965:1129).

Figure 6. Kumeyaay rock paintings, Las Pilitas, Baja California. Sketch by Ken Hedges.

Figure 7. Legless anthropomorph, McCoy Springs, Riverside County, California. Sketch by Ken Hedges.

Figure 8. Phosphene pattern (Walker 1981:176) compared to patterned-body anthropomorph from Renegade Canyon, Coso Range, Inyo County, California. Sketch by Ken Hedges.

Figure 9. Callipene and Lena (Rube) Brown, Yosemite Valley, June 1901. Photograph by H. D. Wulzen. Yosemite Museum, National Park Service, Cat. No. 26964.

Callipene was a renowned shaman among the Southern Miwok at the turn of the century. Lena Brown, who may have been a granddaughter of Callipene's, was the mother of Chris Brown, a Southern Miwok dancer and shaman.

Figure 10. Maria Lebrado Ydrte, 1929. Photograph by Joseph Dixon. Yosemite Research Library, National Park Service, Neg. No. RL-2022.

Maria Lebrado Ydrte was a well-known shaman among the Southern Miwok until her heath at over 90 years in 1931. She was the granddaughter of the Yosemite Miwok leader Tenaya.

Figure 11. Pedro O'Connor, ca. 1920(?). Photograph courtesy of Jennifer Bates. Pedro O'Connor was a Northern Miwok ceremonial leader, dancer and shaman.

Figure 12. Charlie Dick, El Portal, California, 1928. Yosemite Research Library, National Park Service, Neg. No. RL-2075. Charlie Dick was a Southern Miwok poison doctor.

Figure 13. Chris Brown, "Chief Lemee," and young cowboy at the Indian Field Days, Yosemite Valley, 1929. Yosemite Research Library, National Park Service.

Chris Brown often wore stereotypical Indian clothing while performing for visitors to Yosemite National Park, as he is at this celebration designed to increase visitation to the park. Here he holds a Miwok cocoon rattle in his right hand. Most Miwok shamans would not display such objects in the context of tourist entertainment, but Brown did not seem concerned.

Figure 14. Chris Brown, "Chief Lemee," Yosemite Valley, c. 1926. Yosemite Research Library, National Park Service, Neg. No. RL-2026.

Brown, a Southern Miwok shaman, here wears Miwok dance regalia similar to that of the sucking doctor, including a flicker quill band, hairpins, cocoon rattle, and shoulder cape.

Figure 15. Southern Miwok Cocoon Rattle by Chris "Chief Lemee" Brown, c. 1938-1940. Made of mock orange stick, cocoons, commercial cordage and paint, marsh hawk tail feathers, glue. Length 22 inches. Photograph by Michael Dixon. Courtesy of Donald Ewing.

Brown gave this rattle to Donald Ewing, who was a boy

of ten or twelve at the time. Brown apparently saw no problem with presenting such an item to a young boy, unlike other Miwok shamans who did not allow others to handle such objects.

Figure 16. Mountain Travelling. 1989. Acrylic/canvas. 48" x 36". Painting by Frank LaPena.

Figure 17. East. As a Wintu travels he/she starts from the east. Painting east is about the sun and the beginning of a new day. Birds sing before sunrise. Then it is quiet while the sun comes up. Then they sing again. Painting by Frank LaPena.

Figure 18. South. The south gives reference to life. The red is the travelling sun. South is about badger, the obsidian keeper who went south and set the world on fire. The green road is the milky way--the "spirit road." Painting by Frank LaPena.

Figure 19. West. West is oriented toward the jagged edge of the world. You can see it in the evening when the sun goes down--as presented here in the sky. Part of west's orientation is the spirit of moving up and facing west. Painting by Frank LaPena.

Figure 20. North. North is the "main one" and the orientation of *Bohem Puiyuk* (Mount Shasta). LaPena's auntie is in direct association because she lived as close as you can get. Painting by Frank LaPena.

Figure 21. *Olelbis* is a spiritual force. *Olelbis* is neutral and not static. It is responsible for the creation of all life. Painting by Frank LaPena.

Figure 22. "House of Six Directions." In this we see the green spiritual road. In the blue above world we see the stars. At the bottom of the earth is green, and the red has mountains. Painting by Frank LaPena.

Figure 23. Bag of Bones. Photo by Frank LaPena.

Figure 24. Bag of Bones. Drawing by Frank LaPena.

Figure 25. North Mountain (*Bohem Puiyuk*). Acrylic/canvas. 1989. 48" x 108". Painting by Frank LaPena.

SOURCES

The Shamanic Experience by Lowell John Bean and Sylvia Brakke Vane is a revised version of Shamanism: An Introduction, first published in Art of the Huichol Indians, edited by Kathleen Berrin, and published by the Fine Arts Museums of San Francisco/Harry N. Abrams, Inc. in 1978. It is used by permission of the Fine Arts Museums of San Francisco.

Power and Its Applications in Native California by Lowell John Bean is reprinted by permission of The Journal of California Anthropology.

California Religious Systems and Their Transformations by Lowell John Bean and Sylvia Brakke Vane is a revised version of "Cults and Their Transformations," first published in Handbook of North American Indians, Volume 8: California, edited by Robert F. Heizer and general editor, William C. Sturtevant; published by Smithsonian Institution Press. c. Smithsonian Institution 1978. It is used by permission of the Smithsonian Institution Press.

California Indian Shamanism and Folk Curing by Lowell John Bean was originally published in American Folk Medicine: A Symposium, edited by Wayland Hand, and published by the University of California Press. It is used by permission of the University of California Press.

Notes on the Wintu Shamanic Jargon by Alice Shepherd. This paper was originally published in Report #1 (1981) of Reports from the Survey of California and Other Indian Languages, and is used by permission of Leanne Hinton, Director, Survey of California and Other Indian Languages.

Dancing on the Brink of the World: Deprivation and the Ghost Dance Religion by E. Breck Parkman is used by permission of the author.

The following papers, used by permission of the authors, were presented at the 1990 California State University, Hayward Conference on California Indian Shamanism:

Shamanistic Aspects of California Rock Art by Ken Hedges

The Shaman: Priest, Doctor, Scientist by Florence Shipek

Sierra Miwok Shamans, 1900-1990 by Craig D. Bates

Yurok Doctors and the Concept of "Shamanism" by Thomas Buckley

Wintu Sacred Geography by Dorothea J Theodoratus and Frank LaPena

Ridge Walkers of Northwestern California: Paths Toward Spiritual Balance by Jack
Norton

Ajumawi Doctoring: Conflicts in New Age/Traditional Shamanism by Floyd
Buckskin

INTRODUCTION

Lowell John Bean

This volume presents knowledge about various aspects of California Indian shamanism and the religious and philosophical contexts in which it exists. The authors are scholars who have devoted many years to addressing the research needs of California Indians and anthropological disciplines. All have had uniquely close relationships with the communities about which they report, and have been able to report accurately on religious phenomena that are of interest to scholars and Native Americans alike. Three of them, Jack Norton, Floyd Buckskin, and Frank LaPena, are themselves members of Native California groups.

As a celebration of California Indian religion and shamanism, this volume is particularly appropriate at a time when Native American religious values are impacting the general public's consciousness more than ever before, primarily because of environmental and historic preservation laws and regulations. As concern for the protection of these public resources has increased, the more important it has become to achieve an in-depth understanding of California religions and the world view from which they have sprung.

The articles in this volume assume a broad, and not always consistent, definition of shamanism. Shamans are seen as not just specialists in particular activities, but as much more. They are seen as intellectuals; as artists; as healers par excellence; as managers of the physical and biotic environment; as psychics; as philosophers; and as the boundary players of the cosmological and social universe. The shaman's actions in the ancient past, the post-European world, and the ethnographic present are seen as continuously providing over thousands of years actions as vital to a community today as they have always been and always will be.

These essays are also about power, ideas of reality (world

view), cultural continuity and change, the management of social and physical environments, medicine, visual arts, painting, sculpture, drama, poetry, oral literature, costume, and astronomy as demonstrations and conduits of the spiritual and philosophical energies available to people, and especially to California Indian peoples. All of these are arts and sciences that shamans routinely employ in order to serve the people who depend on them for guidance through the vicissitudes of life on earth. They assist people to manage personal relations, emotions, and physical health. They demonstrate aspects of the use of supernatural power to manage the seasons and the landscape, and encourage the growth and reproduction of plants and animals.

Interest in shamans by anthropologists, scholars, and officials who deal with Indian peoples has a long and interesting history in California Indian studies, dating as early as the 1820s, when a curious priest at San Juan Capistrano queried Native Californians about their religions and wrote a report on his findings that provides our earliest information about the role of shamans among California Indians (Boscana 1846). Other Spaniards who worked among Indian people also commented on Indian religion, usually disparagingly, but nonetheless providing a useful body of data that illuminates the history of California Indian shamanism before 1840.

When Americans came to California they were often met by shaman-priests, as were earlier Europeans. Shamans, after all, were responsible for dealing with foreigners, outsiders, or any strange or potentially dangerous elements of the universe. In the late 1890s, when anthropologists finally turned their attention to the study of California Indians, scholars such as David Prescott Barrows, Roland Dixon, and later, Alfred L. Kroeber noted the presence of shamans, and described some of their functions, often, unfortunately, seeing them naively from the narrow point of view of turn-of-the-century anthropology. Nevertheless, these anthropologists recorded important information about shamans and their activities, including supportive oral literature. The directions set by this early work have continued until today.

When Alfred L. Kroeber wrote his classic work, *Handbook of the Indians of California* (1925) knowledge about the status and role of shamans was still somewhat limited, not yet understood as part of a holistic system. In fact, for a long time the academic community as a whole took a rather conservative approach to shamanism, failing to see or appreciate many of its facets. A psychological approach was the most fashionable for a time. According to this approach, the shaman was a psychologically imperfect person whose behavioral patterns were "found" a place in society in order to provide a functional fit for what was different.

As anthropologists moved into a new era and began to focus upon such subjects, or tools of analysis, as sociological categories, status, role, and philosophical concepts, and took cognitive and phenomenological approaches, the role of the shaman was looked upon with another set of lenses. The position of the shaman in society became more clear.

It was not until the remarkable works of Mircea Eliade, focusing on comparative religion, were published in the early 1960s that the study of shamanic religion began to get the attention it deserved from anthropologists and scholars of religion. Perhaps an equally great stimulus to the field was the publication, beginning in the late 1960s, of the books of Carlos Castaneda, himself a reader of Eliade. The fascination of the counter culture with American Indian and other non-Western philosophies was another important stimulus. From that time on the understanding of the shaman's role in society has greatly increased, and many scholars, including Myerhoff, Furst, Harner, Reichel-Dolmatoff, and Johannes Wilbert, have worked assiduously to improve our knowledge.

Yet the literature on California Indian shamanism has remained rather sparse. Some exceptional articles have emerged. These have included Barbara Myerhoff's *The Shaman as a Culture Hero* (1966), Ray White's *Luiseño Social Organization* (1963), and Don Handelman's *Aspects of the Moral Compact of a Washo Shaman* (1972) These and other authors have viewed the shaman in somewhat different perspectives than previously.

The interest in shamanism came to peak, however, not only because of Eliade and Castaneda, and not only because of the "hippy" movement (which had an American Indian component as part of its generative power), but also because of the later development of environmental impact studies with their cultural resource components, and the American Indian Religious Freedom Act. It became necessary for Indians, anthropologists, and agencies--federal, state, and local--to address American Indian concerns.

To preserve places held most sacred by Native Americans, it became necessary for religious leaders to assert themselves publicly, to reveal information previously kept secret, and to demonstrate to non-believers the efficacy of their teachings, and their continued use of traditional ways and beliefs. Rituals and beliefs had to be explained in order to save biota and lands from destruction.

Often, understanding these ideologies makes it possible to save, protect or mitigate not only Indian sacred and historical sites, but also historical materials important to the culture at large when they are threatened. The moral guidelines of the Native Americans are among the best "weapons" in the struggle to save the "sacred" past of people here and elsewhere.

Legal restraints that affect us all, both legislative or agency policies, now protect biological resources, protect communities from the careless and dangerous storage of waste materials that could damage communities, and save scenic and recreational assets. American Indian religious leaders have acted as advisors and consultants to persons making decisions about how to implement the laws and regulations. Many of these Native Americans are persons who function in shamanic roles within Indian communities today, or who work closely with shamans.

Within the archaeological community, many of these same restraints, or guiding principles, are preventing, to a considerable degree, careless, destructive, or negligent archaeological research. For example, in many areas in the State of California, agencies insist on direct Native American involvement when archaeological resources of a religious nature may be impacted, even though such involvement is not always mandated by legal requirements. This insistence often results in a better, more intense data collection in areas that otherwise would be ignored, especially religiously significant places. The protection of these traditional significant places, historic or religious, enriches our national heritage.

As a rule, California Indians remain firm in their appreciation, belief, and/or use of shamanism. The shaman is now, among those groups who no longer have shamans, a well remembered and often recalled culture hero.

A recollection of great traditions, powers, and miracles empowers and validates a people's tradition. It has a special value for the young; a sacred past that sets them apart from others. As Essie Parrish, a Pomo shaman, used to say, "You white people are smart (clever); you can build machines that take you to the moon. But we went there without machines, by the use of our special powers."

The loss of these traditions, among those who have lost them, is not unmitigable, because they can, and often do, use the power of shamans of other groups, not only Indians, but also those from India, Hawaii, and New Zealand. In case of illness, they also have access to Western medicine. It is the best of all possible worlds, some say.

It gives them an edge--an advantage with respect to medical care--and spiritual, ethical and psychological advantages over people whose world has become fragmented and separated into church and state, religion and economy, religion and medicine, religion and ethos, and religion and history. Those whose world is not fragmented in such a way retain the magical past (and a philosophically systemic world) that so beautifully connected man with the parts of him that are above, below and beyond, in the past, present and future.

My own interest in shamanism developed when I began, in 1958, to learn about Cahuilla religion from the Cahuilla Indians of southern California. It grew as I worked with the Luiseño, had conversations with Kumeyaay elders, and held discussions about the latter groups with fellow anthropologists Florence Shipek and Ray White, who were working with the Kumeyaay and Luiseño peoples, respectively.

I observed Cahuilla participation in ceremonies and met and "worked" with Cahuilla shaman Salvador Lopez and others. Lopez was the last Cahuilla shaman who specialized in "fire-eating" as a way to demonstrate his power. At that time there were perhaps a dozen Cahuilla shamans, and perhaps as many Luiseño, Serrano, and Kumeyaay shamans. (Sadly, there seem to be none today.) They, as well as shamans from other areas, were called on for curing rituals when someone was ill; for example, the Washo shaman, Henry Rupert, and a Hawaiian shaman, whose name is not recalled, successfully cured Victoria Weirick, then the acting ceremonial leader of the Wanakik Cahuilla, when she fell ill. She first, and most especially, tutored me in Cahuilla religious matters. Her deep faith and extraordinary care were a lesson in the power of shamanic healing never to be forgotten.

Conversations with Ray White, who at that time had recently earned his Ph.D. at U.C.L.A., about his work among the Luiseño helped me understand much of California Indian philosophy and world view. White had worked closely with several Luiseño religious leaders, including Ray Pachito, Henry Rodriguez, and members of the Calac family. This guidance, and his previous training in philosophy aided White in understanding the complex philosophical ways of Southern California Indians and its place in their cultural systems, and allowed him to go well beyond the scope of anthropological wisdom then expressed by his mentors at U.C.L.A.

This publication is the result of the May 12, 1990 conference on shamanism sponsored by the C. E. Smith Museum of Anthropology, located at California State University, Hayward (CSUH). Four previously published articles pertaining to California as a whole--two that I wrote, and two that Sylvia Vane and I coauthored--begin the book. They are followed by articles given by conference participants, and relevant articles submitted after the conference.

The conference, and the concurrently running exhibition entitled *California Indian Shamanism*, were funded by grants from the CSUH State Lottery Fund, the California Council for the Humanities, and the Institute of Museum Services. They were designed to enable California Indians and scholars to share their knowledge. Not for a long time, and perhaps never, have shamans and their traditions, philosophies, and roles in California Indian society been addressed by so many people at one time, and in a venue that included such a significant number of Native Americans.

The recent interest in shamanism has been stimulated in part by what is called, by some, "neo-shamanism," an especially controversial development. In this volume it is addressed by Jack Norton and Floyd Buckskin, who express considerable concern, as Native Americans, about the impact of that public trend on Native Americans.

More significant perhaps than the New Age uses of shamanic concepts is the fact that with the renewed recognition and appreciation of other religions among the public-at-large there is an increasing recognition of the literary complexity, poetic quality, musical elegance, and philosophical sophistication of Native California religious systems contained in these non-Western traditions.

This is the second volume resulting from a C. E. Smith Museum of Anthropology Scholars Conference. The first was *Seasons of the Kachina*, also a Ballena Press publication. Another conference, to be held in November of 1992, will celebrate the culture and history of the Ohlone Indians of the San Francisco Bay Area, and, in due time, will result in a third volume.

THE SHAMANIC EXPERIENCE

Lowell John Bean and Sylvia Brakke Vane

That particular forms of Native American shamanism are still extant should be understood as manifestations of a widespread social phenomenon rather than as something unusual or unprecedented.

Today, the shamanic tradition survives in the midst of a world where the original cultural context in which it arose and functioned is rapidly disappearing, and despite the fact that shamanism has long been misunderstood, rejected, or superficially or romantically idealized by those outside the culture.

There is no consensus among the scholars as to exactly what a shaman is. In *Shamanism*, Mircea Eliade speaks of "shamanism-technique of ecstasy," and then specifies that the ecstatic experience in which the shaman specializes is "a trance during which his soul is believed to leave his body and ascend to the sky or descend to the underworld"; that he is in control of, rather than possessed by, the demons, spirits, and ghosts of the dead with whom he is able to communicate (1964:4-8 *passim*).

Andreas Lommel, in his work on shamanism, takes a somewhat culturally biased approach when he distinguishes between medicine men and shamans:

> Unlike the medicine man, the future shaman acts under an inner compulsion . . . a psychosis that is emerging for some reason or other is so strong that the only way out open to the individual attacked by it is to escape from it into shamanistic activity, that is to say essentially by means of artistic productivity, such as dancing or singing, which always involves a state of trance (1967:9-10).

Taking a more sociological but limited approach, Gerald Weiss, in *Hallucinogens and Shamanism*, distinguishes between the concepts of shaman and priest, suggesting that there may be a continuum of roles which indeed, in California we see there are. The shamanic role, he points out, is associated with direct contact with the supernatural, part-time operation, and with the curing of individuals by means of rituals "characterized by possession, trance, and frenzy"; whereas the priest is a full-time specialist who has had special training and "leads group activities of a ceremonial nature" in which "routine propitiatory acts of adoration, prayer and offerings" are important (1973:41-42).

According to Harner, on the other hand, "a shaman may be defined as a man or woman who is in direct contact with the spirit world through a trance state and has one or more spirits at his command to carry out his bidding for good or evil" (1973:xi).

Eliade's definition is not only useful as a guideline, but is closer to that of Native California Indians.

Our own definition of shamanism, which is implicit in what follows, incorporates much of the above and attempts to describe and explain this poorly understood, fascinating, and useful ancient universal role.

THE ORIGINS OF SHAMANISM

Shamanism was first recognized by Western observers in central and northern Asia. The word "shaman" is derived from the language of the Tungus, one of the many groups in which shamanism is important. It existed in its most "classic" form (that is, the form in which it was first described) in these parts of Asia and in northern North America.

The origins of shamanism are hidden in the mists of the human past, although surely the presence in earliest human groups of individuals with particular skills as healers must have gone hand in hand with the development of human culture. Disease, traumatic injury, emotional problems, and social and philosophical dilemmas had to be dealt with as surely as infantile helplessness, and those who had the power to cope with these problems must have been esteemed. It seems likely that persons with special healing powers were very often shamans.

We can only speculate about the techniques of the earliest healers. It is not likely that they had available to them the full panoply of skills of present-day shamans, which must have been built up over many thousands of years. However, the 1960 discovery of skeletons in the Shanidar cave in Iraq, which were estimated to be about sixty thousand years old, suggests the presence of the role of curer. With these skeletons, one of which appeared to be that of an important man, were found soil samples particularly rich in eight species of flower pollen, seven of which are known to have medicinal properties. It is certain that they were included purposefully, and we know that pollens have not been found in other graves of that period. If they were, indeed, placed in the grave because of their medicinal properties, it is reasonable to infer that this was the grave of a shaman. Beyond this, the antiquity of shamanism can be inferred from the fact that it appears to be a near-universal phenomenon, appearing in the hunting and gathering societies of all continents and underlying the religions of more complex societies. What comes as a surprise to intellectuals is that a social role with such distinctive attributes enjoyed such near universality in pre-agricultural societies. Shamanism, or something very much like it, has persisted in the small societies of all continents until the present, even though it is not always recognized as such.

What is surprising is not the fact that there are people who can go into trance, but that knowledge acquired in a state of trance can be effectively put to work to cure the ill or to restore equilibrium in a group, and that the beginnings not only of medicine and religion, but also of art, music, dance, and literature appear to be intimately associated with revelations gained in states of trance.

ON BECOMING A SHAMAN

The shaman invariably receives a spiritual "call" which indicates that he or she may be a worthy candidate for the role, whereupon the process of becoming a shaman begins. Although this process varies from culture to culture, there seems to be a universal underlying pattern.

The shaman's role is distinct and special in each culture, although it usually overlaps other roles. The recruitment of the shaman is necessarily dramatic enough to emphasize the special quality of the role. The candidate may become ill, have vivid dreams or hallucinations, undergo a severe psychic crisis, exhibit nervousness or instability, or undertake a quest involving extraordinary physical effort, self-denial, or self-torture. Whether the role is hereditary or not, sought by or forced upon the candidate, its assumption begins with some event which calls attention to the fact that the candidate may be set apart or consecrated.

In some cultures shamans reportedly do not seek the call-- it comes to them spontaneously. Usually, indications that the call may come are observed in a child at an early age by the adults in the community; and, in retrospect at least, these early indications are remembered by the shamans. A dramatic event in early puberty often indicates the propensity toward shamanism. At that time the individual may suffer some great psychic trauma or illness and effect his or her own recovery, may perform a miraculous cure, or have a significant dream. The ability to recover, to cure another, or to communicate a spiritual message may indicate a potential for future power which society can channel for its necessary ends. The initiation ceremonies of boys and girls may also serve as a revelation of shamanic propensity.

When the shamanic role is hereditary, it may descend in either the male or the female line in accordance with cultural tradition. There is often considerable flexibility in the rules of inheritance, so that the most promising of a shaman's descendants are "chosen," either becoming manifest through a psychic crisis or through direct inheritance of paraphernalia and formulas.

Superior skill or unusual talent, either intellectual or physical, is sometimes seen as a "sign" of shamanic potential. Thus the best hunter, the fastest runner, or the brightest or most creative child may become the shaman of a group or be thought to have shamanic potential. There are indications in the literature that in the early stages of metallurgy the smiths who knew the secrets of metalworking were assumed to have the supernatural powers essential to shamanism, an assumption also made about alchemists among others. These assumptions are consistent with the idea of shamanism being associated with the transformation of one thing to another. An escape from danger, like an escape from illness, is sometimes taken as a sign of supernatural power. Likewise, the person with unusual sexual proclivities may be a shaman, and it was not unusual in North American groups for berdaches (male and female homosexuals) to be shamans.

In some cultures a person may consciously seek the role by achieving an ecstatic experience. The vision quest was particularly important among many western North American groups, in which aspiring shamans underwent strict regimens of physical and psychological stress in order to achieve the desired spiritual experience. Sometimes all the elite adolescents of a group underwent an initiation into a secret society whose members had quasi-shamanic status.

The shamanic candidate may also become a member of the profession by purchase or transfer of formulas, equipage, rights, or supernatural experience from another shaman. For example, according to Harner, the would-be shaman among the Jivaro of South America gives a gift to a practicing shaman, who administers a psychotropic drink under the influence of which a spirit helper or "dart" is transferred.

The selection process seems to occur at covert and/or overt levels. A youngster who is intelligent, alert, curious, and ambitious is seen as a potential shaman and guided toward the career. The essential requirements for becoming a shaman are the acquisition of a power source and community acceptance. The various kinds of "call" are experienced subjectively as the acquisition of a power source or sources, that is, of guardian spirits, "darts," "pains," and the like, depending on how the group expresses this idea. The would-be shaman enters into a contractual agreement with the power source or sources and undertakes to develop a working relationship with it or them. Either at the time of the call, during initiation, or in the course of training, he or she receives instructions, rules and regulations, and formulas. These responsibilities imposed by the power source must be accepted. Failure to abide by the contract may bring death, illness, or harm to those around the shaman family and community, and of course the loss of power. The contract is binding regardless of the feelings of the shaman. A prominent California shaman (now deceased) failed to practice for several years. During this time, she and her family suffered diseases and other stresses. Another shaman advised them that the former shaman's abdication of her role was the cause of all their illnesses. The "spirit" would not accept this rejection. When the shaman returned to her traditional role, her and her family's tribulations ceased.

Shamans, for the most part, are set apart from the sorcerers and witches of their own and more complex societies in that theirs is a more positive and important role. Community belief and support is essential to them. Shamans may get the call or decide to seek it, but to validate it the "power elites" of the community, as well as supernatural beings, must pass judgment. The shamans must satisfy their future peers, who control recruitment into the powerful and secret world of the highly skilled.

Public initiatory rites usually precede the final acceptance of a shaman. The initiate is observed at some point in his or her development by other shamans and the community in public performances where power is demonstrated or affirmed. It may be a curing session, or it may be a more dramatic theatrical event involving a ritual reenactment of the would-be shaman's death and rebirth as experienced in trance. One of the functions of the initiation is the public proclamation and validation of the shaman's status. This is necessary because the shaman must ultimately have a "congregation"--a group of others who believe he or she is indeed a person of power.

The ritual death and rebirth which the initiate experiences while in a state of trance--i.e., ecstacy--is remarkable similar in a wide variety of cultures. It is intense, far more convincing than

rites of passage that do not involve trance--christenings, puberty
ceremonies, weddings, and funerals. The subject, in trance, may
be killed by spirits or ghosts, have his or her organs removed and
skeleton dismembered. The navel may be pierced by spears or
arrows, and quartz crystals signifying supernatural power may be
shot into the body. The dangers encountered and overcome often
include dangerous journeys marked by difficult passages where
the candidate is in danger of being crushed by great rocks, of
falling from great heights, or of being devoured by monsters. The
mastery of basic human fears--height, darkness, and space--gives
the shaman the self-confidence to make decisions. His creative
energy is opened up, since he is more self-assured and less afraid
of being in error than an ordinary person. In effect, he is able to
make a self-fulfilling prophecy of success.

   Although the initiation rite of a shaman may take only a
short time, the full acquisition of the shamanic role usually takes
many years and is achieved only after many tests or trials, along
with instruction from master shamans. Sometimes the end of an
apprenticeship is marked by an elaborate public ceremony lasting
for days.

   Aspects of the initiatory experience are apparently
repeated, at least in part, whenever the shaman goes into trance;
but having learned to cope with the dangers, the full-fledged
shaman is more firmly in control of the situations he encounters
than is the initiate, and is more likely to increase the intensity of
them as his career goes forward.

   Even though the initiation is so important for the validation of the shaman's status, it does not establish it for all time. A
community may reassess its shamans, and only after a long career
is a shaman likely to be unquestioningly accepted. There is often
a tacit assumption that his or her power is subject to entropic
processes--that it diminishes with age, unless there is evidence to
the contrary; however, in some groups, it is assumed that power
increases with age and the acquisition of more spiritual helpers.
This, also, has to be demonstrated by the individual shaman.

   In addition, the shaman often finds him or herself in
competition with other shamans and the target of envy. In public
performances, shamans may test one another's degree or legitimacy
of power. A shaman may even have his power taken away during
such an event. Shamans may also evaluate each other's ethics.
Power from spiritual guardians may be quixotic, and a shaman's
status in the eyes of both clients and peers may vary accordingly.

   Most societies believe that the shaman's power can be used
for either "good" or "evil." Hence shamans are closely watched for
malevolent or benevolent tendencies. An imbalance in this
dualistic role can lead to a shaman's disenfranchisement and even

death. For these reasons a shaman's career must be carefully managed. In many societies, a clear demarcation is made between those shamans who are "good" and those who are malevolent.

THE ECSTATIC EXPERIENCE-TRANCE

Unlike experiences in "ordinary reality," the experiences of the person in trance are not likely to be perceived directly by others; yet they are, according to anthropologists who have apprenticed themselves to shamans and taken psychedelic drugs under their direction, so compellingly "real" that trance has been called a "nonordinary reality." What the tutelary shaman does is to teach the apprentice the "language" of the visionary experience, to organize it and make out of it a culturally validated "sense."

The shaman does somewhat the same thing with the people in his or her society when leading curing sessions or ceremonials, especially when this involves putting everyone in trance or trancelike states. The shaman organizes and interprets the experience. This is illustrated by the way in which Huichol shamans conduct the peyote hunt, as discussed by Myerhoff and others (1974). As an interesting aside to the Huichol case, some shamanic complexes have disappeared because the world view of the group and its cultural complex were such that shamans could not control the psychedelic experience for the good of the group.

The purposes of trance are several. According to typical shamanic philosophy, trance allows the shaman to travel to other worlds through magical flight, interact with supernatural beings, and discover the nature of life and the pathway to the land of the dead, so that the living may be told and reassured about the future. It permits shamans to find lost souls, catch them, and return them before their loss causes death or illness. Trance also serves as a device by which the shaman breaks through intellectual and cultural boundaries--creating new ideas, seeing "things" in different ways and in new combinations. It puts the shaman at the widening gulf between a world that is and one that may be.

Dramatically, the experience provides a psychological metaphor of tremendous proportions--life, death, creation, rebirth, and transformation. It provides the well-trained shaman with an intellectual dimension that can apparently multiply his or her capacity to understand the world and its problems, but it is so impressive, so striking, so dramatic, that in order to communicate its meaning--usually by means of ritual--shamans have had to improvise means of communication and thereby have given birth to various art forms. Only these can carry ineffable messages; thus the laymen of a society see and hear realities in a way that enforces societal cohesion, reinforces the symbolic representation of their world, and promotes the mental health of the community at large. This process, as Barbara Myerhoff has pointed out, is manifest in such ceremonies as the peyote hunt--individuals come together to become part of timeless, placeless totality, to renew their world through group sharing and individually experienced but culturally understood visions (Myerhoff 1974).

The trance experience is a natural potential of all people, but some have a greater biological and/or psychological predisposition toward achieving it. Various means, including sensory deprivation, are used to induce trance: rhythmic sound or activity as in music, dance, or meditation; electrical stimulation of the nervous system; fasting; and drugs. All these, except electrical stimulation, are known to shamans. Drugs are used in the form of plant roots, stems, leaves, flowers, or seeds. According to Schultes (1972), the most common of these are hallucinogens belonging either to the nitrogen-containing alkaloids derived from the amino acid tryptophan, or to the non-nitrogenous dibenzopyrans, phenylpropenes, catechols, or alcohols.

In several species of mushrooms that are important in this respect the significant alkaloid is psilocybine, a powerful agent that induces both auditory and visual hallucinations as well as physiological changes. Among the flowering plants, the cacti, several members of the morning glory family (*Convolvulaceae*), mints (*Lamiaceae*), legumes (*Leguminosae*), *Lythraceae*, *Malpighiaceae*, *Myristicaceae*, *Rubiaceae*, and *Solanaceae* include species which yield hallucinogenic substances. Peyote, *Lophophora williamsii*, is the most prominent hallucinogenic cactus.

It is very common to use more than one plant in the preparations employed to induce trance, the mixtures varying from group to group and from shaman to shaman. The use of these psychotropic substances is often accompanied by very unpleasant side effects and even lethal danger, since reactions tend to be idiosyncratic and since the amounts contained in each plant may vary. Of course, a skilled shaman is supposed to be able to put together a formula that will yield the desired hallucinatory effects without serious side effects.

Apparently the achievement of trance, whether by the use of drugs or otherwise, can be learned, and a shaman may be able to control the state, adjusting the various levels of the trance to circumstance and need. However, this control is denied by some shamans, who attribute the degree of intensity of the experience to the will of the spiritual guardian rather than to their own conscious efforts.

Several lines of research promise to shed some light on the biological aspects of trance and to explain why the state can be achieved by such diverse means. Both ingestion of psychotropic substances and the other roads to trance would appear to affect the functioning of the automatic nervous system, bringing about second- or third-stage "tuning" of either the trophotropic or ergotropic system and thus altering ordinary cognitive processes.

It seems likely that skilled shamans learn to interpret the state of the autonomic nervous system by observing such signals as the dilation of the pupils, sweating, respiration, nausea and vomiting, muscle tone, and mental alertness, and use the information to adjust dosages and, in ceremonials, to alternate periods of intense activity and of rest to achieve a desired effect.

These observations do not fully explain why by these processes shamans are able to reach for and discover the deep level of knowledge they do, but it is evident that these processes of special cerebration do occur.

SOCIAL ASPECTS OF SHAMANISM

The shaman is a person of power, controlling, directing, and persuading other members of a society, and usually standing at the apex of the power hierarchy. The power is derived not only from the knowledge and wisdom acquired during apprenticeship and initiation, but also from the confidence of the society, from the legitimacy of the role, and the need that society has for his/her skills.

The societies in which shamanism has flourished have usually been small, relatively self-sufficient social systems which see themselves as coping directly with their natural worlds. Like all other human beings, the members of such groups lived in a world of uncertainty. The presence of a person or persons who could maintain contact with the cosmic forces of the universe directly, who could explain and make sense of both the measured order of ordinary times and the catastrophes of drought, thunder and lightening, earthquake, or flood, was of incalculable value.

More complex social systems tend to have "institutionalized" specialists who transmit information from one generation to another without explicit recourse to the supernatural. Such societies have priests and prophets, not shamans, at the overt level. But the line between shaman and prophet is tenuous, a matter of definition. The prophet usually does not enjoy the legitimacy within his society that is granted the shaman. His is a voice crying in the wilderness, not that of the legitimate curer and philosopher. Despite the differences, the prophet can be seen as a kind of shaman, and thus the study of shamanism illuminates some of the obscurities in the histories and doctrines of the great religious traditions.

Shamans are members of the inner circles of their societies, elites able to explicate the implicit aspects of their culture. They are also boundary players between their own and other cultures, since they travel not only into sacred space and time in trance, but also, as members of an international network of elites, move outside their own social groups in ordinary reality. They are often multilingual, and hence able to communicate with neighboring groups; they have access to a great deal of information. They know the concepts of past and present, can anticipate the future, and can share the ideas of neighboring cultures and subcultures. They are the intellectuals of their societies and "brokers" of ideas between the sacred and profane (or secular) worlds, between the past and the future, between their own societies and others.

The social networks of shamans have multiple dimensions. Since they are able to travel between worlds, whatever their number--lower, upper, and middle--they are able to communicate with all forms of life and knowledge. It is generally assumed that whatever has life has intelligence. Thus the shaman may communicate with "spiritual" beings or souls who are in sacred worlds or times and with sacred persons who are in the ordinary world. His or her network may include all living things, and even seemingly inanimate things that may contain life and power. A rock, for example, may be a source of residual power or the location of a spiritual being; so may animals, birds, trees, grass, flowers, wind, or water. The shaman may know the language of these. And with them as well as with persons from the various levels (ranks) of society he or she communicates regularly.

In addition to contacts with other shamans and their congregations, the shaman often maintains an entourage of personal helpers. These are likely to be people trained to assist in the esoteric matters of the profession. Whether the objective is the cure of a patient or the restoration of "order" in the social "universe," the shaman's various public and private performances encompass a wide variety of dramatic presentations--singing, dancing, music, magical acts, and ritual recapitulations of cosmic creations. These performances often require assistants who may perform purification ceremonies, protect the shaman's privacy, or care for his or her personal needs during the performance. They may gather special herbs or minerals or make special equipment. The singers, musicians, and dancers who often provide ritual accompaniment need to know the unique musical and poetic repertoire of the shaman and be able to perform correctly while the shaman is in trance or undergoing a transformation or magical flight.

These assistants may be members of a shaman's immediate family--husband or wife, child or sibling--apprentice shamans, or, as in the case of one tradition we have observed, they may be deliberately selected from different families within the community in order to provide the shaman with immediate ties to a number of families and a greater network of supporters for his or her position.

The shaman's social sphere often includes other practitioners, who may be either assistants or independent specialists. For example, diviners, who may or may not be shamans may be employed to tell a client what kind of shaman to call upon for specific service. Herbalists may have the responsibility for herbal cures or may supervise the care of the patient in the absence of the shaman. The shaman in such an instance serves as the physician, instructing the patient and those who assist or collaborate in the patient's care in the procedures necessary for the cure. The shaman often understands the skeletal structure, musculature, and other parts of the human body, especially in hunting societies where butchery of game provides empirical data. This kind of practical knowledge is combined with legerdemain and skilled diagnosis, and these in turn reinforce the trust of the patient and the group. Thus, the shaman may show the conquered disease as an object that has been sucked from the patient--the object being a representative of the disease's cause or of the patient's pain--or may demand that the patient or a member of the community confess to acts that may have caused or aggravated the illness--the violation of taboos or cultural norms.

THE SHAMAN IN TODAY'S WORLD

Shamans and their modern counterparts are still found in many societies. Despite the pressures upon the institutions of shamanism--missionaries, Western medicine, governmental proscription, theft or displacement of their specialties--it is alive and well throughout the world. Among California Indians there is a resurgence of shamans and their influence in contemporary political movements. Many political organizations, among them the American Indian Movement, use the wisdom and political skills of shamans. Even those shamans primarily dedicated to serving their own small communities have been called upon and visited by major political leaders in the American Indian community. Pomo shaman Mabel McKay, for example, served on the Native American Heritage Commission by appointment of

Governor Brown. There is also now an annual conference of shamans, or people of power, from the native American community, a movement that began in 1970--a North American Indian ecumenical movement.

In various communities the shaman also serves a wider congregation. Many non-Indians come to shamans with a reputation for special mystical power and healing (part of our own *indigenismo*). The authors, in their public appearances (lectures) with shamans, have invariably found students and others suffering from psychological or physical pain turning to the shamans for help.

On the reservations where shamans live, it is common for strangers to appear at the door seeking aid. Many have a large following bridging their ethnic backgrounds and classes. Their success as healers and their acceptance by non-Indians is testimony to their communities that the Indian culture has retained uniquely attractive, mystically powerful characteristics. This assuages the pain of the stigma of being exploited by a dominant culture.

Within their own ethnic sphere the shamans continue many of their traditional roles--as philosophers, as psychological advisers, as psychiatrists engaged in group therapy, and as curers using traditional methods of healing for ailments, often those which they define as "Indian" rather than "non-Indian" diseases. This interesting diagnostic dichotomy occurs among many North American Indian groups, where shamans automatically refer certain ailments to non-Indian doctors. Some enlightened members of the medical profession in the dominant culture reciprocate. Where this occurs, as among the Navaho, a very valuable and creative collaboration can exist between experts of the two traditions, each learning from the other.

The shaman's role is difficult today, more difficult than in an earlier time. There is, despite the survival value of shamanism, less community support, less economic and political advantage to the individual shaman, and always the nagging doubts of people within and without the culture who, out of ignorance or perhaps fear, negate the ancient role.

Those shamans who have continued to practice their roles in recent years have been personally strong and deeply committed to their professions. But the extraordinary new support that has developed in recent years because of the American Indian Movement, the renaissance of national interest and concern for the Indian culture and community, and a new interest in non-Western religious traditions, has been a significant catalyst for shamans, who can now be placed in context by reference to characters such as Castaneda's Don Juan, familiar to readers to popular literature.

They have a new cross-cultural legitimacy among literati and among Western therapists who are anxious to learn from a study of shamanism and its methods for maintaining and restoring mental and physical health.

POWER AND ITS APPLICATIONS IN NATIVE CALIFORNIA

Lowell John Bean

This paper presents a general description of supernatural power as it was perceived and used by California Indians prior to European contact. The principal existential postulates relating to the concept of power that were shared by most native California peoples are outlined, and the normative postulates (values) that regulated the use of power are briefly discussed. Specific ways in which power might be acquired and the conduits or pathways to its acquisition are reviewed. Finally, some of the social implications deriving from the concept of the presence of power and beliefs about its characteristics are suggested. The description of power presented here is cross-cultural, and the author fully recognizes that not every aspect of power described in this paper can be strictly applied to each ethnic group in the state. Beliefs about power varied from group to group, but for the most part the ideas presented here were widely shared.

THE SOURCE OF POWER

The source of power is sometimes clearly explained in native California cosmologies, and sometimes it is not. Nevertheless, two principal patterns emerge in the cosmologies: (1) power is created from a void in which two forces, usually male and female, come together in a cataclysmic event that forms a creative force; or (2) power and creators appear simultaneously in the universe without explanation, and a creative force begins thereupon to form or alter the world. In both cases, various acts are accomplished through a use of power by a creator or primary creators that leads to a series of creations--among which is man. The outcome of these acts (narrated in dramatic episodes in the native cosmologies) is the creation of a hierarchically structured social universe--a cosmological model in which the nature of power is defined and rules are established for interacting with power sources. Although accounts in individual cosmologies may vary considerably from group to group in depicting this universe, throughout California there appears to be at least a tripartite division of the universe into upper, middle, and lower worlds.

The upper world is occupied by powerful anthropomorphic beings--usually seen as the primary creators--with whom humans can interact to their own benefit. The upper world may also include astronomical personages such as the Sun, Moon, and significant stars or constellations, theriomorphic creatures who are the forerunners of animal species, and other spirit beings who have no counterpart in the real world. Often the dwelling place of the dead is associated with the upper realm, although it is sometimes located in a distinctly different place.

The middle world is inhabited by both men and various non-mortal beings with considerable power. Most native Californians view the middle world as lying at the geographical center of the universe. Usually, it is conceived as circular, floating in space, and surrounded by a void or by water.

Finally, the underworld is inhabited by superordinary beings who are usually more malevolent toward man than those of the other two realms. Such beings take many forms and are often associated with water, springs, underground rivers and lakes, and caves. Frequently, they are reptilian or amphibian in nature (e.g., serpents or frogs) or have a distorted humanoid appearance (e.g., dwarfs, hunchbacks, giants, cyclopes, water-babies).

THE NATURE OF POWER

The nature of power in the universe is best understood in terms of four basic philosophical assumptions shared by most native California groups (Bean 1972; White 1963; Blackburn 1974b; Halpern 1955). These assumptions are as follows: (1) power is sentient and the principal causative agent in the universe; (2) power is distributed differentially throughout the three realms of the universe and possessed by anything having "life" or the will "to act"; (3) the universe is in a state of dynamic equilibrium in relation to power; and (4) man is the central figure in an interacting system of power holders.

First, power is assumed to be the principal causative agent (energy source) for all phenomena in the universe. Power is sentient and possesses will. At the beginning of the universe or some later stage in the creation, power was apportioned throughout the three realms in various degrees or quantities. Thus, power is potentially extant in all things. Power may remain quiescent and neutral, choosing its own time or place to manifest itself. Some things possess more power than others, but anything in the universe that has "life" or demonstrates the will "to act" possesses some amount of power. Even seemingly inanimate things may possess power. A rock that suddenly moves downhill may thereby demonstrate an ability "to act," and therefore reveal itself to be a power source. An animal may be normal or possess some extraordinary degree of power, or, most awesome of all, prove to be a were-animal. Nothing can be judged to be without power until it has been tested by empirical indicators. Since man is never absolutely certain whether or not anything is a power source until it is tested or reveals itself, he lives in a constantly perilous world fraught with danger. Power sources remain a continuous threat of advantage to man until his soul enters the land of the dead, where presumably all is well, and power vis-à-vis an individual soul is permanently controlled.

All power beings are personalized and akin to man in their nature (capable of such emotions as anger, love, hate, pity, and jealousy). Because power beings are capricious, unpredictable, and amoral, they may manifest themselves in many ways that perform for or against man's benefit. It seems that only in historical times has power been viewed as disparately good or evil. Although power is omnipresent in the universe, it is not always omniscient, which means the beings possessing power can be deceived like humans.

The universe exists in a state of dynamic equilibrium with power. While there is constant opposition between power sources and a struggle among them to acquire more power, no one source of power has the ability to obtain ultimate superiority or to alter the condition of the universe irrevocably so long as man conducts himself in a manner that aids in maintaining the equilibrium.

Man is viewed as the central figure in an interacting system of power holders. As the articulating link between all expressions of power, man has been provided with guidelines for acquiring, keeping, and wielding power. Since power is sentient and personalized, man can interact with power or conduits of power much as he would with humans. Power can be dealt with rationally through a system of reciprocal rules (expectations), which were established or handed down to man in early cosmic times. Without individual or community action by man through such rituals as world renewal ceremonies, the balance of power in the universe would be upset, and one side of the system might be disproportionately favored over another. Individually acquired power (knowledge) and traditionally acquired power (held by priests or shamans) must continually be employed by man to maintain the dynamic equilibrium or harmony of the universe.

Since man occupies the geographical center of the universe, he is in an ideal location for bringing power from the upper and lower universes into play in the middle world. Religious persons such as priests or shamans are extremely important socio-political figures in native society. They are the boundary players of power, since they possess knowledge that makes it possible for them to travel safely to distant and hence dangerous places--often in any of the three worlds. Men possessing a knowledge of the rules governing power are capable of receiving, manipulating, and controlling power throughout the universe with various degrees of success.

Form, space, and time are mutable and malleable under the influence of power. During rituals, when power is being exercised, past, present, and future may be fused into one continuous whole. A shaman may use power to bring sacred time into the present so that he can interact with beings from that time. He may transcend space, shortening or lengthening distances through the use of power. Or he may draw a land form toward him or travel speedily across space transformed into another creature, such as a bird, bear, or mountain lion.

Within the middle world of man, power can exist anywhere, and anything occupying space may contain power and be beneficial or dangerous. For this reason, the central place occupied by an Indian group--the village--is more sacred and safer than anything beyond its perimeter. Such a central place is viewed as "tame" or safe because it is controlled by men of knowledge who can protect the inhabitants from other power sources (Halpern 1955; Blackburn 1974b).

If security, predictability, and sociability are associated with one's home base, everything beyond is associated with danger. The forest and other places not inhabited by man are unsafe because they are defined as uncontrolled--as are the other two universes. Thus, travel away from one's home base increases the chances of encountering danger. The danger of uncontrolled power is believed to increase in a series of concentric circles the farther one moves away from one's immediate social universe. For this reason, the presence of strangers in a community may represent a source of danger and must be viewed with suspicion. They may, because they live at a distance, possess greater power for ill use than one's own people.

Although power operates in a dynamic equilibrium in the universe, one of its major characteristics is that it is entropic (Blackburn 1974b; Bean 1972; White 1963). Power has gradually diminished since the beginning of time in quality, quantity, and availability. Such a diminishment of power has occurred because man has at various times treated it or its conduits improperly, failing in his reciprocal responsibilities within an interdependent system. Consequently, as man struggles to reestablish the power balance of the universe in the face of forces seeking to create disequilibrium, power always seems to be restored at a lesser level than in the past. A very rapid loss of power is believed to have occurred after the European contact as knowledge concerning the means of regulating power was lost. Nevertheless, power is always partially retrievable as new rules are established for obtaining and maintaining it.

VALUES AND THE CONTROL OF POWER

The concept of power is integrally related to several normative values concerning its use which are common to most California Indian groups. To maintain a viable world, it is considered mandatory that man acquire knowledge about the universe. Knowledge has value for its own sake as well as for being an instrument in the manipulation of power. Thus, persons who acquire knowledge are considered powerful and treated deferentially. Often it is assumed that knowledge is in part a product of advancing age. Very advanced age (without senility) among south central and southern California groups is an indication of greater power. In contrast, power decreases in north central California with advanced age (loss of physical strength before the onset of senility), and offices associated with power are passed on to younger adults.

In order to acquire power, one must behave honestly, prudently, moderately, and reciprocally in relation to others, and possess the ability to maintain confidences. Honesty is qualified by the understanding that deceit can be used by the weak when dealing with powerful beings or persons who have an unfair advantage. Self-restraint, industriousness, self-assertion, and self-respect are other qualities necessary for the proper use of power (Bean 1972; Blackburn 1974b).

The rules for handling power and using its conduits (such as ritual paraphernalia) function to control the power holder and prevent his misuse of power in two ways. First, power can be used only at proper times and in proper places, and it must be used in accordance with set procedures (e.g., in combination with various power acts such as smoking tobacco). A failure to exemplify in one's conduct those moral values associated with the use of power (such as reciprocity and prudence) leads to automatic disenfranchisement for the power holder and possibly punishment from a tutelary spirit or other persons of power. Secondly, persons having power and knowledge may withhold from unworthy candidates information on procedures for acquiring and maintaining power. Thus, if a candidate's deportment in daily affairs is such that it is believed he will not use power safely or productively, he is kept away from the principal conduits of power. Sometimes, however, among certain groups a "troublemaker" was drawn into the circle of power to "tame" him. It was thought that his acquisition of an awesome responsibility might transform him into a better man.

In addition to the moral virtues described above, men of power adopted an eclectic and highly pragmatic view of the universe. Because power was seen as omnipresent and completely malleable, all phenomena were potentially useful as sources of power. The fact that potential power residing in an object was not immediately obvious could simply signify a failure on the part of an observer to have the requisite knowledge to recognize and use it. Thus, it was important to preserve an empirical attitude toward all new phenomena or ideas and cautiously test them against the framework of cultural realities which were already known. To the native Californian, the diversity and unpredictability of power was consistent with an ecosystem that was equally diverse and unpredictable, although often kind and bountiful in the resources provided by nature. Because it was understood that the sources of power were so diversified, an eclectic and experimental attitude toward power existed in California. Man was not dependent upon one source of power, but attempted to acquire power from as many sources as possible. Since power was unlimited in its potential for acquisition, one shaman might have as many as ten or more guardian spirits.

Finally, because this empirical and eclectic attitude toward power was pervasive throughout California, new ideas developed and spread rapidly and were readily molded into unique, culturally specific styles of power control by different Indian groups. One example of such a diffusion of new ideas was the Chingishnish religion, which appears to have arisen in the late eighteenth century either on Santa Catalina Island or among the Gabrielinos (White 1963:94). This religion spread south to the Luiseño and Diegueño, who uniquely grafted it onto their own religions, and even reached as far into the interior as certain Cahuilla groups, who adopted specific features of the cult.

POWER FROM OTHER WORLDS

Power that existed in the here and now of man's middle universe was viewed as left over from the sacred time of creation. This residual power (White 1963) was conceived as lying about, rather free floating, obtainable and manageable by those born with sufficient innate abilities to handle it or those who otherwise had acquired the requisite knowledge. The principal sources of power, however, lay in the upper and lower worlds, residing in the "sacred beings."

Among some Indian groups in California, every individual sought a connection with power. In other groups, only specifically recognized persons or those who wanted extraordinary power sought it out. Since power was believed to be ubiquitous and continually available, its presence and influence in the events of daily life were constantly appreciated by all members of a culture.

Man was connected with the power available in the upper and lower worlds in very specific ways. Direct contacts were possible with tutelary spirits who instructed one in the use of power; souls and ghosts transcended the space between worlds and could be contacted during ghostly visitations to the middle world; and some humans--through ecstatic experiences--were able to transport themselves to the other worlds or to bring from them supernatural power. Some of the means through which power might be acquired include the following: the vision quest, the calling upon of power sources, dreaming, the inheritance or purchase of knowledge or ritual equipment, and prayers and offerings. Individuals might be instructed in the knowledge, acquisition, and use of power by a power giver itself (sacred being), or they might receive such knowledge through training from a shaman or other ritual specialist.

Various techniques also existed for making the individual more open to the acquisition of power by altering his mental or bodily sensibilities. These included the use or combined use of hallucinogenic plants, the handling of power-containing objects, and various forms of sensory deprivation or acts designed to concentrate attention, such as meditation, fasting, imposed periods of sleeplessness, isolation, induced sweating, listening to music, singing, drumming, chanting, and hyperventilation.

One of the principal routes to acquiring power was the vision quest, and the induction of an ecstatic condition to receive spirits having power was a common preliminary act. Several means were used to induce ecstasy on the vision quest, the most dramatic being the use of hallucinogenic plants with or without accompanying ritual. In California, the most frequently used plants containing hallucinogens were *Nicotiana* (tobacco) and

Datura (jimson weed). The California poppy and formic acid from ants may also have been used by some groups. It was believed that such hallucinogens altered the user's perceptions and level of awareness, making him more receptive to perceiving sacred beings and other power sources.

Power could also be tapped and acquired through many channels that brought it into the human sphere of activities. These included rocks (such as quartz crystals) and other unusual objects, human and animal bones (especially predators among animals), human and animal hair, various animal parts (such as the heart and entrails), non-mind altering plants (such as angelica and pepperwood), and all ritual paraphernalia.

Any unusual phenomenon or event might serve to bring power into the middle world of man or prove to be an omen that could be read for predicting the future (e.g., astronomical events, any peculiar behavior of humans or animals, multiple births, people with unusual marks or physical characteristics, etc.). Power could also be concentrated in specific places in the environment, such as in a pond (water being the great transformer), on a mountain top, or in a particular tree or grove of trees. Power might also be put into a place by those having power. A shaman, for example, might protect a sacred place outside his village where ritual paraphernalia was stored by putting power there.

Within the community, power was invested in or accumulated at various private and public places, most commonly the ritual center where the religious, political, economic, and social lives of the people came together. Such ritual centers were considered sacred places where cosmic or sacred time and space and spiritual beings met with secular time and space and human beings. In such ritual centers, elaborate rites of intensification were carried out as necessary to maintain the equilibrium of the universe or to aid in cosmic rebirth at the end of each year or when the balance of the universe was endangered. Such rituals were particularly critical during times of cosmic imbalance, usually the result of man's failure to perform rituals properly or to act reciprocally with other beings in the universe.

Sacred places could also be divested of power, however, and some places contained power only at appropriate times, such as during religious ceremonies or on those occasions when supernatural powers were closer and more accessible to man. During certain times or periods (such as at night or in winter), power was considered closer to man than at other times and simultaneously more dangerous unless checked and kept under control. In particular, during times of life crises (such as menstruation, birth, illness, and death), power might be in a highly chaotic state and very dangerous to the community. On such occasions, malevolent outside powers entering the village or emanating from the individual experiencing the crisis could harm both the individual and the community. Thus, ritual action, both public and private, was necessary on such occasions.

SOCIAL AND POLITICAL IMPLICATIONS OF POWER

The nature of power as described in native California cosmologies provides an explanation for certain socio-cultural organizational modes only recently becoming clear to researchers (Bean and King 1974; Bean and Lawton 1973). One of these modes is reflected in what Blackburn (1974b) has called an assumption of the inevitable and inherent inequality of the universe. Just as power is distributed differentially and hierarchically throughout the universe, so is it distributed for acquisition and use by human beings.

Inequalities in social rank, intelligence, social prerogatives, wealth, and skills can all be explained by reference to the differential distribution of power. Certain individuals are naturally born with power or inherit it, others possess the capacity to seek it out, and in some instances power itself seeks people out. In a hierarchically ordered universe, it is not surprising that a hierarchical ordering of power is also accepted as part of the structuring of man's middle universe. In the middle or "real" world, some humans have more access to more power than others, and humans in general have more access to power than other species. A similar hierarchy exists in the plant and animal kingdom. Carnivores, for example, are more powerful than plants. In most California Indian cosmologies, there is a clear-cut chain-of-being in the biotic world in which man stands near the top of the power pyramid in the middle universe. He is also at the center of the entire universe, receiving power and using it to maintain the universal equilibrium.

Society itself is similarly hierarchically structured-- characterized by the presence of classes of people with inherent power and with its privilege and wealth. Like cosmological beings, humans with power are regarded with ambiguity by others in their community. Power holders are "necessary evils" performing vital functions. They are treated with respect and awe, but also with considerable caution, since they are potentially amoral in their relationships with others. Their allegiance is to power, both the maintenance of power and the acquisition of more power, and thus primarily to other persons of power, even as much as their allegiance may be to the community they serve as administrators and boundary players. In effect, men of power stand somewhat above and outside the social system in which they live--not entirely responsible to the claims of the local social order. For example, a shaman may not be as dependable in his conduct toward his relatives as ordinary people would be. His higher calling sometimes transcends his secular obligations.

In societies fraught with uncertainty, a person who can control, acquire, or manipulate power is absolutely necessary. While the social price required for his presence may be great, it is necessary to pay it. Generally, throughout California, chiefly families were those that had many priests and shamans. In economic matters, the elite families controlled the principal means of production and distribution of goods, owned monopolies on many valuable goods and services (e.g., eagle down and ritual positions), possessed the power to levy taxes, fines, and establish fees to support institutions, and were able to charge exorbitant interest on loans, thus amassing further wealth. In legal matters, they were the final judicial arbitrators with the power of binding decisions involving life and death within the community.

Just as there was a constant conflict between those with innate power and those seeking to acquire it in the myths and cosmologies of the California Indians, so did such a conflict exist in human society between the elites holding power and newcomers seeking to acquire it. The elites, with their inherited power that brought wealth and privileges, were in continual conflict with individuals from beneath their ranks who sought to acquire power, since power was potentially available to anyone. The elites, however, possessed control mechanisms for the licensing or sanctioning of power such as secret societies, initiations, and inheritance of rank, knowledge, and control of ceremonial equipment. These mechanisms provided a means by which persons of lower rank, possessing skill and ambition (sometimes even those who were socially disruptive), might enter the system. Through such a licensing of power, bright young people of lower ranks were able to move upward, yet the power structure was always kept safe from serious disruption by malcontents with talent.

Since power could always be destroyed, men of power who misused their abilities or endangered the community could be reduced in rank or power through ritual disenfranchisement or, if necessary, assassination.

Empirical indicators of status held by elite families, such as symbols of political office (e.g., ceremonial bundles), were also cosmological referents to the most powerful supernatural beings in sacred positions of the upper world and therefore symbols of power as well. The main social implication of power was that elites lived a life and shared a knowledge that clearly separated them from their people.

Chiefs and to some extent shamans and other specialists were usually men of conspicuous wealth, who had inherited their offices--patrilineally in southern California and bilaterally in Northern California. They wore expensive clothing, lived in larger houses than ordinary people, often were polygamous (certainly having greater sexual access to women), and married within the higher ranks (usually within their class, thus compounding wealth among ruling families.) Such people were relieved from the day-to-day routine of hunting and gathering life and were often totally supported by the populace. This was also generally true of the higher ranking craftsmen. Unquestionably, the elite families received better medical care (because the best medical practitioners were in their ranks), the best diet, best living accommodations, and the least amount of risk in daily life (since they weren't required to carry out sometimes dangerous activities such as hunting or fishing). Such persons were generally relieved from fighting during warfare, serving instead as the arbiters who determined who would go to battle and as negotiators of peacemaking.

Thus, the distribution of power within a community played the primary role in determining all social acts and interrelationships, whether these were between close kin, members of the community, or between different political groups. Even warfare and conquest could be justified in terms of the need to acquire or maintain a power balance. Understanding this allows us to better appreciate the complexity of the social, economic, and political institutions of native California.

CONCLUSIONS

We have seen that understanding assumptions about power is central to understanding the nature of man and his relationship to the universe in native California. Power explains the operations of man's social universe within which all beings are potentially hierarchical, but competitively and reciprocally. Each part of the system through man's intercessionary role at the center of the universe performs a task vis-à-vis the other parts that will create or strive for a state of balanced equilibrium and the maintenance of a viable ecosystem.

The congruency we find between the philosophical assumptions in native California culture about power and the social realities by which the culture functions should encourage us to delve further into the nature of "power" as it is defined by other cultures. We should take seriously each culture's cosmological view of the universe and the role of power within the universe, because this may tell us more about the social rules for behavior than any other aspect of a cultural system.

In further studies of native California. I hope to explore the assumptions concerning the role of power in the universe and the rules for using power as they vary from one ecosystem to another. Clearly there are differences from group to group which I have glossed over in this generalized sketch. In particular, the different sorts of strategies for using power should be examined for all hunting and gathering societies to determine what rules (and I suspect they are very few) equip man to cope with specific types of ecosystems, levels of technology, and social and political conditions.

In another context (Bean 1974a:13), I suggested that native Californians achieved a level of socio-cultural integration not unlike that of many horticultural and agricultural societies--a level that may be more indicative of the normal levels reached within the limitations of hunting and gathering technology than those contemporary hunting and gathering societies that anthropologists have studied in the twentieth century. The California case continues to suggest that our evolutionary models for hunting and gathering societies are inadequate. It also suggests that the process by which cultures switch over to more advanced forms of economic achievement are yet to be understood, since native Californians had the opportunity and knowledge to make such a shift, but in most cases failed to do so. Such an opportunity existed in California because the philosophical assumptions about power provided for *all* possibilities of change. And, especially, they provided a justification for centralized and hierarchically structured power, for the exploitation of individuals and other societies, for conquest, and for other variables necessary to political and economic expansion.

CALIFORNIA RELIGIOUS SYSTEMS AND THEIR TRANSFORMATIONS

Lowell John Bean and Sylvia Brakke Vane

The major religious systems of native California are commonly known as the World Renewal, Kuksu, and toloache (*?antap* and Chingichngish) religions. The Ghost Dance, the derivative Bole-Maru and Dream religions, and the Shaker Church were developments after European contact. The philosophical concepts underlying these traditions are not dealt with directly in this chapter since they have been described elsewhere (Bean 1975; Bean 1976; Blackburn 1975; Kroeber 1925; Loeb 1932). Many local smaller traditions of tribes not included in these prominent traditions, such as bird cults (Gifford 1926), Peyote religions, ancient prehistoric religious systems, girls' adolescent rites, war dances, funeral rites, or the basic shamanistic tradition that underlies all the native religious systems are not discussed in detail, nor are the effects and adaptations of Christian denominations, such as Roman Catholicism, Methodism, Mormonism, and Pentecostalism considered except briefly. All these continue to bridge the old and the new among many native California Indians in the late twentieth century.

The major religions mentioned above established common philosophical assumptions that served to integrate large numbers of people into social, economic, political, and ritual networks of considerable dimensions, including many thousands of people and sometimes hundreds of communities. In most of the groups that participated in these networks, initiation into religious secret societies was a *sine qua non* for elite or leadership status. Initiatory rites, accordingly, served as formal educational institutions in which the existential and normative postulates of these societies were imparted to each generation of elites. These religious-political leaders served as administrators and statesmen of early California--boundary players in the broad-ranged network of social systems encompassing many political and several language groups.

Entry into and status within these religious societies usually correlated with the wealth and the social background of an individual as well as his or her social, intellectual, and technological skills. In fact, some religious societies (e.g., *'antap* among the Chumash) controlled professions and displayed some of the characteristics of craft or guild associations, determining who could enter certain trades or have usufruct and possessory rights to certain property (Blackburn 1974a; Goldschmidt 1951).

These religious systems were intimately involved in the economic aspects of California societies in that ritual events were usually associated with the production and distribution needs of each group and its neighbors. Rituals prescribed by the rules of each system served as interchange events where goods were transferred or exchanged and rights and privileges to economic goods and services affirmed (Bean 1972; R. C. White 1963; Bean and King 1974; Kroeber 1925). These same ritual events, of course, demonstrated to all in splendidly dramatic fashion the religious and philosophical assumptions of each individual society, thereby serving as ethnicity maintenance devices that separated each group from its neighbors while binding many groups together as ritual congregations.

As these religious systems developed through time the institutions associated with them became increasingly complex and formalized, more efficiently integrated both within individual political groups and among neighboring groups, and more institutionalized (Kroeber 1971a; Bean and King 1974; Heizer 1964). They may have been in full development as much as a millennium or more before White contact. Intergroup integration was facilitated by ritual rules requiring religious leaders of groups other than the local group to participate in its rituals. Such rules brought about the development of many major religious centers, which were also centers of economic, social, and political interaction. These were found throughout California; for example, in northwestern California, World Renewal rites were celebrated at 13 ritual centers (Kroeber and Gifford 1949). In southern California the Chumash (King 1971:35-36) and the Gabrielino (B. E. Johnston 1962) each had a number of ritual centers. In other areas apparently the centers were not usually permanent ones; rather, each community became a ritual center for the time it hosted the reciprocating comembers of a ritual congregation (Bean 1972).

All these religious systems had strong roots in a shamanic tradition. Shamans, having control of altered states of consciousness, were religious specialists in charge of the relationships between man and the supernatural in all California societies, in effect philosophers. In some societies, especially those where religion was less formally organized, their vocation was theoretically thrust upon them, and their knowledge was acquired by direct communication with the supernatural. In fact, of course, traditional knowledge provided basic formats upon which individual creative shamans worked. A priestlike role for religious specialists, in which knowledge was acquired by formal education, was more common in the great religious systems described here (Kuksu, ʾantap, World Renewal, Chingichngish). Where these religious systems were not operative, there were networks or informal associations of religio-political specialists cross-cutting cultural and political boundaries and involving social, economic, and political behavior similar to that of the major religious systems. Among some groups (Atsugewi, Achumawi, Tübatulabal), these networks were informal, with little visible structure; in areas of clan and lineage structure (Miwok, Yokuts, Cahuilla, Serrano, Kumeyaay, Maidu), they were more institutionalized, serving to create socioeconomic ties in less favorable ecological settings, the degree to which these systems were institutionalized correlating markedly with economic and ecological potentials. In the most favored environments the formation of the great religious systems was possibly one of the ways in which economic and political interchange between more populous groups competing within the most favorable eco-niches was established, and thus was a factor in the establishment of social systems that could maintain dynamic equilibrium over long periods of time.

To some degree these major religious systems may also have been devices for political expansion, the fear of competing neighbors bringing about the formation of ritual, political, and economic alliances (ritual congregations) in order to reduce potential conflict situations over scarce resources, particularly after population density reached optimal levels. By providing for routinized peaceful interactions between groups of differing and disparate ecological potentials, trade agreements, marriage alliances, and other intergroup institutions were maintained, so that goods, services, and wealth were more equitably or at least more predictably spread among neighboring groups (Bean and King 1974).

WORLD RENEWAL

The World Renewal religion and its rituals were the most striking aspect of the religious practices of the Karok, Yurok, Hupa, Tolowa, and perhaps of the Wiyot, whose culture had

largely disappeared by the time ethnographers appeared on the
scene. These rites were imbedded in a religious system that
extended to the north among the peoples of northwestern American as far as Alaska. It was characteristic of this larger group to
have status explicitly based on the possession of wealth and its
reciprocal exchange in a complex of ritual feasts, and to maintain
a rigid philosophical system comparable to the Protestant ethic
(Goldschmidt 1951). The World Renewal system was an aspect of
this larger system that was in its details unique to California, even
though the basic ideas upon which it was based were more widely
distributed (Kroeber and Gifford 1949).

The Tolowa, Karok, Yurok, Hupa, and Wiyot lived along
the northwestern California coast from the mouth of the Mad
River to that of the Trinity River and along the rivers and streams
as far inland as Inam on the Klamath River. They resided in small
villages, hemmed in by forested mountains, an environment with
a wealth of plant and animal resources, but one in which unpredictable floods, earthquakes, and forest fires were as threatening
to humans as a whole as disease and accident were to individual
humans. In these nations, a network of male priests officiated at
annual cycles of rites that were considered essential to the
maintenance of world order; the health of individuals; productivi-
ty and availability of plants, animals, and fish; assistance from
spiritual beings; prevention of natural disasters; and the like.
Women shamans acted in curing capacities, especially for psycho-
somatic phenomena (Kroeber 1925; Kroeber and Gifford 1949).

Floods, earthquakes, fires, disease, and accidents were
alike in being manifestations of power wielded by extra-human
forces, often as a result of improper actions on the part of humans.
Tradition decreed that only the performance of appropriate rites
could restore the world to an orderly and predictable state, with
man in some degree of control. These rites had been established
or demonstrated by the Immortals at the time of creation. Their
teachings were incorporated not only in the language, customs,
and ritual lore of the people, but also in the esoteric narratives and
dialogues that prescribed for the sacred ceremonies and had the
power to recreate what the Immortals had originally done. These
formulaic narratives and dialogues were repeated by a priest in
each ritual center, acting out a story of what the Immortals had
done in early times of creation in several precise locations,
sometimes separated over some distances, where the original
events had occurred, and in the exact fashion prescribed by
tradition. The death and rebirth of the world were in part
reenacted in the rebuilding of sacred structures (sweathouses,
ceremonial houses, dance arenas), the creation of the sacred fires,
the erection of stone walls related to shamanic power acquisition

rites, or the sacred pile of sand in which priests might stand for part of the rite. Kroeber and Gifford (1949:128) reveal the traditional "rites of passage" structure of the ritual when they note that "at Rekwoi and presumably at the three other Lower Yurok Jumping dances which rebuild the 'ancient' sweathouse, the new timbers are buried and otherwise treated like a corpse." That is, separation and liminality are indicated. After the ritual, both the priest and the dancers who helped him, in part by stomping the "newly created" earth to firm it, went through rites of purification, retiring from public view and dancing before reappearing as their profane selves (Kroeber and Gifford 1949).

The rites conducted by priests and their assistants were esoteric, sacred, and secret parts of the World Renewal cycles. They were accompanied by one or both of two major dance cycles: the White Deerskin Dance and the Jumping Dance. The former involved the ceremonial use of an elaborately decorated hide of the rare albino deer, apparently a condensed symbol of birth (whiteness), the male principle, and the beneficent spirit of the deer. The dance lasted as long as 16 days and worked up to a stirring climax of dancing and an elaborate display of wealth, where potential power became active, kinetic (Kroeber and Gifford 1949).

The Jumping Dance participants wore woodpecker-scalp headbands and carried sacred dance baskets. As in the White Deerskin Dance, the performers were men, usually young, and they danced in place standing side by side, with two or three of them who sang well doing the singing from their places in the center of the line (Kroeber and Gifford 1949).

The dance host invited neighboring peoples to the ritual center, thus integrating thousands of people from several language groups into large ritual congregations. The host needed wealth, power, and networks of wealthy friends and followers to organize the event. He needed to own or borrow requisite ceremonial costumes and regalia used by dancers (who displayed them) and sufficient dentalium bead money and other resources to provide food for the feasts that accompanied the dances. The wealthy came into their estates by inheritance or personal acquisition, often by legal suits. The dance houses themselves were inherited (Kroeber and Gifford 1949).

These rituals not only had first-fruits rites implications, but also provided a time when the recently deceased were remembered and mourned. First Salmon rites were part of the World Renewal system at several ritual centers, as was the Acorn Feast, with a woman priest officiating among the Hupa. The *kepel* dam-building ceremony, at the peak rather than the beginning of the salmon season, was a World Renewal rite of the Yurok

(Kroeber and Gifford 1949).

In the dances, it was customary for the downstream village peoples in the vicinity of a ritual center to alternate with and compete with upstream people, the upstream and downstream directions being the predominant ones in northwestern California, as they were in the San Joaquin Valley, where these directions were involved in moiety characteristics (Kunkel 1962). The northwestern peoples may have had an incipient moiety system reflected in this competition during dances. The dances were timed so that the dark of the moon coincided with either the end or the climax of the dances (Kroeber and Gifford 1949). It should be noted that this orientation was also a characteristic of bead-money exchange and exchanges of women in the area (Gould 1966; Chagnon 1970).

Priests represented Immortals in some of the ceremonies but did not impersonate them; that is, there was no thought that they were transformed into deities; however, during the rite the priest went through extensive purification before and after performing the ritual by separation and fasting. During the rite he abstained from water, since drinking interfered with his esoteric function of world renewal, and avoided sexual encounters, as sexual behavior was antithetical to wealth acquisition (Erickson 1943). Social distance was maintained between the priest and the people; it was also taboo to look at him or make loud noises near him.

Karok and Yurok priests had male assistant priests, and the downriver Yurok had both male and female attendants as well, perhaps a measure of the various groups' relative stratification. The assistants, attendants, and the Karok sweathouse singers seem to have been incipient secret-society members. Priests, and possibly their aides, had to come from families who "owned" secret formulas. The individual who put on the dance was paid. Tobacco, "incense," and the powerful angelica root were used during the rites. Apparently, tobacco smoke and dancing were equivalent to "cooking," symbolizing transformations to new forms (Kroeber and Gifford 1949).

Curing shamans were usually females who sought power by fasting, abstaining from water, and prolonged dancing to attain a trance or dreaming state and a spiritual guardian who provided the power to diagnose and cure. They were assisted by experienced shamans, or "doctors," often their mothers or grandmothers; this form of shamanism also ran in families. Part of the ritual included procedures requiring heat, just as the girls' puberty rite did. Spott and Kroeber (1942:155) suggest that the pain had to be "cooked." It is possible that the "cooking" was also directed at the shaman, who was being made into a higher-status being (Levi-Strauss

1964:334-338). In northern California the sign that a shaman had attained power was bleeding from the mouth or nose, orifices in opposition to the vagina from which came the blood that signified the women's elevation to adult status. It is significant that the shaman, dance leaders, and others of high status were assumed to go after death to join the Immortals in a pleasantly ordered "heaven," whereas the ordinary person after death went to an underworld or to the west where he or she ate rotten salmon and other unfit food and engaged in brawls or fights, that is, his or her afterlife was disordered, having the same high entropy as menstrual blood (Kroeber and Gifford 1949).

KUKSU

The religious system that anthropologists have generally referred to as the Kuksu cult was an interwoven cluster of subsystems common to the peoples in the San Francisco Bay area and the Sacramento and northern San Joaquin valleys and adjacent hill area. It included the Pomoans; Coast, Lake, and Plains Miwok; Patwin; Valley Nisenan; Hill and Valley Maidu; Cahto; Yuki and Huchnom. These peoples developed secret societies of learned men (and occasionally women) who underwent complex rites of passage and formal instruction to signify their elevation to and warrant their holding of leadership positions. They administered and led cycles of rites and ceremonies, usually including curing, singing, and dancing, in which elaborately costumed members of the society or societies represented transformed divinities, ghosts, or spirits. They thus recreated sacred time and in one way or another restored their people to the unsullied state that had prevailed at the time of creation (Loeb 1932, 1933; Kroeber 1932).

There were few activities common to all peoples in this area, since a variety of religious customs and beliefs, many of them prevalent in adjacent areas, were interwoven to create a complex recognized by all its constituent members. Available data suggest that the religious customs and beliefs of any given people within the Kuksu area varied considerably over time, although the Kuksu religion generally may have been several thousand years old. What distinguished the religion was its complexity and formalized organization rather than any given ritual feature of it. Most of the peoples who practiced it had one or more secret societies (ghost, Kuksu, Hesi, Aki) whose members were socially, politically, and economically superior to nonmembers (women, children, and many male commoners were excluded from membership). Most of them had ceremonies in which gods, spirits, or ghosts were impersonated (returned to earth) and some of them, notably the Cahto, Yuki, Huchnom, Eastern Pomo, Valley Maidu, Hill Maidu, and Mountain Maidu, maintained a concept of an anthropomorphic creator that was otherwise found only among the Wintu and Nomlaki directly north of the Kuksu area. The religion as a whole had no native designation and is called Kuksu because the god most widely impersonated is called *kuksu* in Eastern Pomo and similar terms in other languages--an indication of the fundamental identity of the various forms of the religion (Loeb 1932, 1933: Kroeber 1932).

The individualistic character of the religion as practiced in any local group meant that the religious system provided boundaries that bolstered individual group identity. At the same time it was an open system in which traits were exchanged with some neighboring peoples. It was mandatory to invite neighboring groups to ceremonies, a custom whereby ritual reciprocity requirements alleviated the stress of competition for resources and helped reduce conflict. In addition to the reciprocity, which took the form of gifts both received from and given to the guests at ceremonies, it was customary to engage in gambling, trade, and other social activities during the course of ceremonial events (Loeb 1932, 1933; Kroeber 1932).

The secret societies that were so prominent in Kuksu religions were a mechanism identifying persons and the privileges they enjoyed. In some areas a man could not function fully as a member of society without belonging to at least one secret society. In groups where not every man was a member, those who were had access to more power, information, wealth. The same applies to women where they were secret-society members. Membership in the societies was conferred upon chosen young people on the basis of both birth and achievement, but there was a tendency for membership to run in families, often passed ambilineally, a possible indication that the secret societies were used to strengthen affinal relationships and thus constitute intervillage alliances.

The explicit purposes of the secret societies varied. In some areas the initiation of young people and their training seems to have been a major stated goal; in others the goal was "world renewal," first-fruits recognition, curing, or initiation of economic activities appropriate to the time of the year (Loeb 1932, 1933; Kroeber 1907, 1971a; Swezey 1975). Whatever these ritual goals the primary function was administrative.

The most elaborate versions of the Kuksu religion were to be found among the most heavily populated river valleys where there were the most abundant supplies of material resources and the greatest access to information brought by traders and other travelers (Loeb 1932, 1933; Kroeber 1932).

Kuksu was impersonated by a secret-society member strikingly costumed, including a special headdress that varied from group to group, sometimes being a crown or top-knot of eagle or buzzard feathers and sometimes, apparently, a basket headdress with projecting feathertipped wands that was the precursor of the so-called Big Head of the later Bole-Maru cult. These were frequently symbols of valuable food products, such as acorn or manzanita, that were bestowed as gifts each year to the leader of the group giving the rite. Kuksu's body was painted black among the Pomoans and other western peoples, and covered with black feather capes among the central valley peoples. He was more anthropomorphic among the western peoples, where he was associated more often with a divinity than in the east, where he was to a degree associated with the moon (Loeb 1932, 1933). In the east he also had more birdlike attributes. In peripheral groups, where he was known by other names, he took only minor roles in rituals. In the Sacramento River valley and the Sierra foothills, Hesi and Aki societies replaced or existed alongside Kuksu societies. These had incorporated Kuksu traits, and almost always had vestiges of Kuksu impersonation, but were more complex than Kuksu societies (Kroeber 1932; Loeb 1932).

Over most of the area where the Kuksu system prevailed, there also existed a lower ranking society, perhaps from an older tradition, whose members impersonated the spirits of the dead. These spirits, or "ghosts" were considered to live in the area where they had lived as human beings, but in the forests and with the order of things reversed; they slept in the daytime and worked at night, for example. To see a ghost was dangerous and a cause of illness, especially for uninitiated young persons, so that one role of the ghost impersonators was to cure illness so caused. Ghost impersonators wore feather decorations (sometimes representative of disease-causing beings) and carried long black poles; their bodies were painted in red, black, and white strips (Loeb 1932). They were thus condensed symbols of life and death, and mediators between the dead and the living, as indicated by the color symbolism and the allusions to heaven and earth. The dances, in another sense, were a way of opposing the relatively uncontrolled power of the spirits of the dead with the relatively uncontrolled power of adolescent boys under orderly, rhythmic conditions that brought both under greater social control. Thus, both boys and ghosts became "civilized."

Ghost societies seem to have served some of the same functions as annual mourning ceremonies in other parts of California and did not occur where annual mourning ceremonies for the dead were held. In the Sacramento River valley the River Patwin had "running spirits" who went into ecstatic trances and behaved in extraordinary and erratic fashion, perhaps being possessed by the ghosts they represented (Kroeber 1932).

The major public role of ghost societies was usually the initiation of young people, that is, the conduct of the rite of passage to transform adolescents into fully participant members of the tribe.   This was true of the Yukian peoples, most of the Pomoans, the Maidu, and the Coast Miwok. The ghost societies of the Northern and Northeastern Pomo and the Wappo did not initiate all boys and thus were more clearly involved in the formation of an elite class (Loeb 1932; Kroeber 1932).

Initiation into the Kuksu was more dramatic and often included dangerous experiences or the acquisition of dangerous knowledge. In groups of the northwest and southeast boys were initiated, and where the Hesi society was the strongest, girls underwent Kuksu initiations. Within the society there were ranks and many positions associated with ceremonial roles to be achieved, there being at least three ranks of Kuksu membership: novice, initiate, and director. The last was apt to have a high rank in secular as well as sacred society (Kroeber 1932).

In some groups the ghost and Kuksu societies were merged; among other groups traits common in adjacent areas were merged with the Kuksu system. For example, the bear "imperson-ation" that occurred in the Northwest was represented among some of the Pomoans, the Coast Miwok, and the Patwin where Bear society initiations were held annually. In Patwin groups Bear or an analogous "north spirit" society was sometimes a third level of elite secret society (Loeb 1932; Kroeber 1932).

In the Sacramento Valley there were Hesi societies into which all or most boys were initiated. The name may be from Nomlaki, for the Valley Konkow word *hési* was borrowed, with the ceremony, from the Nomlaki (William F. Shipley, personal communication 1976). Within the Hesi society there were as many as 10 or 12 ranks to be achieved by payment and performance. Members were paid for enacting ceremonial roles, the acting not requiring the acquisition of esoteric knowledge; they paid to learn the esoteric knowledge that permitted them to direct performances and for the right to sit in a hierarchy of seating sections within the dance house. Where the Hesi religion was practiced, the dance costumes were extremely elaborate and a bewildering variety of dances was performed in a series of ceremonial events. The dance leader in a Hesi ceremony impersonated a bird divinity; he was termed *mo ̓ki* in Patwin and, from that, *mó ̓ki* in Konkow. Kuksu was often only one of many other animal-spirit imperson-ator performers (Kroeber 1932).

The Hesi society not only celebrated the usual seasonal events, such as first-fruit rites, but also conducted a cycle of dances to animal spirits. The esoteric information that might have clarified the meaning of these song and dance cycles has for the most part not appeared in the anthropological literature. The last members of the secret societies who knew it may have taken it to the grave with them (Loeb 1932, 1933).

The Hill Maidu, instead of the Hesi society, had the Aki society (Loeb 1933); the Valley Konkow word was ʔáˑki (William F. Shipley, personal communication 1976). The northwest Maidu at Chico had both Hesi and Aki cycles. The foothill and valley Nisenan and Maidu had annual mourning ceremonies and no secret ghost societies.

The most sacred Kuksu society dances were Coyote, Condor, and Hawk Dances. Coyote figured in the myths of many peoples as creator, usually one of twin creators, the younger brother of a more remote creator figure. He possessed attributes of intelligence, cleverness, and positive creativity, as well as negative attributes. The Condor and Hawk, as well as other predatory birds, were power symbols, and in the south central valley and in southern California they often were considered as powerful deities. Bean (1975) has pointed out that such members of the animal kingdom are often at the high points in the cosmological order of native Californians.

The Kuksu rites also served as a recruitment process for medicalists, but not uniformly or universally. There was generally more than one kind of medical specialist, at least one of whom was a sucking doctor. The training of doctors was often a function of the secret-society initiation rite; in other instances, sucking or other kinds of doctors received their training solely through individual spiritual experience (Loeb 1932, 1933; Kroeber 1932).

TOLOACHE

The use of narcotic plant materials to facilitate the acquisition of power from sources accessible only in altered states of consciousness is widespread in the Americas. In California, the ritual and ecstatic use of tobacco was almost universal, and even among people who practiced no other agriculture, tobacco was diligently planted and cared for (Kroeber 1925).

Another plant with more dramatic narcotic properties, *datura metaloides*, commonly known as jimsonweed or toloache (from the Nahuatl *toloatzin*, through Spanish), is native to large parts of the Americas. In California, as in parts of Mexico and Central and South America, toloache was used in ritual hallucinogenic and medicinal contexts. Physiologically, any part of the datura plant is toxic as well as vision-producing. It was used with

due safeguards since its use can result in coma or death. Even
when taken in safe dosages, the psychedelic state that results can
be frightening, and those who took it needed to be watched and
guided carefully through the experience. The development of the
uses of this plant for medicinal and psychedelic purposes was a
significant technological achievement (Gayton 1930; Bean 1972;
Kroeber 1925).

A precise delineation of its use in California is difficult,
since societies that use it were no longer fully functioning by the
time ethnographers investigated them. The fullest description of
the datura-based religion designated the toloache cult in the
anthropological literature are for the Yokuts (Gayton 1930),
Luiseño, and Cahuilla (Strong 1929; C. G. Bu Bois 1908a). This is
apparently a very old religion common to the peoples of south-
central and southern California, while the datura plant itself was
known and used (but apparently not in a toloache cult complex) by
peoples as far north as the San Francisco Bay region and thence
eastward into the Sierra Nevada. Among those ethnic nationalities
known to have used datura in religious or medical contexts are the
southern Californians Kumeyaay, Luiseño, Juaneño, Serrano,
Gabrielino, Cupeño, Tübatulabal, and Kitanemuk plus various
other groups (Miwok, Costanoans, Salinan) (Gayton 1930), and,
outside California, the Chemehuevi, Kawaiisu, Quechan, Mohave,
and Cocopa.

Two major religious subsystems developed out of the
toloache cult in coastal California: the Chingichngish religion
among the Luiseño-Juaneño, Gabrielino, and Kumeyaay peoples
and the ʔantap religion among the Chumash (Kroeber 1925;
Blackburn 1974a).

The use of datura was frequently correlated with leadership positions and almost always with professional orientation or
social rank. For example, the Cahuilla páxaʔ, Serrano paxa ʔ, and
Luiseño paxáʔ was an official whose major role was the adminis-
tration of the boys' initiation ceremony. He and the shamans
(whose assumption of shamanic powers was accomplished through
the mediation of datura) were important members of the men's
council that controlled the affairs of the tribe. A young man's
initiation ceremony was held when a number of uninitiated young
men, the accumulated food resources, or the development of
internal social stresses stimulated this ruling group to undertake
the necessary preparations (Strong 1929; Gayton 1930; Kroeber
1925).

Prior to initiation the young men were separated from
their families and taken to a secluded place. After appropriate
purification rites, they were given an infusion of datura root, then

encouraged to dance until falling into an unconscious state. When they awoke, they were in a trance state in which they saw colorful, symbolic, and emotionally meaningful visions under conditions controlled by the *páxa?* and his assistants. During the ensuing weeks the boys were taught clan songs and dances, and at the end of the week a ground painting depicting cosmological concepts was made and explained. The datura drinking was the esoteric part of longer rites, which varied in detail from group to group. Such ceremonies were the core traits of the toloache religion of the Luiseño-Juaneño, Cahuilla, Kumeyaay, Cupeño, and Gabrielino. Among these groups the ceremonies were performed for all boys, while among their northeastern neighbors, the Serrano, only boys of "elite" families were so initiated (Strong 1929).

Toloache was drunk by shamans as part of most of the religious ceremonies in the southern California tribes; it gave access to sources of power needed for healing, divining, diagnosing, dancing, and singing for long periods; for long hunts; for sharper vision; and for sorcery. Shamans in several groups tested their powers during the Eagle Dance by engaging in a contest to see who could kill the sacred eagle by "shooting" it with toloache. In these particular instances the toloache appears to have been personified power (Strong 1929; Harrington 1942).

The Monache and Yokuts who lived in the San Joaquin basin and the southern Sierra foothills took toloache in group rites held in the spring. To take it was an individual decision and its use was not confined to boys and men; women also took it. Before the ritual the participants fasted for 40 days. A professional "pharmacist" prepared the toloache drink and administered it. Those who took it in this rite were also kept dancing until they were unconscious. The visions experienced upon "awakening" gave information about what was causing illnesses or trouble as well as about the location of lost objects and a guide to them (Gayton 1930; Kroeber 1925:504).

These same groups occasionally used datura on an individual basis to assure luck in gambling, to cure certain illnesses, and to attain personal visions (Gayton 1930). In the south the use was more a "part of a ritual which initiated the participants into a ceremonially and politically self-conscious unit" (Gayton 1930:57). The farther away from the southern California center of the toloache religion one went, the less distinct and important the use of datura became. Among the Central Miwok, Gayton (1930) reports that sungazers, a species of ritual participants, engaged in "contests" in which they "shot" each other with toloache, each side seemingly "dying" in turn.

ʔantap

Among the Chumash, toloache use in the protohistorical period centered in the secret society, ʔantap, which takes its name from that of its members. All tribal leaders were ʔantap. This society presided at ceremonies in which the sun, as a male and threatening deity, and the earth and her three aspects (wind, rain, fire) were worshipped (Blackburn 1974a:104). A symbolic association between such powerful deities in whom power was concentrated and the ʔantap who had a monopoly on the sources of power and wealth among the Chumash can be discerned. In fact, a major Chumash deity, a female one, bore the same name as the Chumash word for toloache (Blackburn 1974a), momoy in Ventureño and Ynezeño.

The Chumash had important ceremonials of the world renewal type at harvest time and at the winter solstice, timing them by means of a lunar calendar reset twice a year at the time of the solstices. An astrologerlike official named newborn children, reported problems to the chief, and administered toloache (Blackburn 1974a:104).

Shamans used toloache for mediating with supernatural sources of power in various contests. For example, they were thought to have used charmstones in connection with toloache rites having to do with curing, bringing rain, or assuring success in war or fishing (Grant 1965:66-68). Such rites apparently were also common as far north as the Santa Clara valley and inland among the Yokuts (Blackburn 1974a:100).

The visions of the participants of toloache rites may have been the basis of numerous cave paintings found in the mountains in the Chumash area and in other parts of southern California, but this is not certain. These are abstract works of art probably representing symbolically various supernatural beings in Chumash cosmology as well as the individual dream helpers employed by shamans. They may also have represented the good and evil aspects of power in forms that were in the visual idiom of the people for whom they were painted. The very presence of paintings in sacred sites increased the power inherent in the place (Grant 1965:91-92).

Chingichngish

A second variation on the toloache religious system was the Chingichngish religion, which may have developed from conditions arising from European contact, perhaps a "crisis cult" developed in reaction to European diseases that were decimating Gabrielino and Luiseño groups prior to 1776. Others have theorized that this branch of the toloache religion developed as a result of contact with Christian deserters or castaways, since many of its central features are reminiscent of Christian themes (R. C. White 1963). C. G. Du Bois (1908:76) suggests that Chingichngish "had every requisite of a conquering faith. It had a distinct and difficult rule of life requiring obedience, fasting, and self-sacrifice. It had the sanction of fear . . . It had an imposing and picturesque ritual. And above all it had the seal of inviolable secrecy . . ."

The religion is traditionally supposed to have diffused from Pubunga (near Long Beach) in Gabrielino territory where a shamanlike hero named Chingichngish taught a new body of beliefs that became syncretized with preexisting beliefs and practices. He was assimilated into Luiseño religious literature as creator of the Luiseño and their laws and ceremonials, after he had transformed the people created by *wiyó 't*, the earlier creator, into spirits. He provided a more explicitly moral normative order than had hitherto prevailed and enforced this order by creating a new class of spirits, the "avengers" (rattlesnake, spider, tarantula, bear, sting ray, raven), who were assigned to watch that people obeyed his laws and to punish wrongdoers. Raven had the special assignment of reporting ceremonial mistakes, disobedience of the rules of life, and incorrect revelation of secrets to the god Chingichngish (C. G. Du Bois 1908).

So well were the secrets of the religion kept that the esoteric knowledge of its dogma and ritual have only come to light after acculturation processes have left so few who practice it that these elderly people prefer to leave some record of it rather than let it be completely lost. That it has lasted as long as it has in the face of great odds means that it provides some bulwark against the encroachment of the invading culture complex, thus helping a people to survive. In the 1970s the religion was active at Rincon and Pauma reservations in southern California.

The Chingichngish doctrine is to be found in the songs of the Luiseño sung during their great initiation and annual mourning ceremonies. It has been blended in with rites common to the toloache religion and the traditional Luiseño religion. Its primary center was among the Luiseño-Juaneño, Gabrielino, and Kumeyaay peoples. These peoples have the most extensive recorded repertoire of sacred music and dances of any California peoples, although their not having developed a comparable complexity in ceremonial regalia deluded early anthropologists into an assumption that they had a simpler religious system than existed elsewhere.

POSTCONTACT RELIGIONS

In the south coastal region of California, Roman Catholicism was introduced beginning in 1769. Although some native Californians were Christianized only by force, others apparently accepted the new religion because the Spanish demonstrated possession of kinds of power that appeared desirable. The acceptance of Christianity did not mean that native religious systems disappeared. Native religious ceremonies persisted alongside Catholicism, often tolerated by the priests under the guise of "secular" events, but sometimes carried out secretly. The extreme decrease in native population in the last part of the nineteenth century and the concomitant "melting pot" philosophy on the part of the Anglo-Americans were more destructive to native religious systems than Catholicism. Protestant missions that were permitted to proselytize within Mission as well as non-Mission groups often were the agents of the prevailing pressures toward acculturation, because Protestant missionaries, like the Catholic priests, tended to equate native gods and culture heroes with the devil, but, unlike many of the priests, were intolerant of syncretism. Many aspects of native religions died out because there were no longer ritualists to organize, lead, and participate in them. Their disappearance was often due to death, especially of the elites, loss of native value systems that defined the ceremonial roles as worthwhile, and pressure from non-Indians who denied worth to native beliefs and ceremonies.

To a greater degree than is generally realized, native religious systems persisted, some of them to the present, having been transformed by various degrees to fit a changing socioeconomic system, largely under the direction of native shamans. The first major event signaling a reorientation of native religious systems came to public attention as the Ghost Dance of 1870, a messianic movement originating among the Nevada Paiute, where a prophet announced the end of the world and/or the return of the dead, along with the destruction of all White people and the return of the world to the Indians. The religion spread rapidly in northern California and Oregon, attracting large numbers of native peoples to dances held at ritual centers, often in the semi-subterranean earth-covered dance houses where Kuksu rites had been held. These structures figured for some groups as the means by which natives would be saved during the predicted world holocaust. When the predicted disaster failed to occur, the Ghost Dance died out except in the area where the Kuksu religion had been practiced and among certain adjacent peoples, especially the Miwok and the Nomlaki. Here it survived in the form of a reanimated Kuksu religion in forms compatible with the new social and economic realities. The Ghost Dance demonstrated that by traveling longer distances, a feat made practical by the adoption of the horse as a mode of transportation, native peoples could reestablish some of the underlying structure of their social system through the ritual. The ritual provided spiritual reassurance, contact with the mythic as well as the sacred past, and contacts with one another across the now-weakened intertribelet ethnic boundaries, so that they could make common cause in a troubled time. The Ghost Dance also legitimized the authority of the individual Dreamer, as opposed to the traditional or hereditary leader, and it was this feature that was directly responsible for the innovative offshoots of the Ghost Dance. Group participation was emphasized by incorporating all members of the community more directly into the sacred order--men, women and children (Du Bois 1939; Gayton 1930).

Shortly after 1870, a variation of the Ghost Dance known as the Earth Lodge religion spread from the northern Yana, where it originated, to the Nomlaki, Hill Patwin, Northeastern Pomo, other Pomoans, Wappo, Coast Yuki, Sinkyone, Lake Miwok, Coast Miwok, Cahto, Wintu, Achumawi, Shasta, and various Oregon tribes. As the new ideology traveled, new Dreamers arose who added some embellishments and deleted others. The original doctrine stressed the importance of earth lodges as an escape from world destruction. At least nine large new earth lodges were built at religious centers in the Pomoan area. The "return of the dead" concept was minimized here, whereas in the northernmost parts of the state, the return of the dead was considered a more important purpose of the rituals (Du Bois 1939).

With peoples from various groups assembled in the Pomoan area in expectation of a crisis, and their adjustment to the idea that any individual might have a dream that would bring information from the creator, the stage was set for further innovations. The most lasting innovation was the Dreamer or Bole-Maru religion. The name Bole-Maru was coined by combining two names for the cult, Hill Patwin *bo'le* and Eastern Pomo *ma'rü'* (Du Bois 1939:1), both of which are used to designate the Dreamers who conducted the ceremonies, and apparently originally also the myth or dream that was recited. Two Hill Patwin Dreamers originated this form of the religion, which spread to the Pomoans, southern Hill Patwin, and the Maidu at Chico. It was most elaborate in north-central California where it emphasized traditional dualistic concepts, which were sometimes integrated or compared with the Christian concepts of heaven and hell, God and the devil. Its doctrine forbade drinking, quarreling, stealing, and disbelief. The dance house pole, important as a symbol of the world's center, a path that connected humans with this ultimate source of power, became more important than in the Kuksu religions; its meaning intensified rather than changed. Its decorations changed; cloth in addition to feather pennants was used. Cloth in addition to feathered costumes was also worn, and clamshell jewelry continued to be important. In ritual costume designs new postcontact elements appeared, such as crosses and hearts (Meighan and Riddell 1972), but they are rigorously defended as truly Indian-inspired by today's dreamers. Bole-Maru Dreamers also assumed some of the healing and diagnostic functions of the shamans of older religions, but more significantly they became practical philosophers adapting a new cosmological scheme for the people of this area.

Another innovation was the ball dance, in which participants threw a multicolored cloth ball back and forth, the ball apparently representing among some groups the sacred colors of the universe. Otherwise, most of the Bole-Maru dances were modifications of Kuksu and Hesi ritual dances. A major change from the past was the diminishing importance of secret societies with a concomitant increase in total community (men, women, and children) involvement. As time passed, the end-of-the-world concept faded, and it became customary for the dream function to be concentrated in the hands of dreamer specialists, who took on many of the shamanic roles of traditional times. In the twentieth century, the Bole-Maru is a striking example of a religion that persists in a form adapted to present conditions.

The Ghost Dance of 1890, which originated among the same group as that of 1870, had relatively little effect in California. A number of people vigorously proselytized for it, but most native groups were apparently "immune" to it, some because of the earlier disillusionment, some because the derivative versions (Bole-Maru) of the earlier dance vigorously persisted, some because traditional religions were still relatively intact. It may have been significant that native Californians in 1890 were in comparatively fortunate economic situations and were well articulated with the dominant society while still maintaining their own ethnicity to a considerable degree. Thus there was little need for any form of nativistic movement (Mooney 1896).

In the 1920s, the Shaker Church, a nativistic movement that originated in Washington in the 1870s, spread to northwestern California (Barnett 1957:75-78), particularly among the Hupa, Yurok, Tolowa, and Wiyot. Its doctrine and practices have changed over the years, being derived from varying accommodations reached between Shakers who have individually received power and messages from God, usually during a trance state characterized by body and hand trembling or shaking. The doctrine has features similar to those in Catholic and Protestant

Christianity. These are found in its ritual, regalia, music, and architecture (Barnett 1957).

The major emphasis of the Shaker Church is on faith healing, carried out in homes or in the church. The broad outlines of healing ritual are somewhat institutionalized, being similar to those used by the traditional shamans of the Yurok, Hupa, and Karok. Participants sing and dance to the sound of bells ringing, the bells being "played" as if they were native instruments such as rattles or clapping sticks. Melodic lines are primarily Indian, and the lyrics are a mixture of Christian and native components (Barnett 1957).

Church services are conducted by a minister or by any Shaker, and usually include an exhortation, confessions, and healing. In all church activities the individual has a great deal of individual freedom to innovate within a structured context. These particular characteristics are much like the traditional northwestern California curing techniques and religious practices (Barnett 1957).

Shaker healers conceive of illness as a "pain," as did the traditional shamans of this area, and they use techniques for curing similar to precontact practices. As in the Bole-Maru religion, healing power is used only for the good of others; the negative aspect of power is played down (Barnett 1957). Significantly, these healers function in a context where traditional types of witchcraft still exist, a phenomenon probably still present in all California groups in the 1970s.

Shaker "big doings" at Easter and in August suggest some of the functions of World Renewal ceremonies in that they are thought to involve the restoration of the world to well-being as well as of the individual to health. The Bole-Maru ceremonies are also variations of world renewal and first-fruit rituals, and Bole-Maru believers hold a Strawberry festival in the spring and an Acorn Festival in the fall. Other groups still maintain a variety of traditional dances and fiestas; in southern California funeral and special rites commemorating the dead are performed among most groups. The Inter-tribal Council of California has begun to put on state-wide dance events. In all of these there are echoes of the precontact religious events, including the World Renewal ceremonies of the northwest, the annual mourning services of the southern California peoples, the First Salmon or First Acorn festivals or rites of many smaller "little" traditions, and the great dance cycles of the Kuksu religion. The world is still being renewed for native Californians, and their identities as native peoples are resurgent.

CALIFORNIA INDIAN SHAMANISM AND FOLK CURING

Lowell John Bean

This paper describes the major sociological, and some of the philosophical, features of shamanism among Native Californians before European contact. Since I have elsewhere (Bean 1975) described the philosophical (existential and normative) postulates central to California shamanism and the place of shamans within the broader sociocultural contexts (Bean 1974a), in this essay I will concentrate on the following: (1) the place of the shaman in the cultures of Native California; (2) the varying degrees of medical knowledge; (3) disease causation and sources of curative power-knowledge; (4) varieties of shamanic roles and malevolent uses of power; (5) the shaman as a professional and his acquisition of the status; (6) postcontact reactions to curing and shamanic roles; (7) conclusions.

THE PLACE OF THE SHAMAN

Shamans (better described for Native California as shaman priests) were the principal religious functionaries among California groups, but they were often political administrators (chiefs) simultaneously. The position of shaman has not been fully appreciated in the ethnographic literature of California. It is necessary to see them as the principal philosophers, poets, artists, musicians, intellectuals, scientists, doctors, and psychotherapists because all of these roles were carried by them. They were invariably closely tied, as they still are on some reservations, to all the major sociocultural institutions. Gayton (1930) was the first to demonstrate just how shamans and chiefs worked closely

together in political and economic affairs, and her
observations among the Yokuts hold for most California
groups. Shamans were integral to the political, economic,
legal, moral, and religious institutions of their societies, as well
as central to the aesthetic and healing arts.

Shamans served as mediators between the sacred and
profane worlds. They defined the cosmology of the people
and the nature of the afterworld. Characteristically, they went
in "magical flight" to gain supernatural aid for their people,
learned about the universe so they could aid the soul of the
deceased in their journey to the land of the dead, and received
instructions from the supernatural world on proper life-styles
in the here and now, as well as diagnostic and curative
techniques. Always they served as philosophers for their
people, composing, interpreting, and performing in dramatic
enactments many of the sacred happenings that served as
cosmological guides for their people. The aesthetic development of poetic myth in southern California, the rich ritual
paraphernalia of central California, and the expert use of
native plants for medical cures found throughout California
point to the crucial position of the shaman; they are also some
of the contributions which served to provide people with
avenues of power, enrichment, creative expression, and social
service. In historic times they were the designers of new
philosophical adjustments to the horrors of European contact
(for example, the Bole Maru [Dreamer] Cult). Even now
(1974) they are the focus of cultural identity for young and old
alike, since they serve as culture heroes, culture brokers, and
philosophers in the context of rapid social change.

Where organized cults appeared in California, membership correlated with shamanic status, and women were
generally excluded from access to the role (for example, in
southern California) or reduced, at least formally, to curative
and divinatory functions as men generally attempted to control
and keep exclusive their access to the sacred. In historic times
in certain groups this changed as people became disillusioned
with traditional forms.

The shaman was seen as potentially dangerous, and any
misfortune might be attributed to his malevolency. This
potential was used politically by chiefs and the power elite in
almost all groups, either to tighten social control in their own
societies or to protect people from the aggressiveness of other
groups.

VARYING DEGREES OF MEDICAL KNOWLEDGE

Among all Native California groups there were clearly separate degrees of medical knowledge and practice available to individuals. There was a common folk medicine available to anyone--the treatment of usual maladies by simple techniques of therapy ranging from the use of herbs, sweating, massage, and bed rest to magical forms (for example, in songs and formulas) privately and/or commonly owned. More specialized forms existed, however; they increased in their degree of specialization as shamanic or doctoring roles were more associated with resources of supernatural power and formal education. Consequently, persons analogous to health aides, nurses, and diagnosticians were recognized, as were more advanced specialists whose occupational roles required years of specialized training, often in schools or through membership in secret societies.

These specializations were logically consistent with Native California concepts of how the universe was structured: power was arranged in various degrees. Hence, all social relationships and the acquisition and use of knowledge were similarly arranged hierarchically. All living things, for example, were organized from lower to higher life (and power) forms. Social classes contained elites, ordinary people, and poor people, and power resources were similarly organized. Consequently, differing degrees of power were available and/or explained by the connection an individual or group or species had with the various levels of the supernatural world (Bean 1975).

Common people had residual power inherent to the species of man; thus they had knowledge of common uses of medicinal plants and medical lore. Higher forms of medical practitioners had connections with increasingly higher and more powerful forms of power and thus had more esoteric and specialized knowledge. The possession of this knowledge was protected by institutionalized procedures of schooling and professional rights and privileges.

Disease causation was also placed in a hierarchy, and the cause was treated by the class most competent to deal with it. Since a natural cause was often coterminously explained in relation to supernatural causes, patients would seek knowledge of cause and treatment beginning at the lower levels of power and power possessors and uses and ascend to higher and more specialized forms of diagnosis and treatment if lower-level forms did not adequately solve problems. Thus, from commonly known attempts at curing, they might have gone through increasingly higher levels to diviners, diagnosticians, lower-order shamans, and higher-level shamans. Finally, they reached the most skilled specialists in their society (see chart below).

Disease Causation and Medical Specialists

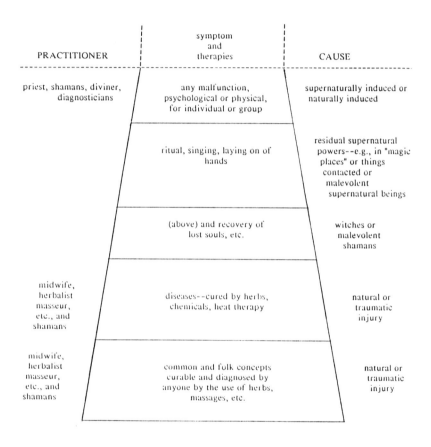

PRACTITIONER	symptom and therapies	CAUSE
priest, shamans, diviner, diagnosticians	any malfunction, psychological or physical, for individual or group	supernaturally induced or naturally induced
	ritual, singing, laying on of hands	residual supernatural powers--e.g., in "magic places" or things contacted or malevolent supernatural beings
	(above) and recovery of lost souls, etc.	witches or malevolent shamans
midwife, herbalist masseur, etc., and shamans	diseases--cured by herbs, chemicals, heat therapy	natural or traumatic injury
midwife, herbalist masseur, etc., and shamans	common and folk concepts curable and diagnosed by anyone by the use of herbs, massages, etc.	natural or traumatic injury

DISEASE CAUSATION AND SOURCES OF
CURATIVE POWER-KNOWLEDGE

Most illnesses and in fact all misfortunes were more likely to be explained ultimately by the absence or presence, use or nonuse, control or lack of control of supernatural forces (power) present in all aspects (persons, objects, intangible forces) of the universe. This power was, according to California Indian cosmology, differentially distributed in both time and space and came from the sacred "dream time" when the universe was created. Through the action of power in the beginning of time, three or more hierarchically ordered worlds were created, each occupied by beings having differing degrees of power. In the upper world lived supernatural beings created at the primordial beginning of the universe. They were beings of very great power who could be utilized by man to control natural circumstances and thus were potential resources for the cause as well as the curing of diseases (Bean 1975).

In the middle world, the natural world in which man resided, all things contained varying amounts of residual power which could act for or against man. In the lower world were a number of other beings (often associated with particularly malevolent power), some of whom man could communicate with for use of their power. They might, however, act independently against man and cause various disasters as well as fortunate circumstances.

It was from the various supernatural power resources in these various worlds that the inspiration and powers of the shamans ultimately derived. The amount of power one received or was able to control determined the nature and degree of curing and the position of the shaman. Shaman-doctors, for example, who were recipients of power from the highest of power resources, were generally considered the most effective doctors, while the lower-level doctors received most of their abilities, and hence world power, from the lesser beings in the middle and lower worlds.

Although ultimate disease causation lay in the realm of supernatural action-forces and most curing forms involved varying degrees of supernatural curing rituals, they were almost always combined with practical medical treatment therapy and posttreatment care. For example, in those cases where there was no apparent natural cause for an illness, herbal remedies were given along with psychic (ritual) therapy, as well as with treatments such as massage, heat, bed rest, surgery, and the like.

The theme which ran through either type of curing, supernatural or natural, was, however, one which stressed the restoration of harmony or balance in nature, in interhuman relationships, (more clearly the case in lineage-structured societies than in bilaterally structured ones). However, because shamans had knowledge of witchcraft, poisoning, and the evil of others, they were in a somewhat dangerous and socially tenuous role. When conditions (medical-behavioral-sociological) became acutely unstable within their community, they were likely to be accused, sometimes placed on trial (where they often confessed and thus relieved the harm they had caused), deprofessionalized by their fellow shamans, or slain.

A lower-level shamanic role, the diviner-diagnostician, found in all Native California societies, was distinguished from that of the shaman on the basis of usability of power. Although these individuals had the power and knowledge to diagnose a disease, discover its cause, and perhaps indicate a cure, they did not have the power or applied skills necessary to proceed with the medical treatment. They were called upon to determine a special course of action, after which a specialist shaman or a lower-order "medicalist" (for example, an herbalist) was called upon to act. These roles were usually reserved for men, but in northern and central California, where power forms were often available to women, persons of either sex might hold this position. The diviner also predicted events and located lost, stolen, or misplaced objects.

In most groups there were those who specialized in the uses of herbs for curative and other nonsacred associated medical procedures (for example, massage, midwifery). These medicalists ranked below other practitioners in status and often assisted other medical practitioners as nurses, acting in postoperative care and carrying out the instructions of higher-order shamans. These roles generally fell to older women who tended to pass the roles on to their daughters. Rarely were these roles filled by men, although many men had considerable medical knowledge and used it situationally in relationship to herbal therapeutics in a nonsacred context. These herbalists, as well as other shamans, charged fees for their services and were usually the first to be called when a family found its home remedies ineffectual.

Rattlesnake Shamans

The most frequently mentioned shamanic specialist in California was the rattlesnake shaman. He controlled rattlesnakes, cured their bites, and protected people from possible snakebite. The rattlesnake was often seen as the symbol of a supernatural "dream time" personage, especially those associated with the underworld of the cosmology. Snakebite was apparently a very common malady in Native California, but the shaman's importance is probably attributable more to the symbolic implications of treatment than to his actual medical functions.

Deer- or Antelope-Shaman

A different type of shaman was associated with animals; the antelope- or deer-shaman usually controlled the large game in his group's territory. Often he had contact with the supernatural guardian of the game. In many groups this role was associated with the ability to transform oneself into another form. This shaman was often an ally of particularly powerful beings (usually masters of the game) and a medical practitioner of considerable skill, as well as a political and economic administrator. Within the category of shamans in the guise of animals, we can place the bear-shaman, a man who could transform himself into a bear in order to utilize the great strength of the bear for various purposes--hunting, traveling rapidly, punishing transgressors of social mores, and so on.

Soul Loss

Since loss of the soul through its capture by supernatural forces, accident, or witchcraft or the like was one of the most common causes of disease and death in Native California, it is to be expected that a class of doctors specializing in soul recovery was recognized. Actually, most shamans were specialists in the care of the soul and in most cultures were likely to have as part of their responsibility the recovery of the soul or the discovery of the circumstances that a soul might encounter following the death of the corporeal body. However, in some groups the soul-loss doctors were specialists whose primary focus of concern was care of the soul. They could send their guardian spirits to restore a soul that had been lost or captured by a malevolent spirit or shaman.

Singing Doctors

Among many groups there was a special type of shaman, the singing doctor. This shaman, usually a male, cured by the power of his songs, obtained from supernatural beings, but was also able to effect cures through the "laying on of hands" and the removal of disease-causing objects. He acquired his original power during visions or dreams by coming into possession of ritual paraphernalia that once belonged to another singing doctor.

MALEVOLENT USE OF POWER AND WITCHCRAFT

Among all groups malevolent uses of power were available not only to legitimate power brokers--shamans and curers--but also to witches or secret poisoners. Invariably, witches were killed if they were discovered and if their executioners had the courage and political power to accomplish the act. Among many groups there was such fear of these persons and perhaps such an awareness of their potential usefulness, that only under extreme circumstances, apparently, did execution actually occur. These executions were usually approved by a chief and other political elites; but among some groups--for example, Yokuts--the poisoner practiced his discipline without fear of punishment if the chief of the group had given his permission for the action.

The methods of poisonings varied, but generally involved the intrusion of poisoned arrow points, a mucous substance, or powdered concoctions made of noxious or poisonous substances. Sometimes sheer power sufficed. Both sympathetic and contagious magics were used; people feared the use of feces, hair, clothing, or the like and the making of images or dolls resembling the intended victim. The ritual usually included the singing of esoteric songs and/or the reciting of formulas which facilitated or generated the magical action.

The disease-producing objects were often placed in a person's house or even in a communal house, where they were directed at an individual. The removal of these objects occupied a considerable amount of the time and attention of the people.

THE SHAMAN AS A PROFESSIONAL
AND HIS ACQUISITION OF THE STATUS

The vast majority of shamans came from families of shamans or were individuals who had been observed by shamans and then, on showing the requisite abilities, had been recruited, trained, and "graduated" into professional practice by other shamans. In either case, a divine call or sign was an early indicator of desire (sometimes ambivalently received) to enter the vocation. Upon receiving this call, the candidate was given a series of tests by supernatural beings, usually while he was in trance states. During these trance experiences, the individual obtained power, ritual, medical knowledge, and a set of rules which guided relationships among the shaman, his sacred helpers, and his future clients. The individual was also tested by fellow shamans, often in a "school" situation. Among many groups secret societies controlled the profession-- recruiting, testing, training, and graduating the young men and women to their professional specialties.

Doctors were guided by the ethical and behavioral rules of their various societies. In those societies having formal schools and/or secret societies, professional recruit- ment, training, and behavior were tightly regulated by established rules of membership and obligations in profession- al activities.

In groups where formal organizations did not exist, professional behavior was controlled informally by shamans who met on regular occasions to compare notes and discuss their activities vis-à-vis one another and their patients.

Doctors were expected to keep secret from the public not only esoteric knowledge, but also much of their practical work. It was important that their public image be enhanced for the good of the profession. This was accomplished by means of extraordinary, extravagant behavior (magicalists), a high standard of living (several wives, better clothing), and specialized clothing and symbols of office (talismans, shamanic costumes, tattoo marks). They behaved like superior persons, often speaking with one another in esoteric languages, which commoners could not understand. They were not supposed to cure members of their immediate families except in the most extreme conditions. Patients were expected to obey the orders (that is, prescriptions: sweating, bed rest, abstention, ingestion of herbal remedies) of doctors, and the doctors were relieved of responsibility for the consequences if these were broken.

Groups varied in their specific rules that defined the doctor-patient relationship, but some general patterns are indicated below:

Doctors were called by patients to treat particular problems. Some doctors received the call supernaturally--that is, they sensed they were needed by particular individuals. Often they dreamed of a specific problem, informed the patient or patients (if it was a group condition), and then offered to provide diagnosis or cure.

Shamans often felt that someone was about to summon them. They were expected to be available to their clients and thus were necessarily specialists, since they were not active in other economic (subsistence) activities.

When a patient called upon a doctor for treatment, a fee was established or the giving of a gift was implied. In most groups, if the doctor was unsuccessful in the cure, he would return all, or at least a portion, of the fee. This was done in part to protect himself from the accusation that he killed or sickened, rather than cured, the patient for monetary reasons and in part because he had failed in his professional assignment. If he could not cure the patient, he might call upon other specialists to help. For that matter, a patient's family might call in two or more doctors simultaneously to provide care. Fees depended on the type of disease, the length and danger to the doctor of the cure, and the rank and economic status of the patient. Usually a shaman attempted to fit his fee to what the market would bear.

Certain life conditions created special medical problems, particularly in the case of warfare. Since warfare in California was frequent (Bean 1974b) and resulted in considerable numbers of traumatic injuries, it was a time of intense activity on the part of doctors. Much like modern medics, Shamans frequently were active on the battlefront, stemming the flow of blood from wounds, removing arrows, providing psychological support to the more seriously wounded. Often they would supervise emergency first-aid operations until the patients could be removed by litter to their home village, where their wounds could receive more detailed attention, both natural attention and the all-important supernatural. Among several groups there were shamans who specialized in removing arrow points, while others would perform the necessary dressings and postoperative care.

POSTCONTACT PERIOD

It is obvious from early mission period reports that European diseases were making serious inroads into Native California population levels well before Europeans arrived en masse. As a result, there was an increased development of cultic beliefs that emphasized a punishing god (for example, the rise of the southern California Chingichngish Cult) and a general outbreak of witchcraft accusations as new, unexplained, and seriously ravaging diseases struck the indigenous peoples. With the arrival of more and more Europeans came new medical procedures that were often more efficacious and more militantly promoted by whites, with the result that many of the medical functions of the traditional doctors were not longer allowed or needed. Suspicion of the efficiency and efficacy of the native doctors by their own people and persecution of native curers by the whites led to some reduction in their status among their own people and in many cases even their death, although a vigorous underground network of native curers continues today.

Various European religious groups (fundamental Protestant, the Shakers) found fertile audiences of people keenly concerned with disease and disease cure. And these religions offered a familiar conceptualization of supernatural curing based upon faith, not an unknown or even unfamiliar concept to most native groups. The difference they allowed was that any member of a cult or religion could receive a spiritual calling, even if for only a short time, and be able to cure with it. Any individual receiving the spirit could become a curer, not just the age-old specialist, the shaman. As these new religious ideas entered California, new concepts replaced old, and the nature of the shaman's relation to the sacred (power sources) changed. In several areas, especially in association with new Indian religious movements (Ghost Dance), the concept of curer changed drastically. A more direct contact with the sacred was allowed to all individuals.

However, it should not be assumed that traditional doctors sat by idly or complacently and allowed themselves to be relegated to oblivion. As the Europeans entered California, they brought with them a new materia medica; and being eclectic and pragmatic in adopting new ideas, California shamans continuously sought to learn these new powers and use them within their medical practices. In fact, the two groups exchanged knowledge of what was useful and comfortably adaptable to each other's cultural pattern.

The more immediate reaction of shamans appears to have been to experiment with old medicines and procedures in treating the new diseases, while at the same time bringing new European medical potentials into the native materia medica. This is a process that still goes on, especially in more recent years, as the number, type, and kind of patent medicines available over the counter have been incorporated into the materia medica of the native curers.

But more important is the fact that the diseases themselves have been redefined into two basic categories: (1) diseases which are the white man's diseases, with their attendant cures; and (2) those which are Indian diseases and have their own proper and efficacious cures and treatments. In addition, native doctors have an edge over their white contemporaries in several ways. They are generally acknowledged to be able to cure diseases which whites cannot or do not often cure or attend to among Indians--for example, cancer, psychic disorders, and alcoholism. Furthermore, Western curative practices have problems that seem insurmountable to some Native Californians: costs, doctors' "negative" attitudes toward patients (that is, impersonal care), inaccessibility to immediate health care, American hospital regimes. Even when facilities and services are available, Native Americans often prefer their own medical treatment. In recent surveys of health conditions and delivery systems among Native Californians, it was discovered that most Indians prefer a doctor who specializes in coming to reservation clinics (a rare occurrence) to those who use off-reservation facilities, even if the degree of care--more medicines, increased technology, immediacy of life-sustaining equipment--is considerably better in such facilities (Bean and Wood 1969).

Moreover, with the increasing concern of the dominant culture about ecological considerations and with what appears to be a renaissance of appreciation for traditional Native American philosophies and life-styles by non-Indians as well as young Native Americans, the status of the native doctor has risen considerably within the past few years. As Myerhoff has pointed out for the Luiseño, the contemporary Indian shaman acts as a culture hero who symbolizes the valuable ethnic background of the Native Californian. He was, and is, the repository of most, if not all, of his people's knowledge of the past, their roots (Myerhoff 1966). But more significantly, shamans still function as the principal creative-active philosophers for their congregation by bridging the oppositions existing between their culture and other cultures. They still cure, direct ritual life, create symbols of ethnicity, draw power from the sacred to the secular world, and act as statesmen advising the secular leaders of Native American peoples.

CONCLUSION

In conclusion I would like to suggest that the term *folk curer* fails to describe the professionalism of medical delivery skills of many medicalists in non-Western societies. The elite medicalists in Native California, and in other areas of this continent, as Vogel (1970) has clearly demonstrated, were in fact highly skilled, well-trained professionals, recognized as such by their own peoples. Thus, the term *folk curer* does not apply universally to non-Western curers. The term should, I think, be used exclusively for those practitioners who operate on the level of "common knowledge and concepts of disease." The fact that there are in most societies medical specialists who have control of medically applicable knowledge, are paid for their services, and are so recognized by their constituents sets them apart from a term such as *folk curer*.

We must also remind ourselves that non-Western medical practitioners do in fact have well-developed medical skills, that they do, despite a symbolic use of "magical" techniques, employ many scientifically validated procedures ranging from surgery, to chemotherapy, to psychiatric skills.

What we know now is but a shadow of what once was. We need more research in the medical functions of Native American peoples. We are still rather ignorant about theories of disease causation as well as curing processes. There is much to be discovered about medical botany, massage, chemotherapy, psychiatric treatment, and the use of drugs among these peoples.

The failure of Western scholars to appreciate and utilize much of this medical knowledge from other cultures surely stems in part from a combination of sources: our own ethnocentrism and cultural arrogance regarding Western medicine is joined with the need of non-Western medicalists (not unlike our own) to keep valuable knowledge secret and limited to an elite class for profit and prestige.

The persecution that non-Western medicalists have received from westerners has further limited our ability to acquire new knowledge, as has the overemphasis of anthropologists and folklorists on the fascinating "magical" conceptualizations of disease and its curing with which most cultures surround their practical methods. Thus, our concern with the esoteric has obscured the scientific contributions of the people we have pretended to understand.

But the situation is changing slowly. Increasingly, medical specialists, anthropologists, and folklorists discover an appreciation of the varieties of medical practice in various cultures. Vigorous debate is beginning. Furthermore, as non-European medicalists become less harassed, as they feel more confident of respectful attention, and as their ethnicity receives greater validation, they will become more open to providing data, so that the exchange of scientific information between cultures will be facilitated.

SHAMANISTIC ASPECTS OF CALIFORNIA ROCK ART

Ken Hedges

There can be little doubt that much of California rock art . . . reflects, directly or indirectly, its creators' concern with hunting luck and the increase of species on which survival depended. But to suggest the derivation of such art solely from the immediate needs of the stomach, as some writers have done, is to perpetuate the myth of "primitive" man as a purely material creature whose intellectual pursuits were focused only or even mainly on sheer biological survival. Anyone who has spent time with such peoples or studied their often highly complex mythology and rich oral literature knows this to be false, or at least simplistic. Certainly no one would deny the primary importance of physical survival. But . . . the goal of the biological and cultural continuity of the society presupposes the delicate interplay and balance of a whole series of material and metaphysical constellations, under the guidance of the shaman. In other words . . . physical survival depends on a multi-dimensional equilibrium of which the shaman is guardian and for whose maintenance he marshals all his gifts.

Not the least of these are special talents of communication, of which artistic expression can be considered the highest level. In contemporary settings the shaman is also often the artist [Furst 1977:12-13].

North American archaeologists often regard rock art as a minor facet of the archaeological record that does not lend itself to the types of analysis applied to more conventional cultural remains like architecture, ceramics, or lithics. Frequently, rock art is seen as a secondary activity that must be associated with some "significant" endeavor such as hunting or agriculture. Seldom is rock art viewed as an activity in itself, nor is it seen as evidence of aboriginal belief in important supernatural forces, the presence of which may dictate the locations where rock art is produced to take advantage of access to unseen powers. In the history of rock art research, there have until recently been few attempts to develop a broad interpretive framework for the study of North American rock art. It is now generally agreed that much of the rock art produced by hunting and gathering peoples is the result of shamanistic activity, including representations of phenomena experienced by shamans in their quest for the spirit world (Hedges 1983, Ritter and Ritter 1977).

In 1958, Baumhoff, Heizer, and Elsasser produced a shamanistic interpretation of the Lagomarsino petroglyphs in Nevada that still stands as one of the best explanations for the enigmatic "abstract" rock art of the Great Basin (Figure 1), relating it to shamanistic practices of Great Basin Shoshoneans who would seek power through dreams at specific power spots, particularly springs and water holes that might be inhabited by the "water babies" from which some shamans got their powers. The authors noted that "the association of the petroglyphs with the permanent spring leads to the proposal that native curing-doctors (shamans) may have been responsible for the rock markings" and that the motivation may have been the acquisition of supernatural powers and the performance of increase rites (Baumhoff, Heizer, and Elsasser 1958:4). In a later version of their paper, the authors replaced this shamanistic interpretation of the rock art with the now-famous hunting magic hypothesis (Heizer and Baumhoff 1962:291).

In 1967, an explicit analysis of the rock paintings of the lower Pecos River, Texas, by Kirkland and Newcomb placed the rock art in the context of a hypothesized shamanistic society: ". . . one can readily imagine that the custom of painting shelter walls in the lower Pecos country may have originated when a shaman emerging from a trance, very possibly induced by mescal beans, attempted to visualize his hallucinations or dreams . . ." (Kirkland and Newcomb 1967:79-80). Recently this interpretation has been expanded in a new study by Shafer (1986) which documents the fact that the Pecos River paintings include splendid representations of such concepts as shamanic flight, animal familiars, visionary imagery, power animals, and a host of other

Figure 1. Petroglyph, Lagomarsino, Nevada. Photo by Ken Hedges.

elements that are perfectly understandable in the light of general shamanistic knowledge.

In 1973, the landmark study of the Peterborough, Ontario, petroglyph site ushered in the era of shamanistic interpretation by using archaeological, ethnographic, and art historical techniques to provide a detailed iconographic interpretation grounded in Algonkian shamanism with reference to shamanism on a world-wide scale (Vastokas and Vastokas 1973). The interpretations are often highly speculative, "but even speculation may provide the general reader with an insight into the problems of rock art research and suggest to the archaeologist new avenues of approach in his efforts to reconstruct the prehistory of North America" (Vastokas and Vastokas 1973:5). The study demonstrates the utility of wide-ranging ethnographic analogy.

DEFINITIONS I: SHAMANISM

Shamanism is the religion of all hunting and gathering cultures, and it forms the basis for many more formalized religions that retain shamanistic elements. The artistic record suggests that the role of shaman has been with us at least since Upper Paleolithic times (Furst 1977:13), and shamanism often can provide the best interpretive framework for an entire corpus of rock art which otherwise resists interpretation.

The core of shamanic practices is the acquisition of supernatural power through the technique of the ecstatic trance, "during which [the shaman's] soul is believed to leave his body and ascend to the sky or descend to the underworld" (Eliade 1964:5). Supernatural power is concentrated in certain places, objects, animals, and individuals. Power can be gained, lost, or manipulated for purposes of good or evil (White 1963:95, 138-139). Since power is derived from the supernatural world, contact with the supernatural world is essential to manipulate and control that power for the common good. The shaman is that individual in a culture who has this ability to enter the supernatural world to gain access to power. Specific duties of the shaman may include divination to foresee future events or find lost objects, curing (Park 1938), weather control, guidance of the soul to the afterlife, overseeing world renewal, and maintaining fertility for human beings, plant and animal food sources, and the world in general.

Altered states of consciousness that characterize the trance experience are basic to shamanistic ritual. The trance state may be induced spontaneously, by sensory or bodily deprivation such as sleeplessness and fasting (the classic vision quest), through techniques of meditation, through intense dancing, by means of rhythmic music, or by the ingestion of hallucinogenic substances.

When the shaman enters his trance, he is transformed. He attains the ability of supernatural flight, and may become a powerful animal or bird and travel to the spirit world. In his mind and in the belief of his people, the transformation is literal. The visual and sensory imagery of the trance state, especially with the use of hallucinogens, is taken as proof that the supernatural world has been attained.

> Dramatically, the experience provides a psychological metaphor of immense proportions- -life, death, creation, rebirth, and transformation . . . it is so impressive, so striking, so dramatic, that in order to communicate its meaning--usually by means of ritual--shamans have had to impro- vise means of communication and thereby have given birth to various art forms. Only these can carry ineffable messages; thus the laymen of a society see and hear realities in a way that enforces social cohesion, reinforces the symbolic represen- tation of their world, and promotes the mental health of the community at large . . . [Bean and Vane 1978b:124].

Features of Native American culture and rock art can be seen as shamanistic without limiting the discussion to practices involving a shaman *per se*. For example, in southern California, young men could achieve altered states of consciousness and obtain a guardian spirit in ritual that allowed some degree of participation in shamanistic activities for all initiates (Kroeber 1925:668-669).

SHAMANISTIC THEMES IN ROCK ART

The best source of data is direct ethnographic information on specific sites. Such information is extremely rare. For the Painted Rock site on the Tule River Indian Reservation, the Wukchumne Yokuts said that " . . . the paintings were generally placed at an important village site, one which was permanently inhabited or at some place where Indian ceremonies were per- formed . . . The Wukchumne stated that such places were Trip-ne (supernatural)" (Latta 1949:179-180). An unpublished historic reference (cited in Hedges 1970:150) to the site of Wikwip in San Diego County tells us that this cave was used by the men to prepare themselves for dances. The ceremonial dancers of the Kumeyaay were shamans. A site near San Jose de Tecate in Baja California is reported to have been the site of ceremonies having to do with the coyote. The original Indian source of this information is no longer living, so the data cannot be further checked. Figures at the site exhibit horns, an important feature in interpretation of the site.

Peter Furst notes that "the great antiquity as well as near-universality of the horn as the symbol of sacred, supernatural or priestly power are well documented" (Furst 1965:47). Horns are "symbols of supernatural power . . . without implying the use to which such power is put" (Furst 1965:72). Among the Huichol, horns represent sacred shamanic power, the "power to speak to the sun and to the other gods" (Furst 1965:53). The Coso Range in Inyo County provides examples of figures with horns or other projections from the head (Figure 2). In some instances, the horns take the form of projectile points (Grant, Baird, and Pringle 1968:37).

Figures with horns and rays coming from the head occur frequently in Tulare rock art of the southern Sierra Nevada foothills, and horned figures are found in Chumash rock art.

Horned figures are rare in Kumeyaay rock paintings. Such figures are known from only two sites, both in northernmost Baja California. The San Jose de Tecate site, a known ceremonial site, has several horned figures, including a figure nearly six feet tall, the largest painted figure recorded in Kumeyaay rock art. At La Rumorosa, one finely painted figure in red bears wavy lines projecting upward from the head (Figure 3). In addition to the wavy lines, this figure has the extremely rare feature of painted eyes, added in black. This figure with its eyes looks at the rising sun at winter solstice through the mechanism of a dagger of light formed by the rising sun. Here the ritual figure has been painted to take advantage of a natural phenomenon revealed only at a sacred time of the year (Hedges 1986). A petroglyph site at Cañon Palmas de Cantu, northern Baja California, exhibits an anthropomorphic figure with wavy lines coming from the head, connecting it with an elaborate flower-like motif (Hedges 1976:132).

Supernatural power is derived from sacred animals and objects, and one widespread source of power is the feline. In classic Eurasian shamanism, the most powerful of the shaman's helping spirits are the spotted panther and the striped tiger (Vastokas 1977:99). For the New World, ". . . the most widespread animal equivalent of shamans in the New World tropics is the Jaguar . . ." (Furst 1977:16).

Of the felines in Panther cave on the Pecos River in Texas, Newcomb says,

Figure 2. Patterned-body anthropomorph with projections from the head, Renegade Canyon, Coso Range, Inyo County, California. Photo by Ken Hedges.

Figure 3. Horned anthropomorph, the "Watcher of the Winter Sun," La Rumorosa, Baja California. Photo by Ken Hedges.

But a hunting-cult hypothesis fails to explain the
presence of cougars in the pictographs, or the fact
that a majority of shamans in all periods do not
have animal associations.   Again,   the
shamanistic-society hypothesis explains these facts.
Cougars . . . are never pierced by darts nor do they
seem to menace human figures. This suggests that
some shamans, or perhaps members of a "cougar
society" received power from this animal.
Drugged perhaps by mescal beans, shamans or
potential shamans may have received supernatural
assistance from these beasts or their mythological
counterparts (Kirkland and Newcomb 1967:79].

This interpretation of feline figures is echoed in the
pervasive animal fetishism of the Southwest.   At Zuni, the
mountain lion is master of the gods of prey, and his fetish is
preferred by hunters (Cushing 1883:31). Zuni art also illustrate a
point of iconography: the mountain lion is usually distinguished
by his tail, long and extending outward or curving back toward
the head. The mountain lion at Petrified Forest, Arizona, is one
of the best known petroglyphs in the Southwest. Other forms are
found throughout the greater Southwest.

The range of mountain lion figures in rock art extends
westward into California, and thence south into Baja California.
In the Coso Range petroglyphs in Inyo county, some mountain
lions are very catlike, while others are rendered more schematical-
ly, retaining the upturned tails. In the Tulare region, a mountain
lion in black and white appears among the Yokuts paintings at
Rocky Hill.

Painted Rock, on the Tule River Indian Reservation, has
a large quadruped painted on the ceiling of the rock shelter, of
which Latta has written, "Sok-so-uh is the name of a bad,
supernatural spirit, and was applied to the large figure on the
ceiling of the Painted Rock . . . This painting resembles the
stretched skin of a mountain lion holding the sun in its mouth."
More recently, Hudson and Underhay liken this figure to Sky
Coyote is his yearly competition with Sun for control of the
coming year; indeed, with his narrow snout and prominent cheek
pouches, the figure looks like Coyote.

In southern California, Bean and Saubel (1972:61) write
that, "for the Cahuilla shaman, datura offered not only a means to
transcend reality and come into contact with specific guardian
spirits, but it also enabled him to go on magical flights to other
worlds or transform himself into other life forms such as the
mountain lion or eagle." For the Kumeyaay, Toffelmier and

Luomala (1936:198) recorded data from a shaman who saw a mountain lion in his datura vision and had that animal as his guardian spirit.

Kumeyaay rock art provides few examples of felines. If we consider, however, that this animal may be depicted not only in profile, as in the examples noted above, but also spread out as suggested for the stretched-skin figure of Painted Rock, then a figure at Las Pilitas in northern Baja California is plausibly interpreted as a mountain lion (Hedges 1975:124). Close by, the site at Valle Seco includes the unique miniature representation of an apparent bobcat--note the feline head, short tail, and round ball feet--ridden by a man.

DEFINITIONS II: PHOSPHENES AND HALLUCINATIONS

Altered states of consciousness that characterize the ecstatic trance may include fantastic visionary images that are taken as proof that the individual has entered a separate world and a different reality (Bean and Saubel 1972:62). The term "phosphene" refers, in a general way, to the images perceived by the human brain as visual images in the absence of visual stimuli. Such perceptions may originate anywhere in the visual pathway from the eye to the brain. Phosphenes, even those produced by simple pressure on the eyes, can consist of relatively simple design elements or of rather elaborate patterns. With the addition of factors such as fatigue, trauma, disease, sensory deprivation, self-induced trance, or hallucinogenic substances, the images can take on fantastic elaborations of form, animation, color, and detail, with the inclusion of landscapes, objects, and familiar places and people, all imbued with transcendental luminosity (Oster 1970; Siegel 1977:132-133; Walker 1981; see also papers in Siegel and Jarvik 1975 for aspects of hallucinatory phenomena). Simple phosphenes and true hallucinations represent the two extremes of a continuum of visual percepts. In the early 1960s, Max Knoll and his colleagues identified a number of basic visual patterns which recur in electrically induced phosphenes. Controlled small doses of hallucinogens produced elaborations and combinations of phosphenes, with the significant additional finding that subjects produced much better artistic renderings of their experiences when recalling the event at a later time, as opposed to crude and sketchy drawings made while under the influence of the hallucinogen (Knoll et al. 1963).

Oster (1970:83-86) defines phosphenes as "subjective images resulting from the self illumination . . . of the visual sense," characterized by patterns that "must be intimately related to the

geometry of the eye, the visual pathway and the visual cortex."
Oster was one of the first to point out the similarity between
phosphene patterns and prehistoric art. He classifies as phosphenes the geometric images of early stages of hallucinations and
images resulting from causes such as fatigue, sensory deprivation,
migraines, and other medical disorders.

Migraine studies provide a complementary source of useful
data. The classic fortification pattern associated with migraine is
a scintillating zigzag arc bordering a scotoma that blocks a portion
of the field of vision (Richards 1971). Less commonly, a crenelate
"fortification pattern" resembling the top of a medieval castle wall
is reported (Oster 1970). Both types of image are commonly
represented in North American rock art and in other forms of
shamanic art (Figure 4; cf. Reichel-Dolmatoff 1978:33, 50, 55;
Davidson 1985:17).

In the 1920s, Heinrich Klüver defined the form constants
which characterized the visions of his subjects. "If we ignore the
colors and movements as well as the 'meaning' with which the
phenomena are invested by the subject, the geometric-ornamental
structure of the hallucinations becomes apparent" (Klüver
1966:67). The major categories of form constants are "a) grating,
lattice, fretwork, filigree, honeycomb, or chessboard; b) cobweb;
c) tunnel, funnel, alley, cone, or vessel; d) spiral" (Klüver
1966:66). While it appears that the concept of form constant is
intended to describe the underlying form of the hallucination
itself, the statement that "the forms are frequently repeated,
combined, or elaborated into ornamental designs and mosaics of
various kinds" (Klüver 1966:66) allows use of the term on the
design element level as well.

Siegel and Jarvik (1975:125-132) report that hallucinogens
produce marked increases in lattice, tunnel, and kaleidoscope
images. Later stages of hallucination are marked by complex
imagery involving scenes, persons, and places, often combined
with or overlaid by geometric forms and form constants. The
importance of hallucinatory trance states and their role in
shamanism have been well summarized by Noll (1985) and
Winkleman (1986).

In rock art research, we deal with images as they appear
painted or carved on the rock surface. Thus I am concerned not
with descriptions of the actual structure and appearance of
phosphenes and hallucinatory imagery, but with the ways in which
they are represented on two-dimensional surfaces by human
subjects. Comparisons with visual data available in the medical
and psychological literature and in ethnographically documented
aboriginal arts enable the development of an interpretive frame

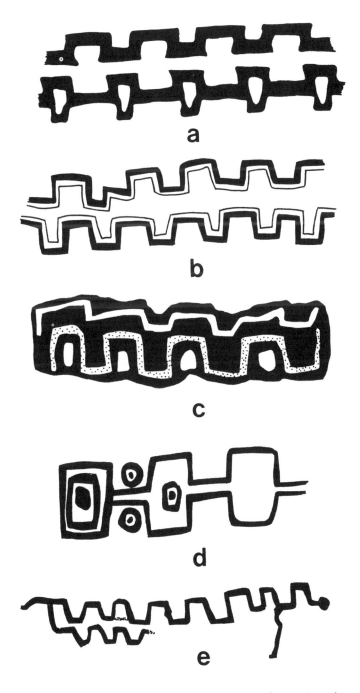

Figure 4. Crenelated fortification patterns in rock art: a) phosphene (Oster 1970:82), b) Tukano shamanic art (Reichel-Dolmatoff 1978: Plate IV), c) rock painting, Montevideo, Baja California (Hedges), d) petroglyph, South Mountain, Arizona (original oriented vertically; Hedges), e) petroglyph, Grapevine Canyon, Nevada (Hedges).

work for the analysis of rock art in North America and elsewhere. Phosphenes are here defined as images interpreted by the brain as visual imagery in the absence of visual stimuli. Form constants are the classes of redundant visual imagery that form the baseline for comparison with aboriginal arts of unknown origin and function. We are particularly concerned with phosphenes and more involved hallucinations associated with altered states of consciousness perceived as trances and visions in traditional shamanistic contexts. Available sources document a perceptual continuum from basic simple phosphenes to fully developed trance imagery.

APPLICATIONS: PHOSPHENES

Basic phosphene patterns tend to recur, as shown by the categories of form constants documented by Klüver (1966) and Siegel and Jarvik (1975). Kellogg, Knoll, and Kugler (1965:1129) isolate 15 elemental forms that provide a corpus of design elements for comparison (Figure 5). The entire range of altered perceptions is marked by a universe of basic forms that underlies such cultural aspects of art as element selection, style, and meaning.

The challenge lies in identifying phosphenes and hallucinatory images as sources of visual imagery (Hedges 1982). Phosphene patterns closely resemble design elements in various kinds of aboriginal art (Oster 1970:83, 87), and it has been pointed out (Blackburn 1977, Wellmann 1978, Lee 1979) that a similar correspondence exists between basic phosphene patterns and Chumash rock art. This observation is supported by detailed comparisons conducted among the Tukano Indians in Colombia, where design elements in ritual art of hallucinatory origin show a close correlation with basic phosphene patterns (Reichel-Dolmatoff 1978:15-34). Similar studies among the Jivaro and other South American cultures have shown that "it is apparent that the powerful images of the visionary experience have exerted a profound influence on ceramic iconography" (Davidson 1985). Jivaro bowls bear classic phosphene patterns, particularly fortification patterns resembling those reported by migraine sufferers.

In South Africa, Lewis-Williams (1985:56-58) documents the presence of geometric forms that he interprets as phosphene imagery in San Bushman rock art and describes the hallucinatory aspects of rock art compositions that combine phosphenes with iconic images of men and animals (Lewis-Williams 1986:173-174). The fact that geometric form constants are combined with the imagery of hallucination simply demonstrates the perceptual

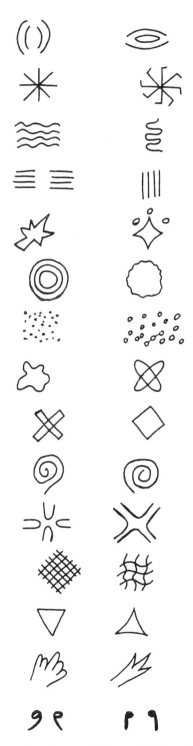

Figure 5. Basic Phosphene designs (Kellogg, Knoll, and Kügler 1965:1129).

continuum that has been noted in both medical and ethnographic contexts. However satisfying it may be intellectually, it matters little if we understand the difference between phosphene form constants and true hallucinations when we are dealing with their perception and interpretations by aboriginal cultures that do not have the analytical advantage of modern scientific knowledge.

Examples of the basic phosphene elements can be drawn at will from rock art. The elementary nature of these elements reveals a basic human trait that manifests itself in similar ways throughout time and space. This observation still provides one of the primary objections to the "phosphene theories" of rock art interpretation: "It also appears that the theory cannot fail simply because there are very few basic shapes that one can draw, whether they come from the mind's eye, hallucinations, or idle doodling . . ." (Bahn 1988:217). This objection begs the question of *why* we draw these basic shapes. The question has been approached from a variety of viewpoints, including analysis of the basic scribblings and first drawings of children. These designs may result from the activation of pre-formed neurone networks in the visual system (Kellogg, Knoll, and Kugler 1965), a hypothesis that suggests children, when they first learn to draw, begin by drawing their own phosphenes. Further support is provided by Anderson's (1975) note that visual pattern preferences reported in studies of newborn children show a "patent relationship" with basic phosphene patterns, including the checkerboards reported as the initial pressure phosphene in many adult subjects (Oster 1970, Tyler 1978, Walker 1981). The implication here is that fetal phosphenes, possibly produced by intrauterine pressure, may provide visual experience before birth. Phosphenes thus can be seen as the basic background of visual patterning that all of us experience on both conscious and subconscious levels.

Explanation in terms of phosphenes and hallucinatory imagery provides an economical interpretation of design element combinations and modes of representation that are not easily explained by other means. In their study of 439 design elements at Lagomarsino, Nevada, Heizer and Baumhoff (1962:293-308) identify 21 definite representational elements, 27 questionable to doubtful elements, and 391 elements that could not be "identified." It is clear from inspection of their data that many *combinations* of design elements were omitted from analysis, and many panels were not recorded. Since their study does not individually identify the elements tabulated, it is impossible to do a direct comparison, but virtually all of their illustrations include at least one basic form constant each, many designs are classic form constants, and nearly all of the designs can be matched in documented examples of hallucinatory imagery. The same can be said for such desert petroglyph sites as the Coso Range, McCoy Spring, Corn Spring, and many others.

Steward (1963:975) suggests an approach to Great Basin Petroglyph studies: "Individual Shoshoneans had dreamed powers, many of which pertained to hunting. If hunters depicted their own supernatural powers at the sites of kills, the wide diversity of element combinations within generalized styles might be expected." Similar explanations apply equally well not only to the so-called "abstract" petroglyph traditions of the American west, but also to rock art in other archaic contexts such as the deserts of Chile (Ballereau, Niemeyer, and Pizarro 1986), where we may infer a similar shamanistic basis for religion and art.

Attributes of hallucinatory images inform our interpretations of rock art. An instructive example is found in an elaborate Huichol yarn painting (Schultes and Hoffman 1979:63) that exhibits classic characteristics of visionary art: a large number of recurring form constants and element combinations, multiple color outlines and implied movement, and the combination of iconic and non-iconic elements. A number of close comparisons can be drawn from Chumash rock art at Painted Rock in California (Grant 1965:Plate 4, 96-97). Before its destruction by natural forces and vandalism, this panel exhibited many of the same characteristics.

In California, Kroeber (1925:938) pointed out that the polychrome painted styles of the Yokuts and Chumash groups coincided with the area of intensive use of *toloache (Datura meteloides)* in shamanistic rituals. To these may be added the southern California groups, especially Luiseño and Kumeyaay (Figure 6). Other authors (Blackburn 1977, Wellmann 1978, Lee 1979) have elaborated upon this theme, and the rock art of these cultures provides prime examples of parallels between the aboriginal art and known characteristics of hallucinatory imagery. Precise ethnographic data have not come to light, however, although the evidence for associating this rock art with datura use is very persuasive. The Yokuts data provide an intriguing example in which visionary imagery covers the interior of a small rock-shelter having just enough room inside for one person to recline. In this example, we have the very real possibility that the artist could return to the rock and re-enter his vision. Chumash rock art is particularly rich in phosphene imagery and examples of what appear to be full-fledged visions. In some instances Chumash designs are outlined with white dots that duplicate a characteristic of datura visions. Chumash and Yokuts rock art are only two of the many styles in which the art meets all of the basic requirements that would enable us to describe it as visionary imagery. No other reasonable interpretation has been offered.

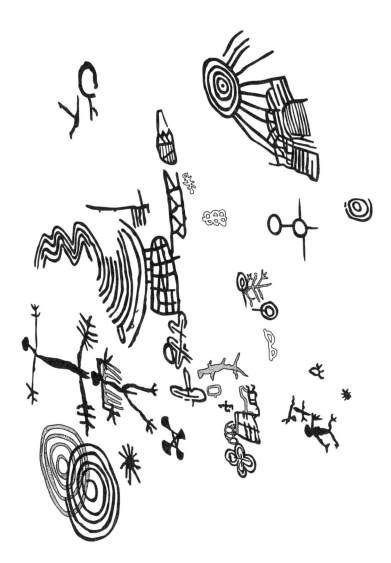

Figure 6. Kumeyaay rock paintings, Las Pilitas, Baja California. Sketch by Ken Hedges.

APPLICATIONS: SPIRIT BEINGS

Several categories of shamanic spirit beings can be identified, beginning with the shaman himself. The shaman may have one or many familiar or helping spirits which, because they frequently take animal form, often are categorized as "animal familiars." A second class includes the tutelary or guardian spirits, often construed as the shaman's alter ego or soul in animal form, which confers on the shaman the ability to transform himself, to become the form that represents the guardian spirit. The third class comprises the divine or semidivine beings invoked by the shaman (Eliade 1964:88-95).

Archaeological and ethnographic arts provide examples of shamanistic motifs illustrating these concepts, and it is not difficult to find analogues of the motifs we find in rock art. The seminal volume edited by Brodzky, Danesewich, and Johnson (1977) provides many examples of shamanistic arts and serves as a useful introduction to the subject. Blodgett (1978) provides an overview of Arctic shamanism with an extensive collection of prehistoric, early historic, and contemporary Eskimo art which illustrates shamanistic concepts, including a particularly vivid depiction of an Eskimo shaman, complete with animal characteristics and horns of power, surrounded by his helping spirits (Blodgett 1978:21). A figure from Big Petroglyph canyon is similarly surrounded by lizards, snake, and bighorn sheep.

Aboriginal artists share long-established traditions which include many verbal and visual representations of individuals undergoing shamanic transformation. The concept is nearly always the same: the shaman passes through stages in his metamorphosis during which he exhibits both human and animal traits, or combinations of human with utterly fantastic characteristics. A fully transformed shaman may retain human features, combined with animal or hallucinogenic images. The metaphor of transformation is supported by research on hallucinogens. Siegel and Jarvik (1975:105-105) quote a particularly vivid example:

> I thought of a fox, and instantly I was transformed into that animal. I could distinctly feel myself a fox, could see my long ears and bushy tail . . . my complete anatomy was that of a fox. Suddenly, the point of vision changed. My eyes seemed to be located at the back of my mouth. I looked out between the parted lips, saw the two rows of teeth . . .

Spirit beings reside on the cliff faces throughout the American West. Little beings, like the dwarves and "water babies" who dwell in myth and legend all around the world, appear in Yokuts rock art of central California--appearing to lead us into the fascinating world of Yokuts rock painting. At Keremeos creek in British Columbia, a guardian spirit watches over an ancient village site. In Barrier Canyon, Utah, giant mummy-like figures without limbs float in space above the mortals who painted them there. Similar images, lacking arms or legs, appear in a wide variety of rock art styles. A figure from the Colorado desert terminates in a wavy line instead of legs (Figure 7), while spirit beings with no legs to stand upon float through the rock art sites.

Lewis-Williams (1986:174) writes of images that combine phosphene elements with anthropomorphic forms, which he interprets as the shaman's identification with his own hallucinations--"In the end, they are what they see and what they feel." This interpretation is supported by self portraits of !Kung Bushman shamans who portray themselves as phosphene-like images which appear to represent their boiling supernatural potency (Katz 1982, cited by Lewis-Williams 1986:174). In a later discussion, Lewis-Williams and Dowson (1988:211) refer to a citation by Klüver (1966:24) which provides the link to hallucinatory experience in the form of a subject who reports, ". . . one of my legs assumes spiral form." A further case cited by Klüver (1966:24) provides an analogue to the truncated, legless figures that are found so frequently in North American rock art: "Before me I see the lower part of my body from the hip down as a large green varnished object which has about the shape of a truncated cone with spiral windings." Since spirit beings are not subject to physical constraints, there is no reason they should have legs, but these examples show that figures thus portrayed may derive not from abstract concepts of what a spirit being should look like, but rather from spirit beings that have actually been seen in the trance state.

Patterned body anthropomorphs are present in many rock art styles, often with patterns of basic form constants, either alone or in combinations. The body pattern of an anthropomorph from Renegade canyon (Figure 8) closely resembles a phosphene pattern of combined and superimposed checkerboards and arrays of triangles (Walker 1981:176). Many other Coso Range anthropomorphs have body patterns of familiar form constants: parallel lines, dot patterns, grids, lozenges, concentric circles, wavy and zigzag lines. Patterned body anthropomorphs in other contexts show similar characteristics. Anthropomorphs in Utah's Barrier Canyon style incorporate not only elaborations on the basic patterns, but also serpents, quadrupeds, or small anthropomorphs

Figure 7. Legless anthropomorph, McCoy Springs, Riverside County, California. Sketch by Ken Hedges.

Figure 8. Phosphene pattern (Walker 1981:176) compared to patterned-body anthropomorph from Renegade Canyon, Coso Range, Inyo County, California. Sketch by Ken Hedges.

(Wellmann 1979:Figures 573-577), suggesting concepts of shamanic alter egos or familiar spirits residing within the shaman. A
similar interpretation might be offered for enigmatic patterned
anthropomorphs of central Wyoming. Figures from Dinwoody and
Trail Lake exhibit wavy lines, circles, and dot patterns characteristic of visionary images, and note once again the companion
dwarf figure.

Body patterns derived from visionary imagery are found
in ethnographic examples. Deities and spirit beings in Huichol
yarn paintings, such as the image of the Mother of Maize, are
drawn with the characteristic fill patterns of this art: enclosed
geometric motifs, often incorporating sawtooth or zigzag lines,
done in multiple color outline (Furst 1969:18). From the Tukano
come two images of the deity Pamurí-mahsë decorated with trance
images. These images have specific meanings on several levels.
The body motif represents images seen during trance, interpreted
as the design of a gourd rattle and, by extension, the gourd rattle
itself, with the deeper meaning of a ritual or the sound of a ritual
(Reichel-Dolmatoff 1978:32, 64-65).

If we interpret the body patterns as representations of
supernatural power manifested in visions of the spirit world, then
the figures might be anthropomorphizations of that power as
embodied in deities, spirit beings, or the shamans who control
power. Moreover, the combination of anthropomorphic figures
with geometric motifs can be explained by direct reference to
hallucinations: "The subject stated that he saw fretwork before his
eyes, that his arms, hands, and fingers turned into fretwork and
that he became identical with fretwork. There was no difference
between the fretwork and himself . . ." (Klüver 1966:71-72). In
a restricted section of Big Petroglyph canyon in the Coso Range is
a collection of patterned body anthropomorphs and related designs
(Hedges 1987:21-22). Here we find a pattern of rows of dots and
variations of this pattern within an outline or with appended
limbs, hands, or a head, and finally a complete figure with the
pattern contained in the body outline. Since none of the other
figures in these panels appears incomplete, there is no reason to
assume that these images are unfinished. The dot pattern is
consistent throughout, with other features of the anthropomorphs
playing optional roles. This is a figure of which it may be said,
"He became identical with dot pattern."

IMPLICATIONS

This analysis of the derivation of rock art imagery from
phosphenes and hallucinatory imagery is first of all an exercise in

finding the sources of the images we see in rock art. As Lewis--Williams (1982:446) has pointed out, for southern San rock art a great deal can be said about *meaning* while *motivations* for the paintings remain obscure. However, he has the luxury of San ethnography to help provide the meaning. A more basic level of interpretation lies with the *sources* of the imagery. For the present, it is possible to develop a generalized but comprehensive model to account for much of the puzzling content of rock art. As we incorporate data from ethnographies of cultures which practice comparable arts, a better model of meaning will gradually emerge.

The importance of what Bednarik (1986) calls the "Phosphene Theory" in the development of image-making and art has yet to be adequately explored, but theories of the mental origins of art need not conflict with other hypotheses: after all, the symbols had to come from somewhere. Whether they came from trance-induced phosphenes is difficult to tell, but there is sufficient evidence to argue that they come from mental imagery, even if we make no recourse to shamanism and trance states. We may feel the need to invoke trance states to explain the enhancement of phosphene imagery; however, just as those of us who live in cities no longer can see the stars, I would suggest that modern man fails to see much of the mental imagery that might otherwise be available. Children, for example, are comfortable with phosphene imagery and tend to express it more clearly than adults: "Phosphenes may indeed be an important part of the child's environment, since he may not readily distinguish this internal phenomenon from those of the external world" (Oster 1970:83). In a traditional hunting and gathering context, mental imagery would not be suppressed or filtered out. The rigors of a hunting and gathering existence might naturally produce phosphene experiences, and the trance state would serve to control and intensify the experience rather than cause it to happen in the first place.

Art styles continually evolve, and it is not always possible to distinguish primary visionary art from art styles derived from such a source. Reichel-Dolmatoff (1978) perceived the presence of phosphenes in a well established art style with standardized motifs having meaning on several different levels. It was only after this revelation that he was able to communicate with the Tukano on a level that allowed him to elicit drawings of primary visions. In like manner, the recognition of phosphene imagery in Huichol decorative art played a role in the development of yarn paintings that depict actual visions. In the Native American Church, peyote fans and rattles carry beaded designs based on brilliant peyote visions. Our knowledge of these documented cases allows us to begin the long process of defining characteristics of visionary imagery which will serve us in illuminating the meaning of rock art.

CONCLUSION

Much of what has been poorly understood in rock art can be better interpreted in the context of shamanism and visionary images. Most rock art is representational--we simply have to determine what it is that is being represented. Studies in the context of shamanism can provide many insights into the sources of rock art images, and bring us a little closer to an understanding of their meanings.

Shamanism is the basic religion of mankind. Evidence of shamanism is found not only in rock art, but in all the arts of hunting and gathering cultures throughout space and time, and in the art and religious practices of many cultures--including our own--that may be far removed from their hunting origins. The shaman enters a separate reality when he undergoes transformation in the trance state. In rock art we have images from that separate reality that we are only beginning to understand.

THE SHAMAN: PRIEST, DOCTOR, SCIENTIST
Florence Shipek

INTRODUCTION

The Dominican missionary among the Southern Kumeyaay, Fr. Luis Sales, railed against a group of men whom he was sure represented evil. He called them evil old men who deceived the Indians into believing that they could heal illness, protect them from harm, and had control of food resources, such as plants, animals, and fish, as well as the oceans and weather, that these powers had been given to certain men at creation and each passed the power to a descendant. Further, Sales describes them as using "absurd movements" and "strange cavortings" to control food sources, manage funerals and pretense to cure illness, and control the elements. Fr. Sales did everything in his power to disprove the claims of these men whom he termed evil, but to no avail (Rudkin 1956: 38-42). The Indian people still fed these old men, whom he says were called "*cusiyaes* or *quamas*". (*Kuseyaay* is the Kumeyaay term for shaman.) Yet, in the same report, Sales (Rudkin 1956: 52-62) commented on the curing efficacy of the herbs used by these men, even though they did not "use blood-letting or other drastic remedies," but "foolish" hand motions and "sucking". Sales then stated that the Spanish would do well to study the medicinal properties of the plants used by these people for healing purposes.

Among the Luiseño-Juaneño, the Franciscan Missionary, Fr. Geronimo Boscana (1933:29-30, 34; Harrington 1934), described in much more detail the belief that in the beginning certain men (*pul*, singular, *puplem* plural) were given the power to control and increase all foods, manage natural forces and to heal sickness. They were instructed that each *pul* should pass his power to only one descendant. Boscana points out that each man controlled one source of food, or one aspect of natural forces, such as rain or wind, or understood the movements of the moon and stars. Boscana wrote that each kept secret his particular knowledge and maintained the crop by ritual and used a special language unknown to the general populace. The "puplem" maintained all knowledge in ritual song and dance. Boscana also states that the general populace paid each "pul" for advice concerning their crops.

In addition to the rituals themselves, the ritual leaders needed knowledge of the phases of the moon (Rudkin 1956:42; Boscana 1933:65). Ethnographic observations among both groups reveal that rituals were timed by the rising and setting of stars and their position in the sky, and that the yearly calendar was based on the moon. Because life crisis rituals may occur throughout the year, star movements throughout the year must be known. Other rituals were timed in relation to the solstices and equinoxes, thus each village had a *Kuseyaay* who was a "sunwatcher" according to Kumeyaay elders. Boscana (1933:65) also noted solstice observations among the Luiseño and that their year began with the winter solstice.

On the basis of both Spanish records and later ethnographic data (Du Bois 1908; Kroeber 1925; Sparkman 1908; Waterman 1910; Shipek 1977, 1989), the shamans may be sorted into three types which match similar categories in the dominant western culture: priests, scientists and doctors.

PRIESTS

The priestly class were those primarily recorded in the early anthropological literature describing the religion and life crises ceremonies of the Luiseño and Kumeyaay (Diegueño-Kamia or Ipai-Tipai). The priests officiated and managed participation in the rituals relating to life crises ceremonies, such as naming ceremony, puberty initiation, marriage, purifications, death and memorial ceremonies. The solstice and equinox ceremonial leaders also belonged to this class, as did the singers and dancers who performed the rituals, under the direction of the leaders. Bean (1972) found the same types of ritual leaders among the Cahuilla, a neighboring tribe. Boscana stated that the *puplem* and the *noot* (Luiseño captain or band chief) spoke a separate language among themselves, and that all rituals were held in this different language not understandable to the general populace.

Interestingly, these practices have major points of correspondence with the Catholic ritual as practiced in Europe and America until recently. Catholic rituals and ceremonies were performed in Latin, an old language--the original common speech of Rome that controlled the empire during the early spread of Catholicism through Europe. Over time, while the priestly class maintained all learning, writing, reading, and church rituals in Latin, the common people of Europe increasingly spoke the diverse vernacular languages of their own countries. Even the church music, or hymns, were in Latin. Commoners obeyed the priests, but did not understand the ceremonies or prayers beyond doing what they were supposed to do, and making the appropriate responses at the proper times. All knowledge and learning was maintained by the church and the priestly class until after the beginning of the Renaissance and the Protestant reformation in Europe.

SCIENTISTS

The scientists were the *kuseyaay* and *puplem* who specialized in knowledge about the plant and animal foods, and natural phenomena. Each office holder had slowly learned from, and been tested repeatedly during training by, his predecessor in the office. All the existing knowledge about any one food or phenomenon had to be learned perfectly, and was maintained in song and dance rituals (Boscana 1933). For ritual to be effective, it had to be performed perfectly. This requirement for perfection assured that the accumulated past knowledge was passed perfectly to the heir of each specialist. Because, in the past, each ritual took four, five or six days and nights to perform, the apprentice had to have an excellent memory.

In addition to learning the existing past knowledge, the novice was expected to observe and report his observations to his teacher continually. Thus, any change in conditions and new observations could be integrated into the existing body of knowledge, with new songs for the appropriate times and actions. Certainly those who "controlled" weather phenomena, rain, dew, fog and wind, must have been highly observant of all phenomena that preceded any change in the weather, and thus they could predict and with ceremony "bring" the result.

Boscana (1933) reported that the Luiseño *puplem* had the power to increase seeds and animals; and Sales (Rudkin 1956), that the *Kuseyaay* were responsible for good harvests. In the course of claims case research on land use among the Kumeyaay, the descendant of the traditional tribal leader introduced me to plant and farming specialists. Each of the plant specialists described how a grandparent taught them not only which plant foods could be transplanted and which needed to be reproduced by seeds or vegetative cuttings, but also that each plant should be tried in every environment from the coast to the desert. In addition to greens, roots, annual seed plants, and perennials such as manzanita, sage and ceanothus, they reported planting acorns and pinenuts to have more food trees. They also saved seeds of agave and yucca to increase those food and technical sources. Cactus cuttings were planted at every living site. They observed how plants responded to different rainfall conditions and times in the year, such that in drought years, the rare irregularly timed rainfalls would sprout some plant food, sometimes one that might be seen only once in twenty years (Shipek 1989).

In addition to the planting activities, these specialists managed the controlled burning process. They knew that certain plants, such as basket grasses, arrow reed, and bow wood must be burned every third year, in order to continue to provide straight usable material. They described regular yearly burning under oaks, pines, mesquite and the native palm to maintain good harvests and to control plant diseases, plant parasites (mistletoe), damaging bugs, and even the spread of poison oak. Chaparral, such as manzanita, rhus, and ceanothus were burned on ten to fifteen year sequences to improve seed quality and remove parasites, insects, pests such as dodder, and plant diseases. Sage, which was destroyed by burning, was managed on a much longer burning sequence, unless the plants became diseased. Kumeyaay elders described burning around springs, wanting only one tree to shade the spring, but no brush or chaparral, stating that one tree and shallow rooted grass and annuals maintained spring water levels more effectively than allowing brush around the spring. All these activities were originally performed by a Kumeyaay band under the direction of the *Kwaaypaay* (Kumeyaay band chief or captain) and the appropriate *Kuseyaay*. Each burning, seed broadcasting, and planting activity was started and followed by rituals, again with special language, songs and dance.

The farming specialists, both Kumeyaay and Luiseño (interviewed for water cases), knew when and where to plant each crop: corn, bean and squash varieties. They knew the water requirements of each crop, and details of several different irrigation methods. To their original crop knowledge, they had learned new knowledge about the crops introduced by the Spanish and later Americans: wheat, barley, melons, fruit trees, chili, and vegetables.

The Kumeyaay plant specialists knew former animal, bird and fish specialists. Each plant specialist had some peripheral knowledge about those specialties, stating that the animal and bird

Kuseyaay participated in plant management to maintain foods, shade areas and nesting areas for the various animals and game birds eaten. They also stated that the fish *Kuseyaay* knew when a red tide was coming and would inform the *Kwaaypaay* so the band could leave the coast before the red tide poisoned the shellfish and fish for eating.

All told, the surviving specialists described very complex ecological knowledge that had been developed by the observations of generations of specialists and was maintained and taught by song and ritual to each trainee. These plant, animal and weather specialists correspond to our scientists, observing nature, recording the observations in song and also performing experiments by moving plants into a variety of ecological niches, observing and recording the results and integrating management practices into ritual. They even had special language for speaking with each other, just as botanists, zoologist and meteorologists have.

DOCTORS

Interestingly, when the Spanish speak of "curanderos" their extensive herbal knowledge is barely mentioned, instead, the Friars concentrate on describing and decrying their curing rituals and singing over an ill person as useless. But when a person recovered, Sales attributed it to "nature." Fra. Sales mentions that the healers often "suck" the sores of a patient, and describes the extensive use of sweat baths followed by jumping in the ocean as damaging, which it was for the diseases introduced by the Spanish, such as measles, chickenpox and smallpox. For the sweating practice to be used as often repeatedly as Sales describes, it must have been effective for the diseases that beset the Kumeyaay before the Spanish arrived.

Several of the Kumeyaay plant specialists on the claims case work were actually healers, specializing in medicinal plants. Here again, I discovered that each one specialized in certain types of diseases. Formerly when many *kuseyaay* existed, they had referred patients to other specialists as appropriate. Even psychological illness were recognized and cared for by a specialist (Tofflemier and Luomala 1936). Each healer had received the calling in a dream and then had trained with an elder relative who was an established healer. After their training, each told of continuing to experiment with plants, searching for new medicinal qualities, but using the plant directly for teas, washes or poultices rather than refining a healing chemical out of the plant. As we researched repeatedly in the various former Kumeyaay environments that seemed still undisturbed, they often sought plants which we were unable to find, some apparently extinct. Instead, we saw European or Asiatic imports, weeds or deliberate imports, some of which had been here for decades and had already been tested by them for medicinal or food qualities and found useful. Others were new to them, and each healer questioned me about these plants and took samples to test. They also spoke of trying various medicines on the new diseases which affected them after Europeans arrived.

During these years, I was impressed with the healings I saw performed by these medicine people and even tried some of the herbs for myself--to my benefit. Many people told me about the last rattlesnake *Kuseyaay* and his work, describing in detail how the doctor was always on his way to the site of the bitten person when he was sent for. His treatment was described by several witnesses. Upon arriving at the side of the bitten man, the *Kuseyaay* began singing a slow chant and slowly stroking the injured man with a feather. This was the only treatment given, and in a few days the person recovered. This rattlesnake *Kuseyaay* was noted for his cures. Modern medical science recognizes that rattlesnake venom kills by stopping the heart. The shaman, by slowing the heart beat, effectively slowed the movement of venom through the body, thus preventing fatally large amounts of venom from reaching the heart at any one time.

Interestingly, some of the healers' medical treatments correspond to information that modern medical doctors prescribe. When a person came for treatment, the first requirement was that the person stop eating salt, fat, and meat. After that herbs and other treatments were administered. Several persons remembered a special treatment by another elderly medicine man from their youth. The treatment showed his great perception in dealing with a new epidemic. When the flu epidemic of 1918 hit that reservation, the old medicine man went around to all the houses checking each family. Where a family was sick, he hunted rabbits and gathered greens for a stew and fed them. Where not everyone in a family was ill, he told them to get rabbits and greens for stew and forbade the use of all sweets, honey, sugar, agave. None of his patients died in this epidemic, in contrast to the disastrous effects for many world populations.

The ethics of healing *kuseyaay* were very strict. To be successful in the healing profession meant that healers could not perform any evil but must always work for the benefit of people who came for healing. They must think only good thoughts. Furthermore, they could not use their knowledge to heal themselves, nor to gain personal power or wealth.

As among the ecological specialists, when we examine the teachings and experimental practices of the healing *Kuseyaay*, we find comparisons to many modern medical practices: specialization, search for new medicines, and experimenting with new medicines when the tried and true remedies of the past did not work on the new disease, or when some traditional medicinal plant was no longer available due to land loss and environmental degradation by non-Indians.

In recent years, with the loss of their own healers, the Kumeyaay have been looking for other sources of help. A Mexican curandero moved into Tecate and advertised among the southern Kumeyaay reservations. Two women went to test his ability. One was ill, complaining of an upset stomach. The curandero asked her symptoms and then palpated her stomach and sucked a rotten seed from her side, telling her she would now be well. The women left and laughed at the curandero because he was incompetent; anyone could see that the woman was several months pregnant. Furthermore, they said a good healer does not need to ask symptoms nor touch the sick person, but should know what is wrong by just looking at the person.

In this paper, I have not discussed the bad or evil *Kuseyaay* or *Pul*, although everyone has assured me evil witchcraft actually exists. The healing and plant *Kuseyaay* stated that evil witchcraft against a healer or any one who was only doing good could not hurt the intended victim, but would rebound and injure the evil person.

SELECTION CHARACTERISTICS

While all sources agree that these different types of positions were primarily hereditary and normally passed from father to son, in the case of Kumeyaay healing specialties could pass from mother to daughter (Shipek 1982). Knowledge was kept secret and passed to only one heir. Therefore, which son or daughter was chosen? Sometimes a grandson or nephew might be chosen, in preference to a son.

White (1957) has analyzed the qualities necessary to acquire knowledge among the Luiseño. He found that the ability to recognize and proceed on vague clues or hints, fearlessness in learning and then in using the knowledge at the appropriate times, and keeping knowledge secret otherwise were essential. Similar attitudes toward fearlessness in learning and using new knowledge exist among the Kumeyaay who are specialists.

On the basis of information from several families in which an immediate ancestral elder was some type of specialist and had asked a young relative to become a trainee, several characteristics could be discussed in those who were asked to train and in those who had inherited and trained for various positions. One person spoke of being asked by two relatives with different specialties. The outstanding characteristics of those chosen were curiosity about everything, willingness to try new things or new ways of doing something. Further, they were doubters, and tested statements made by their elders or by the healer or specialist. In their society, such doubting actions would normally not be tolerated. Therefore, in early childhood, these individuals must have shown intelligence, curiosity, and reasoning ability to be allowed to question aloud or doubt the statement of a specialist *kuseyaay*, or even to test one of his statements. Well above average intelligence, excellent memory, and proven ability to reason were essential for maintaining extensive ceremonial knowledge and ritual songs requiring several days almost continuous performance, and for maintaining the astronomical knowledge necessary for correct performance of rituals. Observational, reasoning and synthesizing powers were also essential.

To conclude, we are describing an intelligent, highly educated, and also practical class who, prior to the arrival of the Europeans, managed the personal relations, emotional and physical health of their people, and all aspects of the environment.

SIERRA MIWOK SHAMANS, 1900-1990

Craig D. Bates

Shamanism among the Northern, Central and Southern Sierra Miwok of the Central Sierra Nevada is firmly rooted in the legendary past. In stories of when the world was inhabited by the animal people, the Southern Miwok tell of the coyote, prairie falcon, nuthatch and red-headed sapsucker shamans (Merriam 1910: 35,179,188). After the animal people left the world, Miwok men and women became doctors. Doctoring among the Miwok changed over time and continues to evolve today.

The mission and gold rush periods of California history left a profound impact upon the lives of Miwok people. The drastic reduction in population, changes in lifestyle, and assimilation of other Indian and non-Indian people into Miwok families must have altered the Miwok peoples' view of shamanism during the 19th century. Information about Miwok shamans, in the form of oral traditions or written data, does not extend much before the 1880s. At that time, there were many kinds of Miwok doctors, each a specialist. Some were malevolent shamans. Other doctors took care of common ailments, and some treated diseases caused by supernatural phenomena, by displeasing spirits, or by supernatural poisoning. The Miwok people considered treatment by shamans essential when a person's health was threatened by serious physical or supernatural danger.

The Miwok have always lived in fear of supernatural power: of wood spirits which started wildfires, water spirits who lived in rivers and consumed fish, evil spirits in certain waterfalls, lakes or places in rivers (some half fish and half woman, and called *husepi* by the Central Miwok or *Ho ha' pe* by the Southern Miwok) (Berman 1982:28-33; Chisum 1967:205; Cox 1974; Gardner and Madsen 1976:492-493; Gifford n.d.b; Hudson 1901; Merriam 1910:228-229; Parker 1974; Taylor 1932:6-7), rock giants,

called *che-ha-lum'-che* by the Northern Miwok (Merriam
1910:232), one-legged imps (Berman 1982:34-37), and ". . .
fetishistic spirits who assume the forms of owls and other birds,
to render their lives a terror by day and by night" (Powers
1877:348). Central Miwok children were warned of spirits in the
forest, such as the small *Nenakatu*, who was two feet tall and had
hair hanging to her heels; *chihalenchi*, a bad, hair-covered man
who ate people who ventured into caves, as would *Ettati*, a snake-
like creature who also lived in caves (Chisum 1967:205; Gardner
and Madsen 1976:488,492; Fuller 1971; Merriam 1910:231-232).
Central Miwok children also feared the *hohoho*, a huge bird which
snatched   away   small   children.[1]   Quartz   crystals   and
archaeologically associated artifacts, such as arrowheads, were to
be avoided, as their possession by anyone but shamans could cause
illness. The spirits of the dead were also feared, as their singing,
crying, talking or appearance could cause bad luck, illness, or even
death (Broadbent 1964:182-189; Cox 1974; Fuller 1971; Stanley
1974; Wessell 1971).

The Central Miwok called nature spirits *suchuma*. They
had the power to roll rocks down on an individual, cause rain,
violent windstorms, or whirlwinds (*pukiyu*). If any of these
manifestations happened, the person affected had to pray
(*kumtubaksu*) immediately, and then sprinkle himself four times
with water to prevent violent illness, or possibly, death (Chisum
1967:204).

For good luck and protection against evil, people had many
devices. Southern Miwok people wore roots of an unidentified
rare plant on string necklaces to protect themselves from sickness
(Clark 1904:58-59). Another root used by the Northern Miwok
kept rattlesnakes away (Cox 1974). Wormwood (*Artemesia
vulgaris*) was used to keep away ghosts, purify and protect those
who had come in contact with evil forces, and to "doctor" dancers,
protecting them from the power residing in dance regalia (Cox
1974; Hudson 1901). Amulets (*wep'-pah*) that were worn around
the neck by the Southern Miwok were usually special stones,
shells, forked jay feathers, or a feather of the *o-lel'-le*, a bird that
lives under water in cold springs (Merriam 1910:221).[2] Some
Central and Southern Miwok kept *mole*, special strange-shaped
natural stones, or broad obsidian blades, to give them luck in
hunting.[3] People contributed stones or sticks to already-existing
piles along some trails for luck and/or for relief of muscle
soreness.[4]

Herb doctors were most frequently consulted for common
physical ailments. They cured by using only herbs and medicines,
and did not invoke supernatural power (Merriam 1955:70). The

Miwok used many medicinal plants to treat a variety of illnesses and injuries (Barrett and Gifford 1933:165-176; Powers 1877:354).

For serious problems and for ailments that were diagnosed as having supernatural causes, the Miwok required specialists-- shamans whose training and connections with the supernatural gave them power to gain favor from the spirits and thereby to help people. The general term for these doctors was *koyabi* among the East Central Sierra Miwok, or *alini* among the West Central Sierra Miwok. Individuals gained shamanic power in different ways. Often it was hereditary and aspiring shamans were taught by a parent or grandparent. Others gained their power by dreaming of, or living with animals such as bears, rattlesnakes, condors, coyotes, deer or salmon, or their spirits. Sometimes a Central Miwok boy sucked up a polliwog or another sort of strange, small black object from the water four times with a hollow stick. Many boys played with hollow reeds, but only a few caught such things. Afterwards he told no one what he had done, but went home, went to bed, and dreamed that he could cure people by sucking. He might then go looking for sick people, and would become known as a doctor after he had cured a sick person. He had little power as a boy, but by the time he was 20 or 25 he would become a powerful doctor (Dixon 1903; Gifford n.d.a:2-3).

Some Central Miwok doctors at Groveland, often women, were self-appointed. They were educated by observing other shamans and by dreaming of the falcon and observing the falcon's advice. In difficult cases they also sought the advice of the eagle. They studied these bird-patrons and observed other shamans for three years before beginning their own practice. These doctresses, called *osa' ka' yabi*, literally "female doctor," generally built up large followings--much to the disgust of other shamans who despised them (Hudson 1901)[5].

Sucking doctors were among the most common of the curing doctors. Very powerful individuals, they usually cut the affected area and sucked out the cause of disease, often manifested as bits of wood or bark, a stone, coffee berries, a sizzling black rock (*tshila* in Central Miwok), a flicker tail feather, a hummingbird's beak, claws of a martin, a fish bone, a metal nail, a worm or even a piece of knotted invitation string. A sucking doctor might sometimes use a small bone whistle, made of red-tailed hawk or owl wing bone, and blow and suck the whistle over the affected part without cutting. When the whistle was plugged up, the doctor sucked the cause of the sickness out of the whistle. Some sucking doctors were known by the way in which they had gained their power: for example, from supernatural interaction with spirits of the condor, coyote, deer, or salmon.[6]   These

sucking doctors were often able to reverse evil that a poison doctor
had done. One woman shaman, upon removing a black, sizzling,
rough stone from the back of a young girl who had been poisoned
by another shaman, told the girl that there would be times in her
life when her back would still hurt her. She assured the girl that
she could always be cured by calling again upon the shaman,
whether she was alive or dead (Aginsky 1943:466; Clark 1904:58;
Dixon 1903; Gifford n.d.a.:3; Hutchings 1888:433-434; Madsen
1976:446; Merriam 1955:69; Steinbach 1963:8, 1965).

Among the Central Miwok at Groveland, the sucking
doctors outfit consisted of a flicker quill band, hairpins, hair
plumes, a 10-inch baton-like cocoon rattle, feather wand, abalone
shell necklace, two strips of buckskin covered with crow feathers
(one passing along the outside of the arm from the wrist across the
shoulders to the other wrist, and another passing from wrist to
wrist across the chest), a belt of buckskin, buckskin clout,
necklace of small perforated stones, a double whistle, eagle or
hawk down stuck to the face and hair (stored in a bag made of a
hawk-leg skin turned inside out), red paint stripe from ear to ear
across the upper lip (sometimes including the face below this
stripe), vertical bars of red, black and white paint on the chest,
and similar horizontal rings of paint on the arms and legs (Hudson
1901). This description is very much like dance regalia worn by
Chris Brown (Chief Lemee) in Yosemite, and in a photograph of
Lemee wearing it, this regalia was identified as a Yosemite
Medicine Man's outfit (Latta 1936:127).

Singing doctors, somewhat like sucking doctors, cured by
pressing the patient's body with their hands, singing and blowing
an elderberry whistle (Barrett and Gifford 1933:249; Gifford
n.d.).[7]

Dance Doctors, called *Kalang'i* by the Central Miwok at
Bald Rock, cured by dancing. They did not give medicine or suck
out evil. For four days before treating a patient the doctor was
required to abstain from both meat and sexual activity. He wore
a woodpecker-tail head plume, headnet filled with eagle down,
abalone necklace, eagle-claw necklace, back cape of hawk tails,
baton of hawk pinons or roadrunner tails, and a double-bone
whistle. The doctor would circle the patient, singing and dancing
to each of the four directions. He would shoot at the seat of pain
with a medicine bow and arrow and shake a cocoon rattle (*so'ko
sa*) filled with small quartz pebbles.[8] Often he would also use an
8" obsidian knife smeared with medicine, and four sticks. He
would set one stick on each side of the patient, one at the head
and the other at the foot. The poison or evil that the doctor blew
off the patient passed out through the sticks (Hudson 1901;

Merriam 1955:79-70).

Curing doctors were always paid in advance for their work. Common forms of payment were a fresh deer, or yards of shell money. If a patient died, the shaman returned the payment to the patient's family. A shaman could be killed however, if he or she lost several patients in succession, as people then feared that the shaman had come under the control of evil influences. Such shamans were usually killed by violent means (i.e., shooting), but occasionally they were murdered by sorcery (Clark 1904:57; Gifford n.d.a:11; Powers 1877:354).

Other shamans had special power or control over certain plants, animals or natural phenomena. A rattlesnake shaman was an individual who had had a supernatural experience with rattlesnakes. He could not prevent rattlesnakes from biting people, but he could save them once they had been bitten. The treatment often included having the bite rubbed with a long string of rattlesnake rattles (Gifford n.d.a). The lost article shaman could make missing objects reappear; they did this by singing (Gifford n.d.a:27).

An acorn shaman predicted crops of acorn and could sometimes make acorns appear out of season (Gifford n.d.a.). Similarly, the rain shaman could call rain to come and last for four days and nights, and could also make vegetable foods appear out of season. These rain shamans got their power through dreams, and sang songs to the accompaniment of cocoon rattles (Gifford n.d.a.:14-15)[9].

Bear shamans, *Tshipamulu* in Central Miwok, were men who had been captured by bears, usually when they had been out hunting. When the men were grabbed by the bears, they fainted and were taken to the bears' lair. There they were cut open, had their insides replaced with down, and then danced over by the bears for four days. The men then returned home, invulnerable to fire. They sometimes demonstrated this power at dances in the roundhouse by standing in the middle of the fire (Freeland and Broadbent 1960:59-61; Gifford n.d.a.).

Poison doctors, *tu yu ku* in Central Miwok, were greatly feared.[10] They often kept their poison (*crakano* in Central Miwok) wrapped in wormwood leaves or in ear tubes made of sandhill crane bones. The poisons were from many different sources among the Central Miwok: pieces of dried *kolesu* (a water creature that looked like the skin and bones of a man) wrapped in braided owl feathers, a big toad (*olasaiyi*), dried rattlesnake head, bear fat, various bear body parts or claws, and *wuh-keh-ah*, which was made by burning abalone shell and putting the ashes on a grave. A person could be killed if the doctor's poison was put in

contact with a person's saliva, feces, nail clippings or hair.
Poisoning could also be effected if the doctors's poison was rubbed
on a pin-like stick, porcupine quill or grass stem section and then,
by magical means, the poisoned dart shot or thrown a great
distance at a person, sometimes from as far away as fifty miles.[11]
Sometimes the poison doctor hid and poisoned people as they
walked by, or poisoned dancers during a dance, hitting the
dancer's knee and causing him to fall down. By any of these
methods, the victim became sick and died.   Some died
immediately, and others suffered lingering illnesses.

Poison doctors often obtained their power hereditarily;
they were taught by a parent through the use of quartz crystals
and by eating roots of poisonous plants, and they were encouraged
to practice hitting a feather stuck in the ground as a target with
porcupine quills so that they could then successfully hit people
with their darts. The doctor often called the name of the person
being poisoned and said, "go to his head!" or "go to his breast!" as
he released his poison. Apparently it was painful for the doctor
when the doctor let go of his poison.

Poison doctors always denied their occult powers and
deeds, and were very careful not to create suspicion. They knew
that the penalty for using their power was death: when accused of
poisoning, these doctors strongly denied everything (Hudson
1901). To avert suspicion, the poison doctor cried and grieved
more than anyone for the one he killed.

The fear of poison doctors affected many aspects of
Miwok life: when women cut their hair short as a sign of
mourning, they were careful to either bury it with the corpse or
hide it so no poison doctor could use it to cause them illness or
death. The Central Miwok believed that the Southern Miwok were
most adept at poisoning, and hence seldom associated with these
southerners; instead, they associated primarily with groups to the
north, west and east. Southern Miwok people to the west of
Yosemite feared the Yosemite Miwok, saying there were many
"witches" (i.e., poison doctors) among them. This fear of poison
doctors extended to the distrust of all classes of doctors. It was
common for doctors to despise one another and to speculate on
who among them might be poison doctors. At least on some
occasions among the Central Miwok, poison doctors vied with each
other in contests to test their powers at the *Pota* dance (Barrett and
Gifford 1933:222, 226; Bunnell 1911:43; Chisum 1967:204;
Freeland and Broadbent 1960:65, 66; Hudson 1901; Kelly 1968;
Madsen 1976:445; Powers 1877:354).

CHANGES IN MIWOK SHAMANISM

Although changes must have occurred in Miwok shamanism due to the tremendous disruption of Miwok life during the gold rush, little information is available to document those changes prior to 1900. Sometime prior to 1859 the *Hiweyi* dance originated at the Central Miwok village at Knights Ferry in honor of the shaman *Sigelizu* (also recorded as *Chiplichu*). *Sigelizu* was probably a Costanoan originally from Pleasanton who lived at Knights Ferry. The *Hiweyi* dance commemorated *Sigelizu's* communication with spirits that allowed him to predict that the smallpox epidemic at Ione would not reach the Central Miwok at Knights Ferry (Gifford 1926:399; 1955:301-302). The class of shaman called *Alini hiwe'yi*, disease diviner, may have originated with *Sigelizu* (Gifford n.d.a.:15, 24).

Miwok doctoring had changed greatly by the turn of the century, as had Miwok life, and continuing acculturation to western life ways left few Miwok with the inclination or time to train as shamans. Speaking of the Southern Miwok of Yosemite, Galen Clark claimed:

"After the Indians were given their freedom from the reservations in 1855, the old ones, subdued and broken-hearted, sickened and died very fast, and most of the men doctors were killed off in a few years. There are none known who now attempt to act in that capacity.

There are still some women doctors who continue to practice the magic art, but as there are now but very few Indians, there is not so much sickness, and very few deaths in a year, so that the doctors very rarely forfeit their lives by many of their patients dying in quick succession." (Clark 1904:57)

Contemporary accounts substantiate Clark's statements. A traveler in Yosemite around 1880 met an aged Indian medicine man hiding in a deep mountain canyon. The Indian had fled from 300 miles to the north, as he had lost a patient and was going to be killed (Lewis 1882:73). In the 1890s, the murder of the shaman Bullock near Wawona was attributed to his losing a third consecutive patient and reportedly left Callipene as the only remaining Miwok shaman in the Yosemite region (Anon. 1903). Other accounts mention female shamans among the Southern

Miwok at that time, including Callipene and Maria Lebrado Ydrte (Taylor 1932:18; Rust 1981). One newspaper article in 1903 prematurely forecast Callipene's death by murder for losing yet another patient; Callipene lived until about 1912, however (Anon 1903; Boysen 1934:2). Perhaps by that time, under pressure from non-Indians, the Miwok had stopped killing unsuccessful shamans.

Miwok leaders lamented the dying out of ceremonies as older generations died, and orations by village leaders at the turn of the century occasionally referred to the lack of ceremonies, or to a particular celebration being the last of its kind (Gifford 1955). A similar case can be seen for shamans, as most turn-of-the-century accounts of doctors seem to be describing doctors in the past, and few of the younger generations showed an interest in Miwok traditions. *Chinita*, at the Central Miwok village of Chicken Ranch, seems to be one of the few practicing Central Sierra Miwok shamans mentioned shortly after 1900 (Madsen 1976:446). Joseph Killeli was a Yosemite Miwok bear shaman (Callahan 1976:108).[12] Pancho Longfellow, originally from the Central Miwok village of Big Creek near Groveland, was rumored to be a poison doctor in the early 1900s. By the 1930s many of these doctors had died, and people who sought this type of treatment had to travel farther and farther. Many relied on herbal cures, consulting the few remaining doctors for serious cases.

Pedro "Petelo" O'Connor, a Northern Miwok doctor and dancer, was perhaps one of the most famous shamans between 1910 and his death in 1942. He lived at Railroad Flat, West Point and finally Jackson, and was well known to Northern, Central and Southern Miwok people.[13] O'Connor, who cured through the use of singing, sucking, herbs and prayers, was also believed to be a poison doctor. In the late 1910s and early 1920s, O'Connor lived in a small roundhouse at Railroad Flat where he had a cocoon tied to a stick and attached to the wall at the rear of the house. When the cocoon began to rattle of its own accord, O'Connor, his wife Mattie, and her grandchildren prepared to go on a trip. Someone would inevitably soon appear to summon him to treat a sick person, often quite far away. O'Connor is remembered as curing ailments that ranged from eating too much fruit, to bad joints, to life-threatening illnesses. He was known to have great power, and Mattie's granddaughters claimed that in the 1920s he took their grandmother's life in order to save the life of another Miwok woman he loved (Bibby and Villa n.d.:39-45; Cox 1974; Maniery and Dutschke 1989:490-491; Stanley 1973-1990; Pruitt 1976).

Other Miwok shamans also had reputations that spoke of great power. Charlie Dick, a Southern Miwok shaman from the Yosemite region, was attending a dance at Ione in the 1920s when a drunken man approached him in the dancehouse and broke wind

Figure 9. Callipene and Lena (Rube) Brown, Yosemite Valley, June 1901.
Photograph by H. D. Wulzen. Yosemite Museum, National Park Service, Cat.
No. 26964.
          Callipene was a renowned shaman among the Southern Miwok at the
turn of the century. Lena Brown, who may have been a granddaughter of
Callipene's, was the mother of Chris Brown, a Southern Miwok dancer and
shaman.

Figure 10. Maria Lebrado Ydrte, 1929. Photograph by Joseph Dixon. Yosemite
Research Library, National Park Service, Neg. No. RL-2022.
          Maria Lebrado Ydrte was a well-known shaman among the Southern
Miwok until her heath at over 90 years in 1931. She was the granddaughter of
the Yosemite Miwok leader Tenaya.

Figure 11. Pedro O'Connor, ca. 1920(?). Photograph courtesy of Jennifer Bates. Pedro O'Connor was a Northern Miwok ceremonial leader, dancer and shaman.

Figure 12. Charlie Dick, El Portal, California, 1928. Yosemite Research Library, National Park Service, Neg. No. RL-2075. Charlie Dick was a Southern Miwok poison doctor.

on him.   Dick is said to have pointed a finger at the man, whereupon the man fell, dead (Bibby 1985).

Chris "Chief Lemee" Brown was a Southern Miwok man who performed dances for visitors to Yosemite National Park from the 1920s to 1953. While Brown was a polished entertainer who sometimes did not hesitate to use Plains Indian regalia in his performances for park visitors, he was recognized in the Miwok community as having some traditional shamanic power, and he talked to park visitors about shamanistic practices.[14]   In 1932 Brown conducted a dance at the Yosemite Valley Indian Village to cure a woman of hallucinations and bad dreams.   In 1949 he traveled to Tuolumne County to doctor Central Miwok people who were about to dance at public performances. Brown made cocoon rattles whenever he could find the cocoons, and, unlike most Miwok shamans, who considered these rattles too powerful for commoners to handle, gave or sold them to friends and park visitors (Alcorn 1932; Cummins 1942; Ewing 1985; Hern 1985; Johnson 1974; Lionel 1985; Steinbach 1965; Wessell 1970).

In 1937, Washoe people introduced the Native American Church and the use of peyote to the Paiute at Mono Lake, just across the Sierra Nevada from Yosemite.   While a few Southern Miwok and Miwok-Paiute people from Yosemite attended these church sessions, the influence of the church and the use of peyote was short-lived in the Mono Lake-Yosemite region. Many people were initially impressed with miracle-like cures, but the death of Young Charlie, an old Southern Miwok man who lived at Mono Lake, and infighting among the Paiute, seemed to have convinced most Mono Lake and Yosemite participants that the church, and its use of peyote, was ineffective (Blaver 1983; Hern 1984; Stewart 1944:75).

During the 1940s and 1950s the fabric of Miwok communities was greatly weakened; fewer young people spoke the Miwok language, and many left the Sierra for jobs in large cities. Most of the old shamans were dead, and almost no one had been trained to take their places.   A few people, usually women, practiced the shamanic calling of deceased relatives. Since the turn of the century there had been a steady increase in the percentage of women shamans among the Southern Miwok, but the virtual disappearance of male shamans among the Northern and Central Miwok and the increasing number of women shamans there was a new phenomenon.

These women shamans did not usually claim to have much power, yet some conversed with owls, were visited by animals that proved to be messengers of death or accidents, and were called upon to doctor their relatives and other Miwok people. Using fresh, dried or boiled plants, they worked to keep people healthy

Figure 13. Chris Brown, "Chief Lemee," and young cowboy at the Indian Field Days, Yosemite Valley, 1929. Yosemite Research Library, National Park Service.
      Chris Brown often wore stereotypical Indian clothing while performing for visitors to Yosemite National Park, as he is at this celebration designed to increase visitation to the park. Here he holds a Miwok cocoon rattle in his right hand. Most Miwok shamans would not display such objects in the context of tourist entertainment, but Brown did not seem concerned.

Figure 14. Chris Brown, "Chief Lemee," Yosemite Valley, c. 1926. Yosemite Research Library, National Park Service, Neg. No. RL-2026.
      Brown, a Southern Miwok shaman, here wears Miwok dance regalia similar to that of the sucking doctor, including a flicker quill band, hairpins, cocoon rattle, and shoulder cape.

and to remove any evil that might have been incurred because of a person's (or their family's) disrespectful actions. Thus, their role was often that of a combined herb doctor and curing shaman.

During the 1960s, at some Miwok settlements, contact with supernatural power was not uncommon. For example, in about 1968 two drunken Miwok men ridiculed Miwok dancers at the Tuolumne Acorn Festival. As they staggered home, owls attacked them, knocked them to the ground, and danced around them, throwing up dust. A young Miwok boy, witnessing the event, got his mother. By practicing the ways of her grandfather, she helped to cure and cleanse the men who had been attacked for their disrespect of Miwok dancing and religion.

The residents of Miwok rancherias feared both supernatural harm and dangerous poison doctors living among them. Every death could be attributed in some way to the family of the deceased not being properly respectful of Miwok ways. The whistle of the gray fox, the late night appearance of a ghostly horse and rider, or a ball of fire rushing across a field, foretold the imminent death of a relative or close friend. One home, imprudently built across an old Miwok trail, was frequently "bumped into" by spirits using the path. The house was also frequented by the ghost of the owner's husband, who died before finishing it, and by the spirits of feathered regalia Chris Brown had brought to the house-site during construction and sung to on visits to the rancheria. Teenagers joked as they fled from a reputed poison doctor at the city park, but their jokes about being

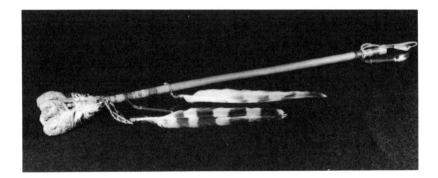

Figure 15. Southern Miwok Cocoon Rattle by Chris "Chief Lemee" Brown, c. 1938-1940. Made of mock orange stick, cocoons, commercial cordage and paint, marsh hawk tail feathers, glue. Length 22 inches. Photograph by Michael Dixon. Courtesy of Donald Ewing.

Brown gave this rattle to Donald Ewing, who was a boy of ten or twelve at the time. Brown apparently saw no problem with presenting such an item to a young boy, unlike other Miwok shamans who did not allow others to handle such objects.

afraid of the old man were a screen behind which they hid their fear.

Since 1970, the attitude of younger Miwok people toward Indian doctors, and of what is considered to be Miwok, has changed. These changes, which reflect new influences, have altered Miwok thought, identity, and religion profoundly. Around 1970, a new religion was introduced to Miwok people, brought from the east by Paiute people. It made use of canvas-covered sweat lodges and, sometimes, catlinite pipes of Plains Indian people. Usually it was most strongly embraced by Miwok people who could not speak Miwok, whose living relatives could not speak Miwok, and, generally, by descendants of families that were not hereditary leaders.

Visiting Paiute shamans have come among the Central and Southern Miwok to teach them this new way, and other religious leaders, including the Zulu shaman Mutwa, have visited the Tuolumne Mewuk Rancheria to share their beliefs with local Miwok people (Anon. 1976:1-2). Today, tobacco offerings, the burning of sage "smudges" at many functions, and the recitation of prayers in English rather than in any Native American language, have become standard practice for many Miwok people.[15] This new religion, emphasizing Indianness, kindness, and brotherhood has helped many people. It has served as a successful treatment for alcoholism for some, and for others, its emphasis on a positive Indian identity has provided a way of gathering with other Indian people.

At the same time, the impact of new-age shamans and the appearance of self-proclaimed "Miwok" shamans who cannot prove their Miwok ancestry have influenced the beliefs of younger Miwok people, as well as those of non-Indians seeking shamanic training. Some Miwok people now practice as new-age shamans, wearing non-traditional crystals and beaded decorations. Some of these self-appointed shamans appear as spokesmen for the Miwok people, and protectors of archeological sites threatened by development. Anxious to identify with a Miwok ancestry, they claim that their practices and beliefs were learned from their ancestors.

For others, among them those who still speak Miwok, weave baskets, or dance Miwok dances, this new sweat-lodge religion is viewed as something not quite right. The comments of two Miwok elders represent this view. "They make a show out of it, smudging everyone, talking in English. They are not doing it like the old people did. They don't know what they are doing, they are showing off," says one older Miwok. Another comments, "Why can't they do like we have always done? They lost their whole culture and don't know what the hell they're doing. Too bad. Too bad. They lost it."

Many older Miwok people are distressed and afraid that the next generations of Miwok children will grow up not knowing true Miwok ways. Perhaps even more upsetting to many is the thought that their children and grandchildren will come to think that the sweat lodge and Pan-Indian powwow dancing *is* Miwok. It is not change that these older folks fear; they often say they know everything must change. Instead, these Miwok elders are disturbed by the prospect of all that they see as Miwok culture being replaced by a new and foreign Pan-Indianism which would not retain anything of what was Miwok.

Miwok shamanism and Miwok life have changed greatly since 1900. The variety of shamans that were an integral part of Miwok life at the turn of the century no longer exist, and it seems unlikely that shamans will reappear among the Miwok to take on the many roles of doctoring. The demands of everyday life at the end of the 20th century, and the influences of Pan-Indian religion and new-age shamanism, seem to have a strong role in shaping Miwok life today. If Miwok people wished someday in the future to resurrect their legacy of shamanism, it could possibly be done by studying songs and rituals in the field notes and recordings of ethnographers such as Hudson and Gifford, listening to the stories of Miwok elders, and by finding the spirits that still dwell in their homeland. While the end result would not be Miwok doctoring identical to that of the past, it would be a new manifestation of Miwok religion centered in and built upon the complex legacy of traditional Miwok shamanism.

NOTES

1. The *hohoho* made a whistling sound much like that produced from blowing through two cupped hands. The *hohoho* is said to have died out when Bill Tadd, a Central Miwok, was young, probably in the mid-to-late 19th century. Bill Tadd did see one some years later sitting in a cedar tree on his allotment on the Tuolumne Mewuk Rancheria. Bill's son, Brown Tadd, thought this bird could have been a condor (Tadd 1984).

2. This bird was perhaps the water ouzel or dipper, *Cinclus mexicanus*.

3. The Southern Miwok believed that certain stones (called *mole*), which could be either naturally occurring stones or items such as large spear points from archeological sites, possessed power which would aid their owners. The *mole* would jump out at the person that it liked. Certain stones would bring good luck in deer hunting. Another stone, shaped like a bear's foot (and called *moleme uhumahti*), would cause its finder to be visited by a bear or bear spirit which, after asking if the man was afraid, would accompany him on the trail. Other *mole* stones allowed their owners to predict rainfall (Crooks, 1980; Gifford n.d.b; Hudson 1901). At Groveland, the Central Miwok *mu'le* were four broad obsidian or flint blades, used to direct the hunter, that were secretly buried together deep in the ground. A hunter would go to this secret place and listen for one of the charms to talk. The *mu'le* would sing and promise game to the hunter, who then pocketed the *mu'le* and set out confidently. The mere possession of one of these charms insured luck in hunting, no matter which direction was taken. The charms were named after the animals whose power they held: *uwuya mulis* (deer), *usumati mulis* (bear), *hilitca mulis* (mountain lion), and *uyimo mulis* (black bear) (Hudson 1901).

 The stone shaped like a bear's foot suggests the carved steatite bear-paw effigy found at a Konkow Maidu site (4-Butte-1) at Chico (Chartkoff and Chartkoff 1983:35).

4. On certain trails there were piles of stones where the traveler placed a stone, asking to have their soreness taken away (Gifford n.d.b.). In one case, the stones in a pile were all obsidian, brought from the Mono Basin across the Sierra, and in this case the pile was for "good luck" (Cole 1935). At one place is a large rock on which a traveler stood to be relieved of fatigue. A stick was cast on a nearby pile of sticks while the traveler addressed the spirit of

the place and said, "Grandfather, here is my money. Take away my soreness" (Gifford n.d.b.).

5. The bird-teachers would seem to be a part of the bird cult, which is thought to have been of great antiquity among the Miwok (Gifford 1926:394-397). Other Miwok consultants have identified the eagle as a "mascot" for shamans, and it was shamans of great power who were visited by the eagle (Madsen 1976:444).

6. Freeland collected a number of narratives surrounding the acquisition of power from different animals and animal spirits. The stories are detailed accounts of individuals receiving their power from the coyote, condor and deer, and power over salmon from a supernatural serpent (Freeland and Broadbent 1960:61-64). Gifford (n.d.a.) also collected a few similar stories, including one about a deer shaman (op. cit.:39).

7. This pressing of the body is similar to the initiation of boys into the dance society among the Northern Miwok, as well as the doctoring of women about to take part in ceremonial dances. The joints of both boys and women are pressed by the hands of the ceremonial leader (Cox 1973; Franklin 1972).

8. The use of quartz pebbles or crystals to fill cocoon rattles is reported for other groups in California as well. Floyd Buckskin reported their use in rattles among his people, the Achomawi (Buckskin 1990).

9. Chief William Fuller, from the Central Miwok village of Bald Rock and later from the Tuolumne Mewuk Rancheria, once told a newspaper reporter that the song to call rain included the word *Howtu*, and that water newts were strung-up as part of the ritual. The news clipping, which was in the possession of a friend of the Fuller family in about 1971, can no longer be located.

10. According to modern consultants and as evidenced by comparing Merriam's names with other recorded Miwok vocabularies, Merriam confused the Central Miwok names of shamans. He identified *Koi'-ah-pe* as witch doctors, *Too'-yu-goo* as dance doctors and *Wen-neh'-hoo-ne* as medicine doctors (1955:69). Central and Northern Miwok speakers in the 1970s and 1980s translated *Koi'ah pe* (or variants thereof) as medicine doctors, or doctors in general, *Too-yu-goo* as poison doctor (probably analogous to Merriam's witch doctor), and they did not recognize *Wen-neh'-hoo-he* (Cox 1976; Fuller 1971; Kelly 1968;

Pruitt 1976; Stanley 1976-1990; Wessell 1970).

Freeland and Broadbent (1960:44) recorded *husi'k-pe* for the Central Miwok word for shaman, *tu'j.uku* as poison doctor, and *?a'lini* as a dreamer shaman. It is interesting that the Northern Miwok and some Central Miwok use this last term for white men. Gifford recorded Tom and Suzie Williams' (Central Miwok) explanation:

> "Shamans in general are classified as *alini*, which means people different from normal human beings because they possess supernatural power. The word *alini* also denotes mana and some people who possess it. Thus, white people are spoken of as *alini* because of their superior equipment and ability to accomplish things the Indian cannot."

It is interesting that, by the mid-1950s when Broadbent worked with the Southern Miwok, the only word recorded for shaman was *tuj.uk*, the word used originally only to denote poison doctor (Broadbent 1964:340).

11. Old people (ca. 1900) saw shamans stick a small peg in the ground, go thirty or forty yards away, and throw sticks smaller than a white man's match at the peg. All the sticks went right to the peg or struck the dust next to it (Merriam 1955:69-70).

12. Killeli was also a close friend of Nancy de Angulo. Jaime de Angulo, her husband, recorded a number of legends learned from Killeli.

13. For example, Chris "Chief Lemee" Brown, a Southern Miwok, remembered learning an eagle dance from O'Connor, probably on one of his visits to Tuolumne from Yosemite (Cole 1935).

14. Chris "Chief Lemee" Brown described curing to a visiting schoolteacher and musicologist, who recorded:

> "The cocoon rattle is the witch-doctors fetish for healing. Four cocoons of the Pandora Moth, large and of a lustrous, natural, silvery color are tied to a stick, supposed to be Seringa [sic]. The cocoon rattle which Lemme [sic] made for me (for $1.50) was trimmed with eagle down and feathers from the side of the eagle tied on (glued underneath) with narrow leather thongs. Had a

leather loop as a handle and four single strips of skin as decorations from which hung two eagle feathers and two tiny white pigeon feathers. It was truly a work of art.

Cocoons are gathered on the sunny side of the slope on the Cyanothus [sic] bush. Lemme had difficulty finding them in fact could not find any although he hunted for them in the territory from Bass Lake up to Tuolumne. These were the last he had on hand.

In Medicine work, the rattle was shaken steadily in an upright position while the singing and circling of the stick was in progress . . . . At the same time the rattle is shaken held upright, while the "stick" is waved over the person lying ill. The healing stick or whatever it is called is about 16 inches long, has a small cross piece, possibly two short branches, near the tip is decorated with a flicker feather and has a horse hair extending from the end. If the hair sticks out straight from the stick after the song, the person will not get well; if it droops down, then the person is going to get well" (Cummins 1942).

15. Sage smudges were unknown to Miwok people, and tobacco offerings were seldom used (Aginsky 1943:448; Cox 1974; Stanley 1978).

ACKNOWLEDGEMENTS

I would like to thank Yosemite Museum Curator, Dave Forgang, for his support while I worked on this paper, and special thanks to Martha Lee, also on the Yosemite Museum staff, for her comments and editing work.

YUROK DOCTORS AND THE CONCEPT OF "SHAMANISM"

Thomas Buckley

There is considerable fascination with mystical practitioners that are referred to, in English, as "shamans." These are people in the religious "elites" of various societies who practice what the comparativist Mircea Eliade called "techniques of ecstacy," realized through trance and, often, possession (Eliade 1964). Shamanism thus defined involves the application of knowledge and power gained through direct contact with spiritual beings toward either benign (e.g., healing) or malign (e.g., sorcery) ends (1964:324). Usually shamans are professionals, specialists who are paid for their services.

As a longstanding interest in shamans and shamanism has intensified, since the 1960s, among individuals in societies whose dominant religions do not incorporate shamanism, there has emerged a tendency to conceive of *all* Native American spiritual practitioners, for instance, as "shamans" (cf. Eliade 1964:3). Yet the category of "shaman," correctly understood, is not necessarily a useful one in understanding a given Native American religious tradition. Wholesale application of the term can obscure, rather than increase, understanding of these traditions by outsiders. The regional religious culture of Native northwestern California provides a case in point.

A. L. Kroeber, probably the best known ethnographer of northwestern California Indian cultures, translated the Yurok word *kegey* (plural, *kegeyowor* [Berman 1982:201]) as "shaman." He restricted shamanistic experience and practice among the Yuroks almost exclusively to the *kegeyowor*, whom he identified as clairvoyant healers, practically without exception women (Kroeber 1925:63, in Elmendorf 1960:247:1; and in Spott and Kroeber 1942:155). Kroeber, who did his most extensive Yurok fieldwork between 1900 and 1907, noted that Yuroks "regularly English kégei as 'doctor'" (in Elmendorf 1960: 504.20).[1] He did note that Yurok men, who attained bravery and fighting powers from spirits and who were called *weskweloy*,[2] or *ploh wichekws*, "big heart", could be considered "shamans" legitimately as well, by dint of their personal encounters with anthropomorphized guardian spirits (in Elmendorf 1960:467.1): guardian spirits appear in person, said Kroeber, only to the *kegey* and the *weskweloy* (ibid., 482.4).

Well-founded in an appreciation of the importance of trance, direct encounters with spirits, and professionalism to shamanism, Kroeber's restriction of Yurok shamanism to these two figures should not be taken to suggest that the two types of actors share a single "shaman" category in Yurok culture, where doctors and warriors belong to quite distinct social and conceptual domains associated with distinct prototypes. Moreover, the *kegeyowor* themselves, while indeed constituting an explicit Yurok cultural category, arise along a continuum of spiritual practitioners; it is a category that often overlaps with many other sorts of specialists, not rigidly defined categorically or hierarchically, who cannot usefully be designated "shamans." So there is a question of whether or not the notion of "shaman" is in fact the most meaningful one in working toward an understanding of the spiritual knowledge and practices of the Yuroks and their neighbors.

NORTHWESTERN CALIFORNIA, CULTURAL CONTEXT, AND ORAL TESTIMONY

Many people, perhaps especially California Indians, are frustrated with the continued representation of *all* native northwestern California cultures, by scholars who have largely followed Kroeber's lead (1925), through Yurok Indian ethnography (see Buckley 1989b). I regret that I must once again do so to an extent, lacking information comparable with that available for the Yuroks on doctoring among Karuks and Tolowas, the two groups most frequently associated with the Yuroks in terms of shared doctoring techniques, let alone the Hupas, Wiyots, or the twelve other groups that Kroeber included in his northwest California culture province (Kroeber 1939: Table 18). This information is available neither in the received literature nor have I acquired it through my own fieldwork;[3] but I take my limited approach on two understandings:

First, I really *am* talking about Yurok Indian doctors and only inferentially and in untested ways about northwestern California in general. But, second, I recognize that doctoring in northwestern California always has had a cosmopolitan or inter-ethnic aspect, doctors of one group--Tolowa say--often treating patients from another--say, Yurok (e.g., Drucker 1937:257)--and doctors of several groups occasionally practicing together as in a famous nineteenth century case involving two Yurok and one Karuk female doctors and a male Tolowa doctor (Spott and Kroeber 1942:164-66).

Cultural particularity and specificity is called for even at the risk of perpetuating undue anthropological fixation on Yurok culture, not only because I lack sufficient information on groups other than the Yuroks, but also because of the tendency in some quarters to deal with putative "shamanism" as a more-or-less universal phenomenon; a thing in itself that might be understood outside of *any* particular cultural context. As I have suggested above, shamanism cannot be well understood when divorced from the cultural (and historical) context within which particular shamans gain and use their powers, and in which their clients find meaning and help. Toward the end of this chapter I will sketch the broader ontological, cosmographic, moral, and metaphysical framework within which the Yurok *kegeyowor* worked, beginning to integrate an understanding of the Kegey's power with an understanding of that religious framework.

To put things in their proper cultural contexts is to attempt to see things from what Malinowski long ago called a "native point of view" (see Geertz 1976). (Today, a less totalizing approach in effect pluralizes "point.") In pursuing this ideal, some anthropologists have increasingly allowed native experts to speak for themselves within anthropological texts, where their voices may enter into dialogue with that of the ethnographer (see, for instance, Clifford and Marcus 1986; cf. Buckley 1987). Whenever possible in what follows I have incorporated verbatim transcriptions of my own--primarily Yurok--teachers' words, introducing them into an ethnographic record long dominated by excellent accounts from the first half of this century that are, however, limited in number and the diversity of cases that they present (e.g., Drucker 1937, Erikson 1943, Kroeber 1925, Spott and Kroeber 1942, Valory 1970). This technique is hardly as modern as the more polemical postmodernists would have us believe. In studies of northwestern California, for instance, John Peabody Harrington's monograph on Karuk tobacco use (Harrington 1932) provides an example of an early "polyphonic" text.

In expanding the amount of available native testimony on Yurok doctors, introducing some entirely new ethnographic accounts and information, I wish to celebrate the knowledge of generations more recent than those with which Kroeber, Harrington, and Drucker worked, and to render individual elders' voices more faithfully than any edited reworking in terms of so-called "standard English," let alone any paraphrase or condensation, might. The truths, the real spirit of Yurok culture, is in these voices, I believe, far more certainly than in any analysis or interpretation that I might make of what they say.[4]

"YOU GO AND SPEAK TO IT"

Many Indian people in northwestern California have had a variety of extra-ordinary powers that have been manifested through the use of purchased or inherited prayers, or what Kroeber called "formulas." As Ella Norris told me in 1976, speaking of practitioners still active in the early years of this century:

> Them days, they pray, everything they do.
> White people, it's different--But Indians it's
> different. Indians, everything they do they pray,
> and they fast--maybe ten days. [Taped.]

For instance, in 1976 while driving together through heavy fog, Dewey George told me about his father, Sregon George's (b. ca. 1870) medicine for dispelling fogs:

> Once I was driving my father and we run
> into some heavy fog like this--couldn't see a thing.
> My father said, "better do something about this."
> I stopped and he got out, made medicine, prayed.
> Fog lifted. I don't know what he did. [From
> notes.]

I have been told of "prayers" used to recover drowned bodies from the river or sea, for turning back epidemic illness, for controlling intentionally set grass fires, and for warding off ill-omens. The power of such "praying" or "making medicine," both usually referred to in Yurok simply as "talking to" (*tergerum-*, *tergum-*), can be dramatic. The following accounts, given to me by Florence Shaughnessy in 1976, offer vivid examples. The first concerns Starwin Bill who was blind in his old age and was often called Blind Bill. He lived with Kitty and Jimmy Gensaw, at

Requa. The time is around 1910:

> If an owl [screech owl, *tekw?es*] came, that
> was one of the things we didn't like because he
> brought a message of something bad, always death.
> So anyone who knows a prayer to counteract the
> message--you say, "You go and speak to it." Then
> you use a special prayer to ward off the message
> that he brings. It brings the message only if he
> hoots, and a special way he hoots--not very long;
> sharp. Always he brings the news of death, and
> that's true . . .
>
> [It was] eleven o'clock at night when
> everyone was in the house singing or telling stories
> or something. And the owl came. And he made
> his call. He was sitting on top of that old
> community hall--it was a big building. So
> Momma [Kitty Gensaw] went in and told [Blind
> Bill] what was happening out there. So he said,
> "bring me rock, one rock." So she found it--it had
> to be a certain shape. She had a lantern, so she
> found the rock. So he took it into his hand and he
> prayed. And then he tossed the rock down, down
> to where the sound, where the owl was.
>
> So early the next morning he was up and
> washed and said, "Go get those kids and send them
> down there" to see if the owl is dead. So we went
> down there and we found a dead owl. We couldn't
> bring it near the house.
>
> Then up at my grandmother's [Ollie Serper]
> the same sort of owl came, and she had a great big
> oak tree by her cabin, her home, just thick with
> limbs. And he came there. And he was making
> his cry just so--he was just bouncing up and
> down, and the leaves were dropping down. So she
> went out and got a rock, and she prayed to the
> rock and went out there and tossed it. So she told
> *X*--he was staying with her--"Go out and bury
> that owl." So he went out and there was a dead
> owl, so he buried it. My grandmother, Ollie
> Serper. See? The same prayer.
>
> I don't know how you would explain that,
> but each time there was a dead owl there the next
> morning. Maybe another owl came along and had
> a heart attack! But it's kind of weird, isn't it?
> [Taped.]

People who knew a variety of such prayers were called *teno:wok,* "educated." Florence Shaughnessy:

> *Teno:wok*--it means he knows all kinds of-
> -he knows all the different ways to pray for
> things, because he has trained, he has been to the
> mountains, he has been to these different rocks.
> So if anything happens you go to this person
> because he's well schooled, he's studied all of this.
> [Taped.]

Such "training" (*hohkep'-*) emphasizes purification through fasting and thirsting (as Ella Norris suggested, above) abstinence from sex, avoidance of pollution, especially through contact with menstruation, frequent sweating and many other specifics, depending on the knowledge or power being sought--often, as Mrs. Shaughnessy suggests, visits to power places, usually in the mountains. Above all, it stresses willfully focused single-mindedness, or "thinking." Harry Roberts told me that when men like his teacher, Robert Spott, who Mrs. Shaughnessy mentioned as being *teno:wok,* trained hard, they naturally acquired some curing powers which they then could choose to develop or not. Aileen Figueroa's reminiscence of her grandfather, which I recorded in 1976, suggests this. (It perhaps relates a practice arising after the coming of European epidemic illness to the area; that is, after 1830 at the earliest.)

> Grandfather [Jones] went out at night to
> pray. He was a medicine man. When the
> influenza was coming [Winter 1918-19] he went
> out at night to pray and it stopped; it didn't come
> any closer. But there's no one can do that now.
>   He also used to doctor people. Not like an
> Indian doctor [*kegey*]--he would just sing and talk,
> pray for people. [Taped.]

The late Dewey George, who was known to have many prayers, also seems to have known how to do some curing:

> There was a Jump Dance at Hoopa [in
> 1972] and *Y* thought he saw a waterdog jump up
> and try to get in his mouth. He tried to pull it out.
> I heard about that and I said I knew how to cure
> him, but my sister didn't want me to. I'd have to
> lock up my house so nobody would come around.

It takes a lot to make Indian medicine. My sister didn't want me to do that because it takes too much. So he went to an Indian doctor in Redding [Flora Jones, Wintu] and she cured him. [From notes.]

Thus, in traditional Yurok culture, people who know or "own" prayers of various sorts meld into people who are able to cure and who are called, in English, "doctors."

DOCTORS

People once commanded many sorts of curative prayers, often used in combination with small amounts of herbal "medicine" (*meskwoh*). Kroeber (in Spott and Kroeber 1942:157) speaks of prayers to cure "snakebite, insanity, sacroiliac slip, cuts, bruises, breaks, puerperal fever, any illness [presumably, of new mothers] within 20 days of parturition, and arrowhead or bullet wounds." To this list I can add boils. Kroeber also notes (in Elmendorf 1960:248.1) that there is no special term in Yurok for such a formula and herb doctors "as a profession." Indeed, in trying to force a rather loose congeries of often multi-talented practitioners into clearly bounded categories of specialists we may risk imposing on traditional Yurok culture a kind of conceptual order not present in that culture itself. Still, there are several terms-- perhaps best understood as designating (occasionally overlapping) prototypal associations rather than rigidly bounded and hierarchically arranged conceptual categories--that are generally translated as "doctor" today (Jean Perry, personal communication 1990) and whose references should be examined here.

An herbalist who held the exoteric knowledge for dispensing the herbal medicines eaten or drunk for curing various simple ills was called *meges*. As such, a *meges* is not attributed spiritual power, although an individual who practices as a *meges* might also command other, esoteric knowledge. (White, biomedical doctors were called *meges*, when they arrived in northwestern California, and were viewed as mere dispensers of medicines, not comparable to the powerful *kegeyowor*, the shamans.)

"Prayer doctors," *kwes?oye?ey*,[5] on the other hand, do have spiritual powers that they exercise in, particularly, driving out or warding off several sorts of dangers (see above). The *kwes?oye?ey* might accompany his prayer with the burning of angelica root or tobacco or use of other medicines. The group once included people who knew how to say the prayers for the dead, to send their spirits off to the next world and to remove the pollution from the houses in which people had died. Ella Norris, in 1978:

> *kwes?oye?ey* means--see, he talks to that roots and you bathe in that roots, when somebody dies in the family. And he talks, he prays over the roots, and they bathe with it, and sprinkle the house to keep the spirit out, like ghosts, and it won't be haunted then . . . Lola Donelly was last one what knowed it . . . That's too bad, its gone away. [Taped.]

Other specialists included midwives who had special prayers (see Weitchpec Susie, in Buckley 1988a:198). Ella Norris:

> The midwife has to know what to do, what kind of medicines to use. Like the deer--deer medicine. Deer has medicine because they have their young anyplace--and a certain kind of grass they eat. So we have to know what kind of grass he chew on, too; got to know that deer song. There's a right way and time when you giving birth why you don't have such a hard time. [Taped.]

(The *kegeyowor* never delivered babies [Thompson 1916:42], probably because of the pollution inherent in the process: "high doctors" had to, by all means, "keep clean.")

A midwife steamed the newborn infant in wormwood and soaproot, I've been told, protecting its vulnerable spirit for ten days, until it had lodged firmly in the baby's body. Thus midwives may have been associated with the Karuk prototype that Harrington called "steaming doctors" (1932:231-34), those who steamed patients placed under wraps with stone-heated infusions of herbs in cooking baskets. It is said by some that the technique of steaming was once the most common and widespread curative technique in the region (Julian Lang, personal communication 1990), and that it possibly belongs to the oldest strata of culture (Victor Golla, ibid.).

Brush Dance (*melo:*) doctors, *?umelo:yik* (?) (Curtis 1924:45) or "medicine women" (Kroeber, in Elmendorf 1960:543.2), also steam their young patients, and may once have been considered protoypal "steaming doctors," but it is also possible that they were originally associated with the *kegeyowor* or, finally, comprised a somewhat unique group. They are better known than many sorts of traditional doctors today as the child-curing Brush Dance is still a regular feature of life in Native northwestern California (e.g., Keeling 1980). According to Aileen Figueroa, Bob Limes, a Yurok man from Serper, acted as a Brush Dance doctor two to three times in the past, but he's gone now and male Brush Dance doctors are seldom heard of: like *kegeyowor*, most have always been women. It is said that Brush Dance medicines are on Red Mountain, near the mouth of the Klamath River. Florence Shaughnessy, speaking of a time around 1910:

> In the old days the [Brush Dance] doctor couldn't have any food, no water. She'd go up in the hills and hide all day--nobody could see her. She'd get the wood for the torches, the salal. If she came from up river they'd send out scouts first, to find where things were because she wouldn't know this country, and they'd tell her where to look. But she had to go get everything herself: fir, and pine to put in the fire.
>
> I went up with the doctor once when I was a little girl--and, Oh! I wanted to come home so bad! I couldn't eat and I couldn't drink and all I could think about was if I ran home then I could get something to eat.
>
> When we came back down we took a burden-basket up to the graveyard and she fastened on a feather in a certain way. You see, the feather stood up straight the way she fixed it. But then she had to go back up and look the day after the dance, in the morning, and if the feather had fallen over then the child would die. But if the feather still stood up, through the whole dance, then the child would get well.

Bad Doctors and Seeing Doctors

Not all doctors worked for the good. There were also "evil doctors" who could be hired to make "bad prayers" against people, to curse them and make them ill. Florence Shaughnessy:

> You stayed sort of away, you didn't dare touch any of their belongings, you shied away from a person that, you know, had bad vibes, let's say. You know by just looking at a person that he cares nothing for you, that he'd just as soon strike you as talk to you. Then you just get away from

a person because you don't want to force yourself
on an evil thing.

So they stayed mostly to themselves, but
sometimes they would throw their weight around
and create a disturbance--a bad fight or
something, because they are agitating, they're
agitators. They want to see something going on.
So like if somebody should be hurt and then they
die from a wound or something, then they come to
you and you say, "We'll pay you so much to make
bad medicine because they have destroyed our
main supporter," or "our third son," or something
in the family. And that's how they got their
power, because they'll be paid for doing this bad
thing. And then they have to go some place to get
more power for being braver and nastier than they
were yesterday. [Taped.]

Frank Douglas:

There was that Bad Place, over by Doctor
Rock. They'd make that bad medicine there, say
"I hope you bind up, I hope you die [of
constipation]--make bad wishes." [From notes.]

People referred to as "doctor" in English today also once
included male *pegahsoy*, "seeing," "wishing" or "confession
doctors," who were clairvoyant and could "see" the "shadows" of
evil past deeds or poisoning attacks that were making people ill.
The *pegahsoy* elicited a confession, *pahsoy*, from the patient or
identified the evil-doer, and then prayed and blew away the
shadow with his breath. (Elicited confessions might be used, at
least among the Karuks, as formulas or prayers for curing future
illnesses of the same nature [Gifford 1958].) Mrs. Shaughnessy,
again:

The evil doctor--you can hire them to put
a curse on a family. That's the bad doctor. They
do that. They learn the bad prayers; they go to the
bad rocks and do this.

And then the doctors ... come in. They're
not necessarily the big doctors [*kegeyowor*]; they
come in and have the power to see, *pegahsoy*.
Your child is sick and he has the same symptoms
every time he's sick, and each time it gets worse.

> Well it means that--maybe there's been bad wishes
> made. And then they come in and they can see
> that, and then you have to confess and talk about
> it. And then, a lot of times there hasn't been
> anything in your family and nothing happens.
> And then its time to go and get the real doctor,
> because it isn't bad wishes--its just sick. [Taped.]

Consideration of the *pegahsoy* brings us into a new realm
or degree of power, however, for they were clairvoyants and they
underwent stringent training (*hohkep'-*) in the high mountains, not
unlike a certain phase in the training (*hohkep'-*) of the *kegeyowor*.
While Mrs. Shaughnessy implied that they were lesser than the
"big" or "real doctors," the *kegeyowor*, at least some of these men
were called *pegerk kegey* (Thompson 1916:42-43)--"man doctor"
or, in Kroeber's terms, male shamans. I return to the *pegahsoy*
below, then, after further examining the concept of shamanism
and its relevance to traditional Yurok culture.

SHAMANS

As Mircea Eliade writes, "every medicine man is a healer,
but the shaman employs a method that is his and his alone"
(1964:5). We have seen that there were various sorts of "doctors"
in traditional Yurok culture that both healed and exercised power
of extra-ordinary sorts, but who were not considered *kegeyowor*--
according to Kroeber, "shamans." The Yurok-English category of
"doctor" is not the same as the anthropological category of
"shaman."

I have argued for ethnographic particularity and contextual
circumstantiality in seeking an understanding of cultural
phenomena, and yet I find in the work of one of the great
comparativists, Mircea Eliade, an at least heuristically useful
definition of shamanism that will, I think, allow us to begin to
interpret the Yurok category of *kegey*. Eliade defines
"shamanism" as "a technique of ecstacy" (1964:4) and writes that,
"shamanism always remains an ecstatic technique at the disposal of
a particular elite and represents, as it were, the mysticism of the
particular religion" (ibid., 8). From this point of view, shamanism
is not a practice--like healing or exercising power--but is the
particular order of technique by which one heals and exercises
other powers. Secondly, and unlike the purchase or inheritance of
formulas or the exoteric learning of herbal remedies, acquisition
of this technique depends upon the personal and experiential,

direct apprehension of esoteric, spiritual knowledge: upon what Eliade calls "mysticism" and what Kroeber identified as the acquisition of guardian spirits (above).

Given such a definition, there are three sorts of individuals in traditional Yurok society that might reasonably be considered shamans: the *kegey*, or "high doctor"; the *weskweloy*, or warrior, and the *?uma?ah*, or sorcerer. All of these statuses are "elite" insofar as they imply control of power, gained through training, that is greater than that controlled by most other people. The *kegey* is associated with high mountain training in the summer, the warrior with bad winter weather and training at lower altitudes.

Warriors

Certain men acquired guardian spirits that imbued them with extra-ordinary bravery and fighting skills through vision questing in power-places.[6] These men were called *weskweloy* (see note 2) or *ploh wichekws*, "big heart," and were considered *Lmey*, "mean," "habitually ready to fight" (Kroeber, in Elmendorf 1960:267.1). They got their powers through questing in the lower hills or mountains at night, in hollow rocks and whirlpools, beneath sea stacks and in other such dangerous, cosmographically transitional or liminal places (see Buckley 1980). There they encountered spirits, most typically one of the ten Thunder brothers (see Spott and Kroeber 1942:227-232), but also various horned water monsters (Kroeber, in Elmendorf 1960:486.1), skeleton-like spirits (ibid., 467.1), and others including, as we shall see, Chicken Hawk.[7] Losing consciousness, they acquired power from their new guardian spirit.

According to Dewey George, warrior training gave one the power to jump extraordinarily high and across very broad stretches from a standing start, and to be very quick, like lightning. They practiced dodging arrows. Harry Roberts told me that these fighters entered a trance when they fought, like the Norse *berserk*, and that, having entered fighting trance, they could only be stopped by being killed. Kroeber noted that they were "semi-professionals" (in Elmendorf 1960:469.13) (there is a mythological figure named Hired Killer [Kroeber 1976]), that they were always more rare than the *kegeyowor* (ibid., 494.21), of lower social rank than these curative shamans (ibid., 473.20), and that they disappeared sooner after massive conduct in 1850 than did the *kegeyowor* so that we lack actual case histories (ibid., 494.21; cf. Spott and Kroeber 1942:167). Nonetheless, in 1976 Antone ("Anafey") Obee gave me this account of an incident that occurred in about 1900:

Training--train [for] combat or duel . . .
We had one relation, I guess he was the best one
there ever was. They call him *mo:lo?ki* ["Old
Lucky"]. They had him cornered in Crescent City.
He jumped on a rail fence. Three or four of them
thought they had him; they didn't get him.

I saw him one time, I seen him coming. He
was a tough old fella. You say, "Watch out!"
"Move aside!" and they did. He was way over
there. He got brushed slightly. He was pretty near
opposite us, say ["Move aside!"]. Jeeze, he went
just like lightning, just start from nothing. He just
swang!

He used to go up in the mountains above
Harry Woods' on windy night. Tenth night he was
up there Chicken Hawk hit him. From then on
they couldn't hit him. A chicken hawk that was
blowing in the wind, must have knocked him
down [unconscious] too . . .

It's in the air: spirits in the air. You go
out in the mountains. [Taped.]

Devils

If shamans are people who acquire power through mystical
connection with spirits and exercise that power through ecstatic
technique, then the Yurok *?uma?ah*, sorcerer, "devil," or "Indian
devil" (Tolowa *t'e?na:gi*, 'at night travels' [Drucker 1937:258])
might legitimately be included among shamans. Indeed, Valory
(1970) suggests that the *?uma?ah* is the exact inverse of the *kegey*,
acquiring evil spirit helpers, dancing and singing in dark parody
of the doctor's dance, *remoh*, and introjecting ("shooting") disease-
causing magical objects, also called *?uma?ah*, rather than sucking
out "pains," *telogeL*, as the *kegey* does. It may be that "deviling"
has always been more an accusation than an actual role. Whether
he is real or imagined, however, the opposition between the "devil"
(*?uma?ah*) and the "bad" or "evil doctor" (above) follows the classic
anthropological distinction between the sorcerer and the witch.
The putative power of the *?uma?ah*, "devil" or sorcerer, is perhaps
comparable in strength to that of the warrior at least, if not of the
kegey. Kroeber called the sorcerer's kit of magical black obsidian
arrows, which flamed and sent out showers of sparks, "the
mysterious thing," and also suggested that the devil was, like the
doctor, a kind of shaman (Kroeber 1925:67; in Elmendorf
1960:525.9,10,11; cf. Drucker 1937:258). Like both the *kegey* and
the warrior, the sorcerer worked for pay. While Valory (1970)

placed *?uma?ah* among the most déclassé in Yurok society (being among the most polluted), the case was not, perhaps, always so simple. Harry Roberts told me that most of the elite "high men" many of whom were, we will see, *pegahsoy*, "wishing doctors," also had deviling powers in the form of "the mysterious thing" for self-protection against envious rivals. It is widely rumored that the famous lower Klamath headman Captain Spott, born shortly after contact (Kroeber 1976:419-20; Spott and Kroeber 1942:144-48 ff.), owned such a fiery kit and that it was inherited by his adoptive daughter Alice (see note 6), who disposed of it in horror--but such rumors about the great families are common.

Like these rumors, however, firm belief in Indian devils and in their magical abilities are also common. Aileen Figueroa told me about a devil she'd seen, probably around 1935, talking about his training in a way that makes it immediately comparable to the training of the *weskweloy* in Anafey Obee's account above and, as we will see, to the training of the *kegey*:

> *?uma?ah*--that's the devil. I've seen them. I've seen several of them, long time ago . . . We was living on the ranch. The little one, he kept crying and crying. We had a dog, and this dog--I went outside and I heard that dog barking down the road. I went outside and I heard that dog running, clear up into the mountains you'd hear him, and then he'd come down. And barking--sound like he was trying to grab at something at the same time. And then he'd come down, his mouth was all wet, he'd circle around, then he'd go back up into the mountains again, not far, but then he'd kind of circle down again.
>
> I was setting down--it was kind of a sidehill--I was setting down kind of on my tiptoes there. I held a three cell flashlight over my head and I was trying to shine it. There's a road runs down below the house. I was shining it and all at once I see a big flame, right in the road there: big flames shooting about that high [three feet]. It was just beautiful, beautiful--you know how fire flames, shaped like that [rounded on the bottom, tapering to a point on top]? Pretty. And right in the middle I seen two green eyes looking right out, right inside that fire.
>
> I hollered, hollered at them [in the house] and I guess finally they heard me--I didn't want it

to leave. Finally they came out and we went down there with the flashlight and looked all over and we didn't see anything. [But] I seen it.

It's a people, it's people, it's--what do you call it? A lot of people don't believe in those things [probably, Indian devil].

I don't know [what they are doing], but I know there is--A lot of time maybe you're mean to a certain person or something like that, and they're trying to get revenge or something like that. Then they'll get themselves into different-- maybe you'll see a great big dog or something like that out there. They can make theirselves into different things . . .

It's the same thing, like with the Indian medicine man. They go a certain time, ten days or something like that, without drinking water or eating, without sleeping with a woman or something like that. They go out and they learn that. You can't do that now because people aren't clean. [Taped.]

There are many difficulties in comprehending *?uma?ah* accusations. First, human sorcerers often seem to be associated, if not conflated with, "Bigfoot," the local gorilla-like sasquatch figure called, in Yurok, *ra:k ni ?uma?ah*, "creek devil," or *ka:p ni ?uma?ah*, "brush devil" (see Buckley 1980), thought to come and go from the spiritual to the material realms at will and from whom human beings are said to have obtained their magical kits. Secondly, while there is clearly an ancient and indigenous putative sorcery technique, emphasizing mystical fire and sparks linked, in myth, with both black obsidian and with rattlesnakes (Kroeber 1976), the attribution of the shamanistic power of transformation- -into dogs, especially--to the *?uma?ah* may well date to the later influences of the Bear Doctors encountered or heard about by Yuroks while among other California Indians during the removals of the mid-nineteenth century (see Valory 1970). Today,"Indian Devils" are most often spoken of as night-running transformers who take animal or bird--especially owl (see above)--forms to "devil" their victims. However, in terms of the present inquiry, the *?uma?ah*, while possibly a shaman in the sense of being a practitioner of a "technique of ecstacy," is not a healer and is not, in any case, in the category *kegey* that Kroeber translated as "shaman." Finally, insofar as we wish to use Mircea Eliade's classic work (1964) heuristically, it is worth noting that Eliade linked shamans both with clairvoyant knowledge of the human soul (ibid., 8) and with a celestial "Great God" whose name may mean "Sky" or "Heaven" (ibid., 9). These attributes, we will see, properly understood in particularistic terms, bring us to focus upon the Yurok *kegeyowor*, eliminating both the *weskweloy* and the *?uma?ah* from further consideration in the present context. Although warriors and devils deserve mention in any complete discussion of Yurok shamanism, mention alone perhaps suffices, here at least.

Indian doctors

The term "shaman" does not correlate with any single explicit, indigenous Yurok category. It may justifiably be applied to three quite separate sorts of individuals who, however, all controlled considerable power acquired through training and may once have been culturally associated to a degree on this basis. They are the *weskweloy*, trance warrior; the *?uma?ah*, transformer-sorcerer; and the *kegey*, variously called in English, "doctor," "Indian doctor," "sucking doctor," and "high doctor." It is time now to consider these doctors--the individuals closest in spirit to what many non-Yuroks conceive of as "shamans." This conception, I think, emphasizes healing as a central shamanic function and thus focus on the *kegeyowor* both attends to a clear native category (which "shaman" is not) and to the non-Yurok concept of "shaman."

There are several excellent accounts of Yurok doctors' calling, training and careers available in the received literature (Thompson 1916, Kroeber 1925, Spott and Kroeber 1942, Erikson 1943, Valory 1970). I will not reproduce these well-known accounts once again. The reader unfamiliar with them is referred to the available sources as given above. Rather than incompletely recapitulating any of these accounts, I outline their common features. More especially, I add new particulars and emphases that I have been given me by more recent experts than those consulted by the authors of the available texts, using verbatim accounts when possible, as in the foregoing.

KEGEYOWOR

Training

Although each recorded case is somewhat different, a general five-step pattern in the recruitment and training of the *kegeyowor* can be discerned (Kroeber 1925:63), albeit with much local and personal variation (Valory 1978:264):

1) The *kegey* receives her potential for power, usually as a mature woman, by one of several means: through inheritance, through what is called "natural design," or calling, and--most dramatically--through a special kind of dreaming, *ka:miL-*("to dream bad" [Valory 1978:76]), distinct from ordinary dreaming (*so:niL-*) (Robins 1958:279). Dewey George:

> A person would go to sleep and dream.
> They'd dream there was something bad working on them, and then they'd have to become a doctor.
> That's the way it used to work--you dream something. [From notes.]

In this dream or in a vision gained through long periods of ascetic training, usually in the hills, the novice meets a guardian spirit, often the spirit of a dead doctor but also Whale, Wolf, Chicken Hawk, and others (Spott and Kroeber 1942:155). The spirit makes her swallow some sort of--often repulsive--object and gives her her first doctoring song, or "spirit song" (Valory 1970:37). The object is a *telogeL*, or "pain." Both the song and this "pain" may be understood as manifestations of the spirit.

The vocation of *kegey* often passed through the female line of families, from mother to daughter (Spott and Kroeber 1942:166), but not everyone who might have wished to have a shaman's dream or first vision was able to do so: inheritance was merely a potential. "Some of them it don't work out; they don't get that dream," said Frank Douglas [from notes].

2) The dream or vision makes the novice sick and she is cared for by an experienced *kegey*. When she is prepared she begins to dance the Kick Dance, *remoh*, in her village's sweat house, perhaps falling unconscious and being supported by her male relatives. She is now "crazy," *keLpey*--like a shaman, however, not *kerpey*, as in ordinary madness--and perhaps foaming at the mouth (Valory 1978:96,249). In this first Kick Dance, which lasts for ten days, she is *che?wish*, "clean spirit dancing" (ibid., 39). She must learn to regurgitate the *telogeL*, "pain," deposit it in a dipper basket, *keyom*, and reingest it from across the room, sucking it in through her mouth or through a pipe, repeating this feat at will, gaining control of the first, and most powerful (Kroeber, in Elmendorf 1960:540.19), pain.[8] If she cannot do so, experienced shamans may seek to get the spirit-pain from her, augmenting their own powers and curing her of shamanic illness--but obviating her chances of becoming a doctor herself (Spott and Kroeber 1942:153-57).

3) When the novice has recovered she is taken in the summertime by her mentor, accompanied by male relatives, to a "prayer seat" in the higher mountains, *chekche?iL* or *chek'weL*, a small, semi-circular stone enclosure (see Buckley 1986). The "seat" is swept and prepared carefully. Florence Shaughnessy was once taken to such a seat in the Siskiyou Mountains by male kin, around 1930, to "make medicine for long life," rather than as a novice *kegey*. She described cleaning the seat as the doctors also must have done:

> They should preserve all of that, over towards Blue Creek; that's all sacred ground. There are many prayer seats there. When I went up there [to Doctor Rock, with Ed Jaynes] we cleaned out the prayer seats. He had a hatchet and he cut the brush growing around the seats. Then we took that and some grasses and we fashioned brooms. And he said, "Now you start in the middle and sweep the old leaves and twigs into the corners, and I'll carry that down later." [From notes.]

Again, in the case of the doctors use of these seats followed considerable training and the initial acquisition of power. Thus, Dewey George told me that doctors had to have a certain degree of power even to go up to the mountain seats:

> The doctors used to walk up to Doctor Rock. They had power, so they walked up. They'd go up there and they'd dance for ten days, ten nights. Then they'd come back and they'd dance in the sweathouse for another five or six nights. That's if they wanted to be good doctors. They'd go up with their relations to dance . . .
> Good doctors go up [to] Chimney Rock, but only the very best ones. Most went up to Doctor Rock, not many to Chimney Rock. The Hupa had their own place, up at Trinity Summit. The Orleans [Karuks] went someplace up in the Marble Mountains, the Smith River [Tolowas] went someplace, too. The Yurok and the Katimin [Karuks] went up to Doctor Rock and Chimney Rock. [From notes.]

Note, here, that the degree of power attained in the mountain "seats" was related to the altitude: Chimney Rock is considerably higher than Doctor Rock. Doctor training may be understood in part as a gradual progression from lower to higher altitudes, from the hills to the mountains, from lesser to greater power. Different spirits and, hence, powers resided at different altitudes and, moreover, on different parts of single sacred site, like Doctor Rock. Dewey George again:

> Up on Doctor Rock there were different parts of the rock for each [power]. I've seen four places where there have been fires. [From notes.]

Occasionally, many shamans would go into the mountains together to train, to augment their powers through new spirit connections by which they learned more, or to assist a novice and test her. Florence Shaughnessy:

> Groups of doctors used to go up there to dance and to train, or people would go up alone, in secret. And they'd keep themselves hidden if anybody came around; they didn't want to be seen. They'd camp off in the brush and they'd just make a small fire so nobody could see them. That was because they were so pure and they didn't want anybody to come near them and spoil it. They kept the unclean people away. [From notes.]

The novice's dance in the *chekce?iL* was a "test" (Thompson 1916:39), an "examination" (Spott and Kroeber 1942:160). Kroeber said that "the function of this act is obscure" (1925:63), but that the novice "speaks things that are not known to other people" (ibid., 64), dancing to the different directions with her arms extended. I have twice been told that doctors dance with such concentration that their feet entirely leave the ground, and they levitate. The dancer listens for the right voices among the many she hears--those singing *remoh* songs. Other voices may offer her evil powers, but she must say, "I did not come here for that" (Spott and Kroeber 1942:161). When she hears the right voices she falls into trance and runs back down the mountain to her village sweathouse, unconscious and "crazy," protected by her male relatives who have accompanied her and her trainer (Kroeber 1925:64) and who may restrain her with a long strap, *(?)weskul*, lest she injure herself.[9]

When the novice successfully passed her mountain test she had attained new spirit helpers and songs, and had "made her path into the mountains," through establishing a relationship with the *wo:gey*, "Immortals," and doctors' spirits there. This meant that she could call on the mountain spirits for assistance in her cures and could also visit her mountain "seat" or sacred site in trance, without leaving her home, gaining control of new pains in this way. It also meant that her route into the mountains where she would live on as a spirit after death, able to help living novice shamans, had been established (cf., Spott and Kroeber 1942:161).[10]

Would-be shamans who could not make the necessary spirit connection, perhaps because they had broken the stringent rules of ascetic training, failed to pass the mountain test. Ella Norris told of a novice going into the mountains with her own aunt, Mary Williams, an established *kegey*, near the turn of the century when it was becoming difficult to acquire the powers of a *kegey*:

> Trail goes along the top, goes to Red Mountain, from Red Mountain to Doctor Rock. So going on that steep mountain, I guess, and on side there, must have been June month because they say there was blackberry vines there where it's kind of damp, way up on the hill there. So-- 'course they been fasting ten days down here, and this cousin was so hungry and those blackberries hanging there looked *good*! So she took two. She put one in her belt and one in her mouth. You not supposed to eat or drink.
>
> So, when they go up there, why naturally that Mary Williams she started in dancing and fasted. And one man goes, he has fire just side of [Doctor Rock], has fire going and talks to it all the time while the doctors are dancing--facing the early morning. They get answers from there. They get their Master's degree. Early in the morning, that beautiful--looks like abalone shell, that blue inside, its a beautiful thing.
>
> So sometimes they get their answers. Someone hollers. Certain sounds: they know they gotten their Master's degree, I call it, to be an Indian doctor. So this one dance, dance, dance, dance--ten days. She never get nothing. So they asked her, "What's the matter? What did you do?" So she confessed. She said I put one in my mouth.
>
> So she never got--see how strict they were? I'm telling you! [Taped.][11]

4) In this mountain test, the novice might acquire her second pain if she had not gotten it before, perhaps in the first *remoh*, for *telogeL* always occur in pairs, *wahpemew* (Valory 1978:44). After she ran down the mountain, the newly tested doctor began dancing a second *remoh* in her village's sweathouse, gaining control of both of her pains and demonstrating her abilities to eject and reingest them. This second dance usually lasted only about five days.

Following the second Kick Dance the novice might begin her practice as a sort of apprentice, often under harsh tutelage, "almost like a slave" to her teacher. A modern "Indian doctor" who underwent different training than that being described here was similarly indebted to his benefactor, Albert Thomas, a Wintu-Achumawi doctor (DuBois 1940), and similarly bound in apprenticeship. He told me that he went with Thomas on all of his cases for a year (probably around 1930) and that the doctor always asked the patient to give his apprentice some little gift--"an old hat or an old shirt"--as well as paying him, Albert Thomas, cash. One night, the ex-apprentice said, the doctor made three hundred dollars from all of the people who came to be doctored, but he got only an old shirt, although he had had to do most of the doctoring work for his teacher. Some nights he did all of the work, the doctor just observing. Still, he didn't get paid.

5) Traditionally, after the new doctor had refined and demonstrated her ability to cure she might be given a final dance, *?ukwerkwer*, the "pain cooking" ceremony, if her family could afford the expense. This took place in a dismantled family house, rather than in the less commodious sweat house where the *remoh* was held (Valory 1978:260, 260.1).

Having done all of this--which might take two or three years--the trainee was acknowledged as a *kegey*--in this sense, a "full" or "high doctor" (cf., Valory 1978:91). Often she acquired the powers of a "tracer," a finder of lost objects, together with clairvoyance and the ability to cure by sucking out pains (Valory 1978:55).

Practice

The doctor's pains are best understood as manifestations of her guardian spirits and/or the powers granted her by those spirits. They both gave her clairvoyance and the ability to suck out disease-causing pains, also *telogeL*, from her patients. Smoking her pipe (Harrington 1932:227-28), dancing, and singing her doctor's "spirit song," she entered trance, got "in the spirit," and "saw" the cause of the patient's affliction.[12]

This might be seen in the form of a "shadow," *sa?awor*, an image of a past deed that was now making the patient sick (Gifford 1958:248), the *kegey* "half seeing the ancient act in shadowy form" (Kroeber, in Elmendorf 1960:505.21). Florence Shaughnessy:

> They'd get the doctors and they'd dance and they'd see a formless thing, they all see this formless thing--it is not an object, just a sort of mass of something. And they know this evil force has something to do with this person . . .
>
> A doctor would have a vision of something, a mass of something, some trouble coming towards them. That was a memory in the family, some terrible secret they'd hidden, a "skeleton in the closet" that was effecting that person--and when it was stated, then it would go away and the person would get better . . .
>
> The whole family, everybody would be there. The doctor would sing in a trance, and she'd tell her vision. If you had knowledge of it you had to tell. After there was a confession the doctor'd fan the patient with a large basket. Then he slept. And he woke up hungry again, and in a couple of days he was well. [Taped.]

After hearing the patient's and family members' confessions, the doctor prayed over the patient and blew the shadow away with her breath (or a fan, as above)--the method identified earlier as *pegahsoy* (Spott and Kroeber 1942:156). (The *kegey* Fanny Flounder was reported to blow water over her patient after eliciting a confession [Valory 1978:265-66]--possibly an infusion of herbs [Drucker 1937:258]. Both *kegey* and male specialists, as we will see, practiced this sort of healing.)

In more serious cases, however, the *kegey*, entering trance, would see pairs of *telogeL* in the patient's body and would suck these out with her mouth.[13] The pains which she had acquired from (or which in a sense *were*) guardian spirits, and learned to control through the Kick Dance, would go out and capture the patient's paired pains with a "blanket" of "slime" (Spott and Kroeber 1942:156), allowing the shaman to extract them. A modern doctor, perhaps voicing a rather contemporary interpretation in 1978:

When the doctor sings it's like he's snake charming. The pains get hypnotized by the songs and start rising in the body to see what it is and when it's close enough to the surface the doctor can take it out by sucking, or with his hands. [From notes.]

Doctors specialized in curing different sorts of illnesses, by dint of the different kinds of *telogeL* that they had ingested and brought under control. According to the same man:

Doctors are like mechanics--specialists. Some mechanics are for radiators, some for transmissions. It's the same with doctors. I have a rather wide range of specialties [see below]. [From notes.]

Sometimes these specialists worked in teams to diagnose and treat very ill patients (cf. Spott and Kroeber 1942:164-66). Dewey George:

Three doctors worked on me when I was young. I was very sickly. That was seventy years ago [in 1976], and there were lots of doctors then. I was sick all of the time. They used to go after the doctors, on the trails, in boats. They used to say, "If you see boats going up-river real fast, they're going for the doctor!" They'd go up pretty fast. We used to have lots of doctors.
There're different kinds of doctors. Some press their mouths on your body. They press their mouth on your belly; they'd suck. I saw a doctor suck out a big ball, round [golf-ball sized], and it had roots coming down from it. I guess it was a cancer. I didn't have that.
They had power. They'd sing, they'd dance, they'd foam at the mouth. The foam would come out of their mouth and they'd grab that in their hand and they'd go outside. Then they'd [shake off the foam]; they'd take that outside. [From notes.]

The *telogeL* that the *kegeyowor* sucked out of their patients took many forms. Florence Shaughnessy spoke of the famous Yurok shaman, Fanny Flounder:

When Fanny went to cure she took baskets.
She'd suck, and she'd draw little things--they
looked like little pieces of rock--from the body of
the patient.

They made a lot of noise when they were
doctoring. We had to sing to help her, but it was
scary and we didn't want to--but we had to.
[From notes.]

Aileen Figucroa added to this picture of the pains that
Fanny Flounder extracted:

I saw her take things out of people, sucking
them with her mouth. Then she'd spit it out in her
hand. I saw her spit out eyes, eggs, lizards,
arrows. That was real. I saw those things breath
and move . . .

[Fanny Flounder] would sing and dance...
Nobody would tell her where they hurt. But she'd
just go and--she'd put her mouth [there] and suck
it out. Then she'd spit it out in her hand and drop
it on the [keyom].

I'd see her when there'd be a bunch of
them in there--they'd dance plumb around; there's
a bunch of them dancing . . . Then she'd spit out
like a little lizard--you could see it just move and
kind of quiver. [Taped.]

Doctors were ranked in terms of the numbers and strength
of the *telogeL* and other powers that they controlled, as well as the
altitude at which they had been "tested." After the *kegey* had
passed her mountain test she could acquire additional pains for
treating various sorts of illnesses without going back to the
mountains physically, although she might demonstrate these new
powers in additional Kick Dances. Florence Shaughnessy
remembered such a dance put up for Fanny Flounder who, it is
said, ultimately acquired five pairs of *telogeL*, making her one of
the most powerful, famous, and wealthy doctors in memory:

Doctor songs had word-pictures in them.
[Fanny] would sing and spew up her vision. Once
in the middle of the night George
[Meldon/Flounder] came out to the [Gensaw] house
and asked us all to come help Fanny, who was in
great pain because of a dream she'd had. We all

had to go down to the Matz [Brooks' traditional plank] house and sing to help her. I didn't want to go because it scared me, but we were made to go to help. Fanny wanted a Kick Dance to relieve her pain, and George came to get us.

Bill Gensaw sang Jimmy Gensaw's song about a bird that had a special stump that nobody else could come near because it was full of his food. He sang and Fanny started dancing. George said, "Don't stop singing!" We sang and sang and she danced. Finally she spewed up a bloody mess into a basin [keyom] we had there. It looked just like a small swallow all covered with bloody slime. I looked and I could see its little beak, the gold stripes on its shoulder. It was *breathing* there--I saw it clearly, sitting there breathing.

George put the bowl on the mantle [storage ledge of the semi-subterranean house]. Fanny got up. She was swinging around, making that sound that doctors make [see below]. Then she drew on her long pipe. There was a *thud*!--I can still hear it, like flesh hitting flesh. Then the basin came swirling down to the floor, empty. She got up.

Z's grandfather and Jimmy Gensaw grabbed her and held her and she calmed right down, and she danced some more.

That bird was a new pain for her, and they said it gave her power over tumors. [Taped.]

The Sucking Doctor's Power and its Limits

Fanny Flounder, who died in the 1940s at close to one hundred years of age, is widely regarded as having practiced a virtually aboriginal mode of doctoring. After massive contact with Euro-Americans in 1850, however, it seems to have become increasingly difficult for would-be *kegeyowor* to fully attain their powers. In the early years of the twentieth century, while several "full doctors" like Fanny Flounder continued to practice, there began to emerge partial or "half doctors"--women who had considerable clairvoyant and healing powers, but who could not pass their mountain tests. When the Indian Shaker Church was introduced on the lower Klamath in 1927, many of these "half doctors" joined, finding in the Shakers' dancing an equivalent to the *remoh* and in the Church a new social context for their work (Valory 1966). I do not examine these historical changes in this Chapter, however, attempting rather to augment, through an evoked "memory culture," the record of a reconstructed Yurok culture at close to the time of contact.

At that time, before the introduction of monotheistic religious concepts, it is my understanding that the power of the spirits through which the *kegey* cured was ultimately attributed to the universe itself, *k'i ?wes?onah*, "that which exists" and, also, "sky," manifested in the individual as *wewolochek'*, "her spirit" (see Buckley 1984). The energy is made visible in the waves and tides of the ocean, which are caused by the edge of the sky (*wes?onah*) rising and falling upon the sea at the western end of the world. Fanny Flounder's first doctor's dream was of the falling sky-edge, which dripped with icicles of blood, one of which was to be her first *telogeL*, given to her by Chicken Hawk. Her song was, "Where the sky moves up and down you are traveling in the air" (Spott and Kroeber 1942:159).

The waves caused by the falling sky-edge go throughout creation. Ella Norris:

> Like I said about Doctor Rock . . . I wish to goodness [the Forest Service] would leave that place alone because that's the last thing we ever own, that's our Holy Land, that's our secret place. That's where they used to go to practice--not only to be a doctor, but there's different places, different little places--like that whale place [see Spott and Kroeber 1942:224-27]. And then another place where the tide goes in and out. Its a hole there. When the tide comes in here [by the sea] it goes up there, and when the tide goes out it's low. [Taped.]

Harry Roberts, who spent time with Fanny Flounder as a young man:

> There was a theory. [Yuroks] thought that the ocean waves went through the body. You know, even in the mountains you can see the creeks rise and fall very slightly? Indians said that the ocean waves set that rhythm and that they set a rhythm in your body, too. That rhythm would come ten or twelve times a minute, or as slow as four when you're almost gone. If there's a lot of tension it might get up to eighteen or twenty--so much tension that you can't relax.

That wave--it's not really in the water, and it's not in the tissue. It's an energy wave, Spirit. It comes up through your feet, all the way up to your head, then back out down through your feet and your fingers. Occasionally it goes out through the top of your head, but I don't know about that: that's information a doctor had . . .

The doctor used this--to create a current. When Fanny [Flounder] was curing I used to see a blue light coming off the back of her head, and I could see it at the end of her fingers. You see that in a dim room. She'd create a low-keyed hum-- "hmmmmmmmmmmmm"--and click sticks together, or clap her hands lightly. She'd go on like that for a long time, like a beehive: keep it up for hours. Then suddenly she'd touch a tension spot on her patient's body and lead the tension off. Then she'd [wipe her hands vigorously].[14]

I don't know how you do those things. You focus your energy. You're a receiver, that's all. All energy is in the air or something, and you gather it in and focus it, make it do what you want. I can't tell you how . . . Once I asked Fanny how she got those baskets [keyom] off the [ledge]. "I just think them off" is what she said. She didn't know how either. [From notes.]

Such power made the *kegeyowor* frightening to some. While Fanny Flounder was well known for her humor, children, especially, were often terrified of the *kegeyowor*, as has been suggested in some of Florence Shaughnessy's testimony, above. Lucy Thompson remembered doctors brushing their hair over their faces to frighten away children and to secure their own privacy (Thompson 1916:41). Ella Norris:

I remember that in 1902 my mother's mother-in-law went up there [to Doctor Rock], Mary Williams. She was *kegey*. How I found out is she always sit with her back turned . . . So I told my mother, "What's the matter with that old woman?" She said, "Shhh! She's an Indian doctor, don't want to be mingled with too many people. She just came back from Doctor Rock." They don't mingle with everybody because they praying all the time, they clean, make it work for everybody goes to him . . .

She had her hair pitched, parted in the middle--that's the way Indians fix it. Wear Indian cap--cap made with just roots, beargrass trimming, no black in it. She'd always have her back turned, because kids get nosey. So I told my mother, "What's the matter with that old lady--she always has her back turned." She said, "Shhh! Just don't bother her. She's an Indian doctor." [Taped.]

These doctors' services, for which they were highly paid, were not limited to curing. They were viewed as spiritual specialists wise in many matters. In 1984 Lowana Brantner, Yurok of Meta, told the anthropologist Arnold R. Pilling that Fanny Flounder had come to her home when she was a girl, to instruct her during her lengthy first menstrual seclusion, at menarche (in Buckley 1988a:207-8). (Other testimony suggests that this act indicated Fanny Flounder's great power, strong enough to withstand menstrual pollution.) Some anecdotes reveal that the *kegeyowor* well knew their limits, however:

Two young girls stopped eating. They were both about sixteen and they lived in a village near Weitchpec. Their parents went around the village asking for help until they had enough money to offer a doctor, and then they took the girls down the river in a canoe to Murek where there were a lot of doctors, each one with a different specialty. They lived there right through the time when my mother [a partial doctor] was alive. They found the right doctor and she accepted their offer and started smoking her pipe and singing. After about half an hour she stopped and cleaned her pipe and handed back the money. "Yes, they both have a pain in them, but I'm not the kind of doctor to remove that sort of pain. But don't worry; in seven months it will come out the same way it got in."

The girls were pregnant. [From notes.]

THE PEGERK KEGEY

A. L. Kroeber insisted that among the Yuroks, "when a doctor [*kegey*] is spoken of it is always taken for granted that it is a woman" (Spott and Kroeber 1942:155). Male doctors seem to have been more common among the Tolowas and Robert Spott, Yurok, discusses a Tolowa ("Tolowil") "pegerk kegei" ("man doctor") in the same volume (ibid., 164 ff.) In an earlier publication (1925:68), Kroeber himself mentioned a Yurok male shaman who had a rattlesnake for a *telogeL* and who specialized in curing insanity. Finally, Fanny Flounder told Spott of being cured by a male doctor, probably Yurok, who she said was a member of the Shaker Church rather than a traditional, non-Christian *kegey*, but who sucked on her (Shaker doctors putatively do not suck) (Spott and Kroeber 1942:164; cf. Valory 1966:78-79). So the situation would seem to have been a bit more complex than Kroeber, with his insistence on rather rigid culture trait typologies (see Buckley 1989b), acknowledged. It may be that Kroeber and other early students mistook a decline in the number of male doctors after contact (Harrington 1932:231) for an immemorial pattern, or simply that male doctoring practices remained more secret than those--perhaps more public ones--of the female *kegey*.

Nonetheless, the Yurok writer Lucy Thompson discusses the "pa-girk-ka-gay" (*pegerk kegey*) at some length, saying that they were often of the "high" or aristocratic families (as were the *kegeyower*), that they engaged in lengthy training that culminated in a ten day mountain vision quest, that they cured patients of ills that the *kegeyower* did not treat and, finally, that they played an important role in scheduling and in starting the world-renewing Deerskin Dance:

> These men doctors help to start and to make the settlements for the white Deer-skin dance . . .
>
> [They] get together about the last of July or first of August and have a talk and settle the questions and give out the announcement that they were going to have the Deer-skin Dance (oh-pur-ah-wah). [Thompson 1916:42-43.]

Kroeber, on the other hand, denied that Yurok men ever got curing powers in the mountains, as did the *kegeyower* (Spott and Kroeber 1942:163), and considered the Shaker doctor who treated Fanny Flounder a cultural "hybrid," doubting that he had danced in the mountains (ibid., 164). Furthermore, Kroeber "never heard of 'kegei' as a term used of men who exercise a function or authority in a world renewal" (Kroeber and Gifford 1949:82.4). He was stumped by the occurrence of a shaman's *chekche?iL*, or "prayer seat," in the Karuk world renewal dance at Ina'm since, "The occurrence of this shamanistic element in a

world renewal is remarkable, because world renewal and doctoring
occupy wholly separate compartments of the culture, and no other
feature shared by them is known" (ibid., 128).

I believe that Kroeber was wrong on several counts. His
errors resulted precisely from his understanding of northwestern
California cultures in terms of discrete "compartments" and his
consequent failure to appreciate the integration of various domains
in those cultures (cf. Bean and Blackburn 1976:9). I have written
elsewhere of the integration of concern with death in the world
renewal ceremonials--concerns that Kroeber viewed as wholly
opposed (Buckley 1988b; contra. Kroeber and Gifford 1949). The
same sort of rethinking is in order in the case of Yurok doctoring.

Clearly, while Yurok men very infrequently underwent the
training of the *kegey* after contact, the *kegeyowor* being virtually
taken for granted by contemporary Native northwestern California
cultural experts to have been women, they did train for curative
abilities in the mountains, as Lucy Thompson claimed. Florence
Shaughnessy:

> I know men go out to the mountains also to
> study and pray for different things that they
> perform, like the *pegahsoy* [seeing or confession
> doctor--see above]. He has to go and have a vision
> and then he has to bring that vision out. When he
> goes to the mountains he generally goes to Doctor
> Rock and then to the men's rock to pray until
> everything becomes clear, and then he's given a
> certain power for what he's been praying for, what
> he wants to do . . .
> If you hurt someone, it's up to you to take
> this force away . . . to restore, to make whole
> again. If you're the one that caused this evil thing
> to happen, then they [*pegahsoy*] come and confront
> you and say, "Now you will have to come forward
> and restore what you have taken away; you have to
> restore health, because you're the one that did it."
> So they know that you have done it, so there's
> nothing for you to do but come and try to help this
> person that you damaged. Try to make whole
> again; when there's damage that you've done,
> bring to life.
> They [*pegahsoy*] don't use their mouths [to
> suck out *telogeL*]--they just sing and smoke their
> pipes and they dance, and then they see this evil
> vision. And then they'll talk it over and they'll

have to see which direction this evil vision comes from, and they'll pinpoint it to some village or to some instance, and they can almost find the person who is guilty of it. Men could go into this trance and see visions: they were seekers of visions too. . . . But not just an ordinary person. You had to go to the mountains and pray for that power. [Taped.]

Frank Douglas talked about such a man:

Pegahsoy--well, there's different ones, you know--man doctors sometimes, you know. Mother was sick, you know. There's Poker Bob lived at Johnson's. We was at Johnson's. And I had two nieces, just young gals, and they was about ready to have their monthlies. Oh, that's a bad thing you know, bad thing. *Pahsoy* [prayer, confession]-- maybe it won't work out, you know, cause he [*pegahsoy*] has to keep clean you know. So he come. He talk to my mother. He was scared of the [*kimoLeni*], pollution], but he did anyhow. [Taped.]

Like the *kegey* using the same technique, the *pegahsoy*, "man doctor," had a vision in which he saw what was making the patient ill, and then elicited a confession (*pahsoy*) to cure. Florence Shaughnessy:

There was a woman that had a child by her brother-in-law, so she strangled it. Then when that woman had children by her husband they choked to death. She lost three children that way. Then the forth one got ill and she confessed. That child lived, and then she had another that lived-- two sons that lived. [From notes.]

Dewey George said that one of his "old-time" relatives had smoke-cured the heart of a kinsman murdered at Sregon, in order avenge the murder through a curse on the killer's family (cf. Spott and Kroeber 1942:185). Mr. George had chest pains and called in a *pegahsoy* who "saw" the long past act of mutilation and magic. Dewey George confessed the family secret, and was cured.

The confessions heard by the *pegahsoy* are not always so dramatic as these. Simpler confessions of human weakness--like eating bear meat, or killing house-pets to be rid of them, or defiling a sacred place--are common.

In 1978 the modern doctor mentioned above, who said he inherited doctoring powers from his mother, a Shaker half-doctor, and from Albert Thomas, as well as having had his own visions in the mountains, making connections with the spirits there, was working cooperatively with a Hupa clairvoyant who, the doctor said, had inherited some of his mother's power, too. He told me:

> When you *pahsoy* a second person has to be there to help: it takes two to do it. Doctoring spirits come to help. The doctor can see them and work with them, and even the patient can feel them around . . . The spirits look him [the patient] over and see what's wrong, what needs to be confessed. [From notes.]

When this man doctored in this way he sat on a stool and prayed, in Yurok, calling on the "sky" (*wes?onah*) and the spirits (*?o?lek'wish?on*) to help him rid the patient of defilement (*kimoLeni*). He burned tobacco and blew on the patient, blowing away, after confession, the "shadows" (*sa?awor*) of misdeeds which the clairvoyant (as well as the doctoring spirits) had helped him see. The patient was left feeling "empty," for the shadows had been "in" as well as "on" him.

Fanny Flounder was, according to most sources, among the last living "full doctors," *kegeyowor*. The modern doctor was undoubtedly influenced by his mother who joined the Indian Shaker Church in the 1930s. While not all knowledgeable people accepted his claims to doctoring power, he seems to have in fact continued the far older tradition of the *pegerk kegey*, the mountain-trained "man doctors" mentioned by Lucy Thompson (1916) and by my own teachers.

Thompson's second claim, that the *pegerk kegey* played a role in the world renewal ceremonies of the region must be examined as well. Kroeber himself noted that certain ceremonial medicine men were called, in English, "doctor" (1976:265, 380), yet did not attach significance to this. Ella Norris, however, seemed to corroborate Thompson's claim, *contra* A. L. Kroeber:

> Four or five medicine men that fast for ten days before they have a Jump Dance, they stay in the sweathouse and pray . . .
> I seen Deerskin Dance in 1904, Requa; Jump Dance in 1905. Each time they fast for ten

days. My Great Uncle, my mother's uncle, was
great medicine man, and that's how I know.
Charlie Williams's dad, Old Charlie: last Indian
doctor. WeLkwew, Requa, Pecwan, Kep'el,
Weitchpec--five place [on the lower Klamath]--
they take turns . . . They fast, and they have five
fires because there are five doctors--Indian
medicine men, one each village--leaders in each
village. They go into the sweathouse, they're the
ones go into sweathouse, men doctors, *pegerk
kegey*--that's right . . .
　　Clean: you don't eat with everybody, you
eat by yourself, you have your own food.
Merwerkserh--you clean, don't mingle with
womenfolks; *merwerksishon*, same thing [pure,
clean, beautiful]. They have their own food, they
don't eat the same acorns. They have special food
for the ones that praying. [Taped.]

　　Harry Roberts spoke of such men, whom he called "high
men," representing all of the dance districts of the region, meeting
together in inter-tribal councils to settle important regional
matters (cf. Kroeber and Gifford 1949:43; Pilling 1978:143) and,
on occasion, to have private emergency Jump Dances in the
mountains (cf. Waterman 1920:264; Kroeber 1976:186, 186.n.). At
least one of these men, George Meldon, also practiced as a
pegahsoy, coming to the sweathouse at Johnson's to "clean up"
Harry Roberts before Mr. Roberts went into the high mountains
for his own training in non-curative specialties, seeking to connect
with the spirit forces there to gain "luck" (cf. Spott and Kroeber
1942:160).
　　George Meldon was the medicine man (*lo*) for the world-
renewing fish weir at Kep'el. He came-down river to marry
Fanny Flounder, losing his power and his position because he saw
the sea, which was forbidden him. In the 1930s he said that he
had been, while *lo*, "Doctor of the World," telling Erik Erikson to
tell his readers that "he [Meldon] is the world's doctor," and that
his prayers were "to cure the world" (in Erikson 1943: 277, 280).
Since Kroeber knew Meldon well, indeed introducing Erikson to
him and publishing the resulting monograph, Kroeber's later
remark to the effect that he never heard the term *kegey* ("doctor")
linked to positions of authority in the world renewals is hard to
understand (Kroeber and Gifford 1949:84.1).
　　Part of the difficulty may have been that Kroeber viewed
"*kegey*" as defining a rigidly bounded category of primarily female

shamanic healers. Indeed, it may be usefully understood in this way, as I trust we have seen. But this sort of categorical understanding may also be misleading. My suspicion is that the "*kegey*," rather than simply providing a linguistic label for a fixed category, as we might tend to view her, comprised, traditionally, the prototype for a classificatory grouping of persons viewed as "like," in some way, the *kegey*, and thus associated with her.

From this interpretive perspective, the *pegerk kegey* was not necessarily a male exception to a general rule that *kegeyowor* were women. Rather, "*kegey*," instead of meaning "shaman," alone, may have signified a person who, through extremely stringent training involving high mountain practice, gained control of the most major sort of power, that associated with the "sky," which he or she commanded, through "clean" living, toward "seeing" and toward healing, as did the *kegeyowor*--whether it be healing of people or of the world itself. Such, I speculate, were the associations of "*kegey*."

THE ONTOLOGICAL AND METAPHYSICAL CONTEXTS OF DOCTORING

When the *kegey* and the *pegerk kegey* went into the mountains they went both *heLkew*, "inland," and, in trance, *wonoyekw*, "up in the middle of the sky," to heaven, *wes?onah hiwonek*. To an extent, the high mountains and the middle of the sky are, in traditional Yurok cosmology, metonymic. The trail leading up the Blue Creek drainage to Doctor Rock, called "the Golden Stairs" in English, is thought to actually go up into the Sky World. Thus, at death, both *kegey* and medicine men go "inland" to the mountains and, from there, to dance in the world of spirits above, where the most wonderful wealth objects, like albino deer that are half covered with pilleated woodpecker scalps, live (cf. Thompson 1916:74; Kroeber, in Elmendorf 1960:520.30). According to Ella Norris, doctors go to "heaven" in trance and see this wealth:

> They go into that where they get their "power," they call it. When they get their power then they can see things, and they can explain it to you. Biggest part of it always come out just about right. That was the same way with that [*wonoyekw*]. [Taped.]

Mrs. [Sregon] Jim, a famous *kegey*, told Kroeber the prayer she said when offering angelica root to the spirits:

"Now this *wo?Lp'e?y*, I got it *wes?onah hiwonek*, right up in the middle of the sky. That's where this *wo?Lp'e?y* grows that I throw in the fire, because all the money and woodpecker heads up there, they all eat that. It is nearly dried out because the dentalia have eaten all the tops. That is the place I got it."
That's the way I would talk when I would throw it in the fire. When I slept in the sweat house I talked the same way just to be sure, for the old people used to tell us, "That's where the best kind grows, *wonoyekw*, right in the middle." It didn't come from there in fact, but one just talked that way and threw it into the fire, so that all kinds of money would come right to this house, as though coming to eat the tops of the *wo?Lp'e?y*. [Kroeber Papers, Bancroft Library, University of California, Berkeley.][15]

In a sense, then, when the doctor established her trail into the mountains (above), she established her connection with the world above, the "sky," *wes?onah*, which is also "the world," *k'i ?wes?onah*, "that which exists." The "sky," in this sense, as "Spirit," is the source of her power, and the power of the doctor--male or female--is called, I am told, *wes?onah kegey*. The power of the *kegey* comes from "the sky," which is at once "the world," "that which exists" or, in a modern doctor's terms, "the created." (Harry Roberts called it "creation.") By the same token, those men who go to seats in the mountains to pray for "luck" (Spott and Kroeber 1942:160), according to Harry Roberts, enter trance and ascend into the Sky World above, where they are taught by the spirits. The most powerful men enter trance in a seat on what is called Peak Eight, rising through an aperture in the sky, directly above. Thus, Peak Eight is both below and *is* "the center of the spiritual world." One is reminded of Eliade's comparative criterion that "the shaman specializes in a trance during which his soul is believed to leave his body and ascend to the sky or descend to the underworld" (Eliade 1964:5).

The kegey's and pegerk kegey's relationship with the sky occurs in distinction to the power quest of the sorcerer--and of the warrior--both of whose powers come from the cthonic realms, the Underworld, home of the Thunders, the warriors' primary guardian spirits, of lightning, identified with the sorcerers' fire, and of death. The underworld is, in Yurok mythology, both the destination after death of the shadows of those who have not lead exemplary lives, as have the *kegey* and the *pegerk kegey*, and the home of Mole and of Jerusalem Cricket, the bringers of death to the world (Kroeber 1976). Power may be sought below, as by the warrior, but the power of the above, *wes?onah*, is higher in every sense. "The high men have creation [*wes?onah*]," said Harry Roberts, "they didn't need beliefs in this one and that one [spirits]; they were for other people."

Kegey, then, and *pegerk kegey*, are those who draw power from the "the world," also called "sky," to cure, in turn, people and the world itself. As *George Meldon* said, "I am the world's doctor" (above). Here we have engaged a paradox, and this paradox becomes more dense. A formula from the Deerskin Dance at Wechpus (Weitchpec), says,

> *ki pegahsoy k'i ?wes?onah tu?*
> *kowicho ko?mi we? no:minahpi?mo?w*
> *heL . . . to? ki skuye?n wero:kwsek'*
> *ki pegahsoyetek k'i ?wes?onah*

> Soon the world will *pegahsoy* and
> don't be too afraid of this!
> Hey! then good will blow here,
> the world will *pegahsoy* here.[16]

(Roughly: "A big wind is going to blow now, but don't be too afraid; it's just the sky doctoring the world.[17])

To summarize: 1) doctors get their power to heal people from the "sky," metonymic with "creation"; 2) some doctors, *pegerk kegey*, identified with *pegahsoy*, doctor creation, or "the sky" itself, yet; 3) creation, "the sky," is also a doctor, *pegahsoy*, who doctors itself and the people in it, through the world renewal ceremonies directed by the human "man doctors."

We enter, through study of the *kegey*, a Yurok metaphysical conception of total ontological interdependency and codetermination quite foreign to the logic of Western dualism. Thus the *wo:gey* Immortals who originally recited the Wechpus Deerskin dance formula say:

> *nekah kelekw numi ?ekonepe?moh k'i ?wes?onah*
> *meL hasek' kowicho ko?mi no:minapi?mo?w*

We . . . well, the world and us pretty much support
each other,
So I think you shouldn't be too afraid of what's happening
here.[18]

The kinds of distinctions between "God," "earth," "spirit,"
and "humanity," common to the Judeo-Christian traditions, are not
present here. Ella Norris-perhaps reflecting her Tolowa heritage
in her focus on the dawn--told me how she called God, "Early-
Morning-Rise," sunrise, *woLkeloh ?ela chi?n wegenoy?o:mom*
("'Morning-Always-Early' you are being called"):

> I do that in the morning when its beautiful.
> You see that beautiful sun rising back there real
> early, you talk to it, you tell it what a beautiful
> day . . . "You watch over me, take care of my
> children, too."   *?o?lekwisho?n*--that means us,
> we're human here, and I'm your child . . . "don't
> deny me, don't think I'm somebody else.   I'm
> related to you."

I asked her, "What's the word for 'spirit,' then?"

> You use the same word, *?o?lekwisho?n*.
> Means we're--I don't know how to explain it in
> English--I know what it means in Indian [Yurok]-
> -we're part of *you*, part of the same thing.
> Because they're supposed to be human too, the
> Creators--they're the Creators. That's the word
> you use. [Taped.]

SUMMARY

The doctors of native northwestern California arise along
a continuum of practitioners and powers--and spirits. Often they
have multiple skills, or techniques, at their disposal: prayers,
herbal medicines, trance, clairvoyance, sucking out of pains. They
are ranked in terms of the number and power of these techniques
that they own or control, but they are also related to two
dimensions, vectors of power or associations of spirits, high and
low.
     The first moves, upwards as it were, from the use of
constructive or benign prayers, to "praying doctors," to clairvoyant
confession doctors, to sucking doctors. Certain ceremonial actors

are associated with this dimension which includes, at its higher reaches, the *kegey*, "sucking doctor," and *pegerk kegey*, the "high man": people associated with the high mountains, with summer, and with "creation," the sky, the world. It is noteworthy that the full meaning of this association is realized in service to the community, as one or another sort of curative "doctor."

On the second, low dimension, the continuum runs from those who control curses, to the "evil doctors," to the devils, *?uma?ah*. Their powers, it would seem, are those of the below and of winter. While the *weskweloy*, warrior, shares in this source of power, however, his ends, and hence the moral theater that he occupies, though "mean" and destructive, are quite different. The poisoners, makers of bad prayers, and devils act against the community--cause, rather than relieve pain, while the warrior, although he may be an assassin, has at least the potential to act in protection of the community.

Within these continua we may specify three categories of powerful people who might legitimately be called "shamans"--the *kegey*, doctors, the *weskweloy*, warriors, the *?uma?ah*, sorcerers. All practice "techniques of ecstacy," all are empowered by direct contact with spiritual forces, all are, to an extent, professionals, paid for their services. And yet it may well be that the category of "shaman" is not one particularly suited to understanding native northwestern Californian spiritual practice. The three figures are very different, one from the other, and the one most readily recognized as a "shaman," the *kegey*, is far more closely associated non-hierarchically, as a prototype, with other, non-shamanic actors--like the *pegerk kegey* and other ceremonial officiants--than with the other two.[19]

I have approached these topics in what may seem a rather anachronistic way, as a problem in description and classification or, rather, association--*somewhat* as A. L. Kroeber and other disciplinary ancestors approached their ethnological work. Yet in doing so I have tried both to respect the truth of the particular voices of those who taught me what little I know of the subject of Yurok Indian doctors, and to integrate their teaching--in itself, highly descriptive--with an interpreted ontology and metaphysics through which the descriptive materials might begin to make religious, rather than simply ethnological, sense.

If we understand religion to be, most often, an empathetic response to human suffering, as I believe we should, then we must understand the Yurok doctors' spiritual efficacy, or power, to be correlate with their own personal suffering--with the sacrifices they made to alleviate the suffering of others. Indeed, while the *kegey* were paid and paid well, they sacrificed much to the demands of purity and of being "crazy" in the shamanic way, *keLpey-*, the consequence of direct intercourse with the spirits. No wonder Florence Shaughnessy and Ella Norris were scared as young girls.   In the tales of Mrs. Norris and others' of the kegeyowor's isolation we must also recognize the vast loneliness of those who delve deeply in the spiritual--a loneliness that Harry Roberts often stressed in his talks with me.

While I have argued that the Yurok *kegeyowor* were indeed "shamans" in a technical, comparative sense, I have also urged caution in the application of such comparative categories. Still, with a final emphasis on the topics of suffering and self-sacrifice, as these pertain to religion, it seems fitting to close with a final reference to Mircea Eliade (1964:13) and his conviction that the shaman's life is one "that is not lacking in tragic greatness and beauty."

NOTES

Acknowledgements

First and foremost, I give my gratitude and respect to the elders, so many of them gone now, who taught me during the 1970s and whose knowledge is represented, however incompletely, in this paper: Frank Douglas (Yurok), Aileen Figueroa (Yurok), Dewey George (Yurok), Georgina Matildon (Hupa), Ella Norris (Yurok-Tolowa), Antone Obee (Yurok), Harry Roberts, Calvin Rube (Yurok), Florence Shaughnessy (Yurok). Thanks, too, to Lowell Bean for inviting me to think about doctoring again, and to Howard Berman for lexical information. Lee Davis, Victor Golla, and Peter Nabokov gave alert and useful critical readings to an earlier draft of this paper, for which I thank them. Jean Strange Perry has been most generous and immensely helpful both in tracking down linguistic information and in her suggestions regarding Yurok systems of classification. I have used her materials and ideas liberally in this chapter, although I have not cited her in every instance, for I wish to take full responsibility for any errors I may have made.

A Brief Note on Orthography

Together with Jean Perry and others, I am working toward a "practical orthography" (PO) for transcribing the Yurok language. In it, most Yurok words are pronounced roughly as they appear to an English speaker. I have modified Robins' (1958) phonemic orthography slightly so that it may be duplicated on a standard typewriter or word processor.

Robins	PO	Effect
•	:	lengthens a vowel, as in "*too* bad!"
ʔ	?	glottal stop, as in "uh-oh!"
k', p', t'	*k',p',t'*	glottalized consonant, as in "ki<u>ck</u> it."
c	*ch*	as in "win<u>ch</u>"
š	*sh*	as in <u>sh</u>ip
*k*ʷ	*kw*	as in <u>q</u>uick
ɹ	<u>er</u>	a vowel, as in h<u>er</u>
ł	L	like the <u>lth</u> in wea<u>lth</u> if you press the tip of your tongue on your pallet.

Tolowa and Karuk words are transcribed as they were in their cited sources.

1. Robins (1958:205) phonemically transcribes the Yurok word as *kegey*--the rendering that I use throughout this paper. Kroeber gave it as *kegeior* (1925:66), as *kegei* (Spott and Kroeber 1942), and as *kégei* (in Elmendorf 1960:247.1). The Yurok writer Lucy Thompson gives it as *kay-gay* (Thompson 1916:43). Howard Berman (letter, 3/31/90) suggests that "*kegeior*" is a variant of *kegey* and should be phonemically rendered *kegeyor*. He has given *kegeyowor* as the plural of *kegey* (Berman 1982:201). All translate the word as "doctor," with Kroeber alternately rendering it "shaman" as well (e.g., Spott and Kroeber 1942: 155 ff.). The elders with whom I worked in the 1970s all used the English "doctor" or "Indian doctor" when speaking of *kegeyowor*. Gifford (1958:251) gives *k:ein* as a Karuk equivalent. Drucker (1937:258) gives *ti':nun* for Tolowa.

2. It is possible that the Yurok word *weskweloy* is derived from the stem *(?)wesk-*, which denotes linearly articulated organic matter, like grass, tree limbs, and hair (cf., Robins 1958:262-63). If so, *weskweloy* refers to--or at least connotes--a particular style of piling up the hair on top of the head in a bun secured by double-ended, pointed bone or hardwood pins that was the prerogative of trained warriors. The matter needs to be further investigated, however, and this note comprises only an hypothesis.

3. I have done fieldwork in northwestern California intermittently since 1970, most extensively and formally in 1976 and 1978 and as recently as 1991. This research in Native northwestern Californian culture and history has been supported at various times, since 1976, by the Danforth Foundation, the Healey Endowment of the University of Massachusetts, the Jacobs Research Funds of the Whatcom Museum Foundation, the Phillips Fund of the American Philosophical Society, as well as other sources. I appreciate the confidence and generosity of all of these funding institutions.

4. Traditionally, Yuroks and other Native northwestern Californians have avoided mentioning the names of the dead. More recently, however, many Indian people have expressed the desire to have the names of people in old photographs that are reproduced identified in captions, for instance, and to have the oral contributions of deceased relatives and friends fully acknowledged in print. I have decided to follow this practice in the present chapter, begging the pardon and forbearance of any

whom I may have inadvertently offended in doing so. (On my use of original, unedited, and often non-standard grammar in transcriptions of Native testimony, see note 15, below.)

5. Robins (1958:214) gives *kwes?oyew-* as a verb, "to treat (used of prayer doctor)." Gifford (1958:251) gives *k:anekiava* as Karuk for "praying doctor." Drucker (1937:258) gives *tcɛːcɛ'* for Tolowa "'talking' or 'singing' doctor."

6. It is said that some women attained warrior powers. Alice Spott, the adoptive daughter of Captain Spott and sister of Robert Spott, is said to have been *weskweloy* and thus to have had the right to tie her hair up as a warrior, as she appears in photographs from the early years of this century (Palmquist 1985:13). Florence Shaughnessy recalled her foster father, Jimmy Gensaw, referring to Alice as "*numi pegerk*," "very much a gentleman" (literally, 'very man'). More complete information on women warriors among the Yuroks, who most likely would have been categorized as sociological males (as were the *kegey*--see below), are lacking, however. More commonly, women armed with fir branch clubs are known to have accompanied male *weskweloy* in armed confrontations and at war settlements, using their clubs to knock down their own warriors' bows, preventing outbreaks of violence until all efforts at negotiation had failed, at which point they used the clubs on the enemy warriors (cf. Spott and Kroeber 1942:184). These women did not have shamanistic powers, however, and the topic thus takes us far afield.

7. There has been some discussion as to whether the raptor/spirit *chpegi-*, referred to by Yuroks, in English, as "Chicken Hawk" is in fact the sharp shinned hawk, *Accipiter striatus velox* or Cooper's hawk, *A. Cooperii*, or both.

8. Note, here, one of Eliade's criteria for "shamans": "the shaman controls his spirits" (1964:6).

9. The use of a strap--reportedly about twenty feet long--to restrain the novice shaman as she ran in a frenzy (*keLpeyew-*) back down the mountain to dance in her family's sweathouse brings to mind the similar restraint of Hamatsa--or Cannibal Society--initiates among the Kwakiutl (see Boas 1966) and reminds us of Kroeber's and others' classification of the Yuroks as a Northwest Coast people (Kroeber 1939, Drucker 1955).

10. I have heard often, from elders, of the importance of keeping trails clean by cutting overhanging brush and removing detritus, especially if the trail is to be used in "making medicine." The spiritual significance of this is perhaps suggested by the range of meanings incorporated in the kegey's "making her path into the mountains."

11. Drucker writes (1937:257):

> A potential [Tolowa] shaman often received her call in a dream, it is true. These dreams, however, were vague and served only to indicate that her quest for power would be successful. One dreamt "about the mountains" (since pains came from the mountains), or "about the sunrise" (whose colors indicate the color of the pains the dreamer will obtain).

12. Compare this with the Yurok writer Lucy Thompson (1916:40), who calls the *kegeyowor* "seers," and with Eliade's generalization that the shaman "sees" the "soul" of his clients (1964:8).

13. In his study of culture trait distribution among western North American Indians, Jorgensen notes that such disease-causing intruded objects, called "pains" in California, are common throughout the American west (1980:296).

14. Harry Robert's account resonates with Aileen Figueroa's account of her mother, the Shaker doctor Maggie Pilgrim, healing Aileen's sore shoulder with her hand, from which Aileen could feel heat emanating (Buckley, fieldnotes, 1976); with Kroeber's statement that upon occasion the doctor, "does no more than touch the patient with her fingertips and blow the cause of the illness away from these" (Spott and Kroeber 1942:158); and with Cora DuBois's report that the Wintu-Achumawi doctor Albert Thomas sent out bolts of power in a long spark, "like electricity," from the tip of his index finger to the patient's body (DuBois 1940:91).

15. In his *Handbook*, Kroeber rendered this transcription as, "This angelica comes from the middle of the sky. There the dentalia and woodpecker scalps eat its leaves. That is why it is so withered" (Kroeber 1925:66).

    In transcribing verbatim testimony from tape recordings and notes entire in the present paper I have taken a different approach, resisting the urge to paraphrase, condense, or to merely incorporate the facts contained within people's narratives as "data." Again, it is my hope that by representing my teachers' particular voices as well as their full narratives I am giving voice to their particular truths, the total of which I myself may not be aware of as I write.

For example, it is interesting that Kroeber edited out, for publication, Mrs. Jim's reflexive statement that she knew the angelica didn't come from the middle of the sky, maintaining her standing, in readers' eyes, as a "confused" religious practitioner (cf. Kroeber, in Steward 1961:1043; Buckley 1989b:22), rather than inquiring what "the sky" might mean to her as a self-consciously metaphorical locale.

16. The formula is from the Kroeber Papers, Bancroft Library, University of California, Berkeley. For a more full treatment of the phrases given here, see Buckley 1984:476.

17. On the tenth and last day of the 1988 Yurok Jump Dance at Pecwan, just such a fierce wind roared down the river canyon from the south, raising clouds of dust and tearing the huge plastic canopy off one of the camps. People that I talked to thought it was a very good sign: that it meant the "prayer"--the days of dancing and fasting--was working. Earlier a Yurok dancer had told me that the object of the dance was to have "The Creator" blow "all the spiders and ticks and bugs away down the river"-- that is, to purify the world of everything *kimoLeni*, "dirty."

18. For a more technical translation and discussion, see Buckley 1984:477.

19. The noun *kegey* would appear to come from the verb stem *key(chek'in-)* 'to sit,' through an infixed *-eg-*, a nominalizing element signifying intensive, repeated action: a practice. Thus, "One who sits as a practice." This possibility is interesting in its connotations. The *kegeyowor* both practiced in mountain prayer "seats," *chekche?iL* or *chekweL*, and sat on redwood stools while smoking their pipes and contemplating a diagnosis. Both smoking and sitting on such stools were male prerogatives among traditional Yurok, as were mountain training, use of sweat houses, wearing feathers in the hair, and accumulating wealth, all of which the *kegeyowor* did. Thus the *kegeyowor* were sociological males (see Valory 1970) or, more accurately, "complete people." The male/female complementarities involved resonate with many other American Indian cultures (where, for example, warriors are often equated with women--see Buckley 1989a), and with local

testimony.   Kathy Heffner McClellan, Wailaki, remembers her grandmother saying, "I know all the man things and all the woman things. That's why I'm a great doctor."

We note that the -*eg*- infix occurs also in *pegahsoy*, both a "wishing doctor" and his curative technique, derived from the verb *pahsoy*, to "pray" or "confess" (thus, one who makes such praying his way of life), and in *meges*, "herbalist," derived from *mes-*, a stem denoting herbs or leafy material (thus one who practices with herbs).

DANCING ON THE BRINK OF THE WORLD: DEPRIVATION AND THE GHOST DANCE RELIGION

E. Breck Parkman

INTRODUCTION

One of A. L. Kroeber's Ohlone (i.e., Costanoan) informants from Pleasanton sang of "Dancing on the brink of the world" (Kroeber 1925:471), a possible reference to the Ghost Dance that had characterized much of California several decades earlier. The Ghost Dance was a nativistic and messianic movement that predicted the destruction of the EuroAmerican world, and a return of the world Native Americans had known in earlier times. The movement appeared in two waves, both originating among the Northern Paiute (Paviotso) of the Walker River Reservation in western Nevada. The first wave spread primarily through northern California in 1870 (DuBois 1939; Gayton 1930), while the second wave of 1890 spread for the most part eastward to the Plains (Mooney 1896). It is thought that the Ghost Dance religion was accepted in the California of the 1870s because of the deprivation being experienced by Native people, and in the Plains of the 1890s for a similar reason.

DEPRIVATION AND THE REVITALIZATION OF CULTURE

Religion is, in part, a social mechanism for controlling the various effects of collective stress. As such, it presents an ideal focus for those studies concerned with culture contact, and the effects generated by conquest. Throughout history, conquered societies have been given to various modes of resistance to or facilitation of acculturation. Analysis of these societies reveals an underlying factor of conquest: the correlation existing between deprivation and religion. The occurrence of widespread deprivation among the members of a conquered society will usually serve as a catalyst to produce a religious reaction to the conquest. The religious reaction, depending upon whether it takes an aggressive or a passive approach, will serve to either hinder or facilitate the acculturation process.

Stress, as a product of conquest, occurs at both the individual and collective levels. When the dominant society is viewed as culturally superior by the conquered society, widespread deprivation will often manifest itself among the latter. Relative deprivation, which has been defined as being the "negative discrepancy between legitimate expectation and actuality" (Aberle 1962:209), might be viewed then as a cause of religious reaction to conquest. Deprivation might be determined by use of certain reference points: 1) one's past versus present position; 2) one's present versus future position; and 3) one's present position versus the present position of someone else (Aberle 1962:209-210). Various kinds of deprivation exist, including those which concern possessions, status, behavior, and worth (Aberle 1962:210). The type of deprivation most fundamental to the religious reaction to conquest is that which is characterized by the comparison of the desirability of the past to the undesirability of the present. This is a character common to most nativistic movements (cf., Galbraith 1982).

Ralph Linton (1943:230) has defined the nativistic movement as being a "conscious, organized attempt on the part of a society's members to revive or perpetuate selected aspects of its culture". The aspects to be highlighted are chosen for their distinctiveness. The more distinct they are in comparison to the elements of the dominant culture, the more important they are as symbols of the dominated culture's uniqueness. The importance that was placed on singing and dancing by Ghost Dance participants is an example of this. Song and dance were viewed by the Native Americans as prime ingredients of their own culture, and were considered distinct from the elements of the dominant EuroAmerican culture. That the buffalo was chosen as a focal point in many of the ceremonies of the Plains Indians indicates their longing for the past, when great herds of these animals shadowed the plains, and their unhappiness with the present, by which time the Whites had all but exterminated the animals.

The Native American Church represents a more recent religious reaction to acculturation (Slotkin 1972; Stewart 1972). Once again, ceremonies involving singing are highlighted, as is the ceremonial consumption of Peyote. Rather than serving as a mode of resistance to acculturation, the Native American Church functions to facilitate the integration of Native American expectations with the realities of EuroAmerican culture. To do this, the Church has combined traditional elements of the Native American experience with certain elements of Christianity. The result has been a religious movement that, while successfully satisfying Native American needs for spiritual guidance, does not pose a serious threat to the dominant EuroAmerican culture.

The Ghost Dance and other messianic movements, as well as nativistic movements, cargo cults, and revolutions might all be considered types of revitalization movements. Anthony Wallace has defined the revitalization movement as "a deliberate, organized, conscious effort by members of a society to construct a more satisfying culture" (1956:264). He finds the basis for his revitalization philosophy in an organismic analogy involved with the disillusionment and redefinition of a cultural *gestalt*.

Bernard Barber (1941) examined the messianic movement as a response to acculturation. In his study of the Ghost Dance, Barber illustrated the correlation existing between the occurrence of widespread deprivation, and the acceptance or denial of the messianic movement. For Barber, the spread of the Ghost Dance of 1870 differed from the movement of 1890 because of the change in loci of deprivation, and was explained in his thesis, in which he attempted to show the correlation existing between deprivation and messianic movements:

> The messianic movement served to "articulate the spiritual depression" of the Indians. Those groups which faced a cultural impasse were predisposed to accept a doctrine of hope. Correlatively, the tribes that rejected the doctrine were in a state in which the values of their old life still functioned (Barber 1941:664).

Therefore, the Ghost Dance spread westward to northern California in 1870 because that is where intense deprivation was being experienced by Native Americans at the time. Relatively little deprivation was being felt in the Plains area at this time, thus the movement did not move eastward. By 1890, conditions for the Plains Indians had become much worse and, as a result, the Ghost Dance moved eastward. This second movement did not affect northern California, the Indians there having become disillusioned by the failure of the first Ghost Dance. In Barber's (1941) thesis, a correlation was proposed between deprivation and messianic movements. In the case of the Ghost Dance, there can be little doubt that this correlation does exist, and that it is the primary factor influencing the acceptance or denial of the religious movement. Whereas Spier (1935) and DuBois (1939) both attributed the spread of the Ghost Dance to deprivation, similarities between it and Paiute culture led them to conclude that the Ghost Dance was consistent with Paiute recurrent ceremonialism. Hittman (1973), on the other hand, has argued that the Ghost Dance of 1870 occurred among the Paiute because of the deprivation experienced by them when early reservation life disrupted their traditional food quest and shamanistic-curing complex.

Anthropologists have used deprivation theory to explain religious changes produced by the stress of colonization, acculturation, and domination. The social and economic inequities produced by such confrontations create the stress responsible for religious change. Such stress, and the religious reaction that results from it, develops out of psychological, social, economic, and political deprivation (Lessa and Vogt 1979:414).

THE DESTRUCTION OF NATIVE CALIFORNIA

Following the initial confrontation with Europeans and EuroAmericans, many California Indians were placed within the missions, where life for them was sometimes a hard one (Costo and Costo 1987). Punishment was dealt out severely, and was often unexplained. People were crowded together, sometimes in unsanitary conditions. The birth-rate of the Mission Indians was very low, and it is thought that there was a high rate of neophyte-induced abortions. Life in the mission served to destroy the Indians' traditional, social, and political organization, and to undermine their native ideology. Indeed, this was a goal of the mission system. There were probably native leaders and shamans in every mission, however, who sought to maintain their traditional beliefs and values.

The effects of missionization on California Indians served to strip them of much of their ethnic identity. Some redefinition of world view resulted from this. In some cases, tradition was adhered to in clandestine ceremonies; nevertheless, a new "way of life" emerged. Much of this new "way" was probably nothing more than a front to please the Franciscans. Following secularization, many of the traditional cultural patterns resurfaced in communities such as Pleasanton. Indeed, recent research by anthropologists has shown what Native Californians have always known: that traditional values and beliefs still exist among the descendants of former Mission Indians.

Following the secularization of the missions in 1834, the life of the California Indians became, in many cases, a miserable one. Although some were able to find jobs on ranches, or as sheep herders, many more remained unemployed. Alcoholism, violence, crime, and all the other forms of social decay manifested themselves among the Indian groups set adrift. The fate of many of the non-Mission Indians was not much better. With the California Gold Rush, and its invasion of miners, the relatively sheltered Indians of the interior were subject to the same cruelty that their western neighbors had been experiencing for years. With the advent of the Americans, however, the injustices committed upon the Indians took a more sinister and genocidal nature (cf., Carranco and Beard 1981; Heizer 1974a, 1974b; Heizer and Almquist 1971; Hurtado 1988; Norton 1979).

By 1870, the life of the California Indian was not an ideal one. The people were in the midst of a time of transition and they were determined to survive it. For those people living in the Sierra Nevada foothills, life was often spent dodging Americans who considered an Indian life worth no more than the expense of the bullet it took to make him a "good Indian". For the former Mission Indians living in such places as Pleasanton, life was deteriorating through the influence of alcohol, violence, and the moral decay of traditional values. In spite of such hardships, however, there were individuals within these groups who insisted on preaching the traditional values, and in whom the former ways were perpetuated. It was similar men and women who had led the original resistance against the non-Indian invaders; it was they who had led the original clandestine ceremonies during the mission internment; and it was they who seized upon the Ghost Dance as a mechanism for regaining their grasp on the people, and for turning back the destruction done to them by the newly arrived, dominant society.

With the appearance of the Ghost Dance, and its doctrine of salvation, the Indians were easily persuaded to convert to the new movement. Their reaction was but one of several options which were available to them, this being one of the underlying principles of Barber's (1941) deprivation/messianic movement correlation. The arrival of the Ghost Dance in Round Valley produced an entirely different reaction than that at Pleasanton, with the Indian people at Round Valley converting to Christianity in record numbers (Miller 1976). The rejection of the Ghost Dance doctrine by other groups often involved a somewhat better living situation, or else a clash with certain traditional beliefs, such as the fear of the dead among the Navaho (Hill 1944). When the Ghost Dance reappeared in 1890, there was no participation in it by the Pleasanton community, nor by most other California Indians. This could have been due to one or more of three factors: 1) the failure to learn of the new movement (fairly unlikely given the improved communication system of the time); 2) improved existence and living situation, invalidating the necessity for a messianic movement; or 3) skepticism based on the failure of the earlier Ghost Dance involvement. The reason behind the denial of the 1890 Ghost Dance in California was probably a combination of the latter two factors.

Although the teachings and predictions of the 1870 Ghost Dance did not prove true, there was an inherent value for all those who participated in it. For a short time during a turbulent period, it organized a people who had been forced into disunity (Bean and Vane 1978a:670).

GHOST DANCE MISSIONARIES FROM PLEASANTON

On August 9, 1834, Governor Jose Figueroa issued his "Reglamento Provisional," which called for the secularization of the California missions. Shortly thereafter, the Mission Indians began to return to their ancestral territories, or portions of them still unsettled by the non-Indians. Following the secularization of Mission San Jose, many of the neophytes settled near Pleasanton, located in the Livermore Valley just south of Mount Diablo. Little is known of this settlement, although it was probably quite large in its early days, with a population perhaps in excess of five hundred individuals. The settlement may have also received neophytes from Mission Santa Clara and Mission San Francisco. There were other smaller communities located elsewhere in the San Francisco Bay Area. About 1872, the dances associated with the old Kuksu or God-impersonating cult were revived by the residents of the Indian community at Pleasanton (Gayton 1930:64). This appears to have been done as a direct result of the Ghost Dance of 1870, which was at that time being practiced in south-central California. The new movement was spread from Pleasanton to the Southern Maidu and the Northern and Central Miwok by three Pleasanton missionaries. However, it is not clear how the Ghost Dance was diffused to the Pleasanton community.

The spread of the Kuksu cult was known to have spread from south (Pleasanton) to north, being diffused to the Miwok, Maidu, Wintun, and Pomo. Working from this, Gayton (1930) proposed two routes of diffusion of the Ghost Dance to Pleasanton: 1) that a wave of the movement diffused southward from the Klamath, Modoc, Shasta, etc., through the Wintun to Pleasanton and then returned northward after having been remodeled there on the old Kuksu cult pattern; or 2) that the movement had a separate and direct entry directly across the central Sierra Nevada by way of the Washo, Southern Maidu, or Northern Miwok. Gayton (1930:64) argues against the probability of either of these routes, instead presenting a third possibility, which appears more likely then the other routes:

> The occurrence of the Ghost Dance among the
> northern foothill Yokuts offers a third and equally
> plausible explanation of its presence at Pleasanton,
> that is, that the messianic doctrine was introduced
> at the coast settlement by northern valley Yokuts
> or Southern Miwok who had relatives and friends
> in the missionized Yokuts-Miwok-Costanoan
> group of Indians there. Since the original form of
> the Ghost Dance was known to all the Yokuts of
> the San Joaquin valley and perhaps to the Miwok
> as well, it seems unlikely that news of the cult
> should fail to reach their relatives at Pleasanton
> (Gayton 1930:64-65).

There is little evidence of the Ghost Dance movement as
it was practiced in Pleasanton. The record, however, does contain
the accounts of three missionaries sent out by the Pleasanton
community to spread the doctrine to their eastern neighbors.
These three men were Tciplitcu, who went among the Central
Miwok, Sigelizu, who went among the Northern Miwok, and
Yoktco, who went among the Southern Maidu. It is from their
teachings that a glimpse of the Ghost Dance, as practiced at
Pleasanton, is possible. It is also their teachings which proved
fundamental to the role played by the Pleasanton community in
the Ghost Dance religion.

THE MISSIONARY TCIPLITCU

Tciplitcu, also spelled "Chiplichu" (Gifford 1955:301; Levy
1978a:412), was an Ohlone from Pleasanton who went among the
Central Miwok about 1872 to teach them the Ghost Dance
doctrine. The missionary settled at Knights Ferry, where he began
to teach the people the *hiweyi* dance. The *hiweyi* was danced on
a hilltop at Knights Ferry when it was first introduced by
Tciplitcu (Gifford 1926:402).

Tom Williams, a Central Miwok informant, believed that
Tciplitcu had first come to Knights Ferry from Pacheco, located
just north of Mount Diablo, when he was ten years of age
(Gifford 1955:301). He gave the following account of Tciplitcu,
and of the *hiweyi* dance he began:

> A Costanoan from Pacheco, Contra Costa County,
> settled near Knights Ferry when he was about ten

years old. He went by the name of Chiplichu, and
when he grew up, he married a Miwok woman of
Knights Ferry. He became a sucking shaman
(*koyabi*). After becoming a shaman, Chiplichu
danced and sang in his home every night, and he
was in the habit of talking with the spirits. His
house was situated half a mile from the ceremonial
house at Knights Ferry.

One day some Northern Miwok from Ione visited
Knights Ferry and said that there was an epidemic
of smallpox at Ione. They said it was traveling
towards Knights Ferry. The Knights Ferry people
were very frightened by this news and many of the
men went up into the hills. The women were left
behind in the ceremonial house, which was closed
up tight. Twelve men sat down just below the
summit of a high hill, where they sang under the
direction of the shaman, Chiplichu, who was
behind them on the summit of the hill. He danced
on the summit, and as he did so, he kept pointing
a large cocoon rattle towards Ione. The singers
who were in front of him were facing Ione also.

He and the singers sang four songs. While he was
dancing during the last song, he kicked the ground
very hard with his right foot and sank into it waist
deep. Then he stooped down and talked to a spirit
in the ground. He asked the spirit if the Ione
people were telling the truth. The spirit replied:
"There is no sickness coming at all. There is no
sickness over there." Then the shaman told the
singers that there was no sickness coming, and the
singers went back and told the people that
everything was all right (Gifford 1955:301).

The informant, Tom Williams, who had been one of the
twelve men on the hill, said that a shaman who practiced this was
called a *hiweyi*. The four songs which were sung on the hill are
called, in the order of their performance, the *chikilmina*, the
hoholoyu, the *hahayua*, and the *hahamaka*, the words of which,
according to the informant, were understood by the people of
Ione, Pleasanton, and Pacheco.

After Tciplitcu performed on the hilltop, a ceremony was
held in the ceremonial house. The ceremony was called the *hiweyi*

dance and lasted for four nights. The ceremony was organized by Tciplitcu, who had learned the dance from the spirit with whom he talked on the hill. The shaman began the ceremony by drawing blood from each of the people in the ceremonial house. This was done by scratching their backs with a small white rock, Tciplitcu then sucking the blood and spitting it into a basket. Following this, the shaman danced, accompanied by the twelve men who had accompanied him earlier on the hill. Each night, the shaman danced from sunset until midnight. He and the people who had come long distances slept in the ceremonial house at night after the dancing ended.

The shaman wore an elaborate costume while performing the *hiweyi* dance. The informant described his dress:

> Chiplichu wore a feather boa called *hichli*, which passed across the back of his neck and was drawn back under his arms from the front, the two ends being joined behind to form a tail. He carried a cocoon rattle, called *wasilni*, in each hand, and a third cocoon rattle was fastened in his hair. He wore a wreath on his head, made of stems and leaves of mugwort (*Artemisia vulgaris*) twisted together, and his hair was held firmly by a net. Four bunches of split crow feathers attached to sticks completed his headdress. Each of these feather ornaments was about two feet long and tied with deer sinew. They were thrust in his hair, one sticking out in front, another in back, and one on each side. The cocoon rattle which he wore on his head was fastened at the back, with the rattles up. A tule mat, said to be six inches thick, with armholes, was worn very much like a skirt and reached to the knees. It was held by a string around the neck, tied in front. Under the mat, Chiplichu wore a piece of deerskin about his middle. He was not decorated with paint.

> As he danced, he held a cocoon rattle upright in each hand. He held the rattles away from him at about the level of his breast and swung them together from side to side. While the ceremony was going on, the people were supposed not to smoke. Whenever Chiplichu saw anyone smoking while he was dancing, he turned around four times, then danced up to the offending individual.

He went on dancing, but rubbed his hands four
times down the arm of the offender that held the
pipe. After the fourth time he took the pipe away
from the man. Then he danced up to the fire,
made four passes with the pipe over the fire, and
finally threw it into the blaze. He did this because
he was told in his "dream" to allow no one to
smoke when he danced (Gifford 1955:302).

The *hiweyi* was danced in curing ceremonies, especially for
those caused by the sighting of a ghost (Gifford 1926:402). Before
the introduction of the hiweyi dance, the *kumtupu* was performed
for the same curative purposes. The *lileusi* was a second dance
which was performed at Knights Ferry, and was thought to be
very old by its performers (Gifford 1926:400). In the lileusi, the
performer impersonated a spirit which was thought to come from
Mount Diablo, probably indicating a Pleasanton origin for the
dance (Gifford 1926:400-401). Certain other dances performed by
the Central Miwok, which were also performed by the Northern
Miwok and Southern Maidu, were attributed by these people as
having come from Pleasanton (Gifford 1926:401). It is not clear
if Tciplitcu was responsible for the introduction to Knights Ferry
of these dances.

A somewhat different account of Tciplitcu is given by the
informant Louis, another resident of Knights Ferry:

Additional but somewhat contradictory
information about Chiplichu was obtained from
the informant Louis at Knights Ferry in 1923. He
stated that Chiplichu was a dancer and *an anlini*
(shaman), and his people were all Yokuts and used
to come to Knights Ferry to dance. From
observing them the Knights Ferry people learned
new dances, of which *hiweyi* was one. When
Chiplichu came to Knights Ferry, Louis was
already a young men. (In 1923 he asserted that he
was eighty years old.) Chiplichu danced *hiweyi* (as
described by Tom Williams) on the tablelike hill to
the west, below which the highway now runs. The
hill is called Choyochoyu.

At the time of his death, which, according to
Louis, was natural and not by murder, Chiplichu
was living below La Grange on the Tuolumne

River. Louis was thirty-five or forty years old at
that time. Louis did not know the name of
Chiplichu's original home (Gifford 1955:302).

The murder of Tciplitcu, which the informant Louis
disclaims, occurred at Knights Ferry. According to the story, his
head was cut off, and his body thrown into the Stanislaus River.
For many years after that, his head was said to be in the vicinity
of Knights Ferry, and was often reported to have "rolled" after
people crossing the bridge there. Tom Williams claimed to have
seen the head, and Louis admitted to having heard of a "rolling
head" at Knights Ferry. According to Williams, Tciplitcu was
murdered by a group of Indians who were jealous of his
shamanistic powers, and disliked him because he was a foreigner.

THE MISSIONARY SIGELIZU

Sigelizu was a Plains Miwok from Pleasanton who went
among the Northern Miwok about 1872 to teach them the Ghost
Dance doctrine (Gifford 1926:401). Although the teachings of this
missionary were a product of the Ghost Dance stimulus, they did
not include any reference to the end of the world, or to the return
of the dead. Sigelizu introduced new spirits to the Northern
Miwok, notably the tula and *hiweyi* spirits. He also introduced
many dances to these people, including the *tula, oletcu, kuksuyu,
lole, sunwedi* (called the *olotcina* by the Central Miwok), *sukina,
kilaki, mamasu,* and the *hiweyi* (Gifford 1926:399). Sigelizu also
introduced a sixteen day confinement for Miwok boys and girls
who were learning to dance.
Sigelizu taught the Northern Miwok at Ione in Amador
County. Here he occupied the position of *temayasu* (dance
manager). The office was a traditional one and was not created by
the missionary. Sigelizu went from one house to the next teaching
the people the various dances. He built a dance house at Buena
Vista, located near Ione, where he taught the western dances to the
local people. He also taught the people who lived north of Ione.
Sigelizu had great "medicine", although he was not a
sucking doctor. He would often talk to a ghost outside the dance
house at night. The ghost informed him that if he did not dance
he would kill him. The ghost was said to have once caused
Sigelizu to become temporarily crazy, and made blood flow from
his mouth.
After teaching the *tula* and *hiweyi* dances to William
Joseph, another of Gifford's informants, Sigelizu carried the

feather paraphernalia used in the dances over a hill each evening at sundown, always going in the direction of the sunset (Gifford 1926:401). This was done for four successive evenings. Sigelizu informed Joseph that the *tula* and *hiweyi* dances were taught by Crow and Meadowlark to a man whom they took down into a pond, and confined for sixteen days. Sigelizu warned Joseph against killing crows or meadowlarks lest he suffer severe illness or death. He was told, however, that he might pick up feathers at the birds' roosting places, and it was with these that he might make the dance paraphernalia.

Sigelizu had the power to detect a menstruating woman by simply looking around the assemblage gathered in the dance house (Gifford 1926:401). After detecting such a woman, the missionary would point at her and order her to leave. If she did not leave, the dancers would be unable to dance properly, and the singers would choke.

Sigelizu became sick and died in 1876 at Comanche, Amador County, after having witnessed the ghost of his dead brother.

THE MISSIONARY YOKTCO

Yoktco was a Plains Miwok from Pleasanton who went among the Southern Maidu, probably around 1872, to teach them the Ghost Dance doctrine (Gifford 1927:220). Many Maidu informants felt that Yoktco had come from Mount Diablo, a place thought by many Indians to be the home of spirits (Ortiz 1989). Although Yoktco lived at Pleasanton, at times he would visit the Sierra Nevada foothills to teach people to dance. The missionary learned certain dances in his youth at Pleasanton, which he later taught to the Southern Maidu. These dances included the *hiweyi*, *kilaki*, *kuksui*, *lole*, *mamas*, *ta*, *tula*, and *yomuse* (Gifford 1927:220). As a child learning such dances, Yoktco had been locked for sixteen days in the dance house at Pleasanton.

The language generally spoken by Yoktco was Plains Miwok. The dances he introduced to the Southern Maidu can not be considered typical of the Plains Miwok, though, but rather typical of the mixed community of Ohlone-Northern Valley Yokuts-Plains Miwok in which he lived at Pleasanton. While dancing, Yoktco ceased to speak Plains Miwok, instead speaking a strange language, which was probably either Ohlone or Yokuts. Yoktco first went to Ione to teach the Northern Miwok the dances, being accompanied by a troop of Pleasanton dancers. He later went to Folsom to teach the dances to the Southern Maidu there.

To the latter, he taught the *hiweyi*, *kilaki*, *kuksui*, *mamas*, and *ta* (Gifford 1927:230). The *kuksui* dance had two performers, who were called *kuksui* and *musil*.

Yoktco was a dreamer, similar to the maru or Ghost Dance dreamers of the Pomo. He made public his dreams, considering them to be divine revelations. Yoktco did not predict the end of the world, nor other such apocalyptic events, but he did present an equivalent idea, dreaming that the world would become filled with white people with there becoming another and separate world for Indians. If they danced, Yoktco told the people, they would live long lives, and never be sick for longer than a couple of days. In one of his dreams:

> Yoktco dreamt of an altercation between Moon and Coyote. The former said people were to die and return in three or four days. Coyote said they were to die and not return, and that people were to cry for them (Gifford 1927:230).

Yoktco died in 1873 or 1874, after naming an old blind man, named Rice, to replace him as dance manager among the Southern Maidu.

THE MISSIONARY ZEAL OF PLEASANTON

During the 1870s, the Indians residing at the post-Secularization settlement at Pleasanton were redefining their cultural *gestalt*, for the second time, as a result of the conflict between their culture and the dominant culture.

If it is reasonable to assume that the loss of the Indians' ancestral land led to their experiencing a high rate of deprivation, and obviously it did, then it is also reasonable to assume that the loss of the land, and subsequent resettlement within a mission structure, and eventually the loss of this structure and subsequent resettlement among the dominant culture as an enclave of non-assimilated individuals, would surely lead to a high rate of deprivation, as well. These two types of deprivation might be termed SINGLE LOSS and DUAL LOSS, and are defined as follows:

1. SINGLE LOSS: A level of deprivation experienced from the initial redefinition of the cultural *gestalt*.

2. DUAL LOSS: A level of deprivation experienced from

the secondary redefinition of the cultural gestalt.

Faced with the gradual increase in the absorption of their territory by the dominant culture, and with the physical atrocities committed upon them during the process, the Indians of the Sierra Nevada foothills, as well as those of other areas affected by the Ghost Dance movement, experienced a level of deprivation of the SINGLE LOSS type. With the appearance of the Ghost Dance of 1870, and its inherent doctrine of salvation, the Indians were easily convinced to convert themselves to the new movement, an action which was necessitated by and resulted in the redefinition of their cultural *gestalt*.

Having already lost their ancestral lands, and imprisoned within the structure of the mission system, the Indians who were later to settle at Pleasanton were subjected to a higher level of deprivation (DUAL LOSS) by being turned out from the surrogate cultural system (the Missions) they had been forced to accept. This naturally required that they perform a secondary redefinition of their cultural *gestalt* at the time of secularization of the missions, which was probably as traumatic as the initial redefinition of the *gestalt* at the time of their arrival at the mission. Turned out into a hostile world in which they found it difficult either to return to their traditional ways, or to assimilate the ways of the dominant culture, the Mission Indians tended to congregate in enclaves similar to that at Pleasanton. Thus, their ability to adopt missionary zeal at the prospects of improving their condition is explained by the condition itself.

Relatively little is known of the Ohlone prior to missionization. Their territory extended from the Bay Area south to Monterey, and included the location of the Pleasanton settlement. Seven missions were established in their territory between 1770 and 1797, the last one being Mission San Jose, which was to later supply most of the neophytes to the post-Secularization settlement at Pleasanton. The analysis of mission baptismal records indicates that the last Ohlone tribelets ceased to exist by 1810 (Cook 1957). Before conquest, the number of Ohlone speakers probably ranged from 10,000 to 12,000 individuals, living in approximately 50 different tribelets (Levy 1978b).

Many of the Ohlone were brought to Mission San Jose, where they were kept with Indians of other tribes, including Northern Valley Yokuts, Plains Miwok, Lake Miwok, Coast Miwok, and Patwin (Levy 1978b:486). The Indian population of the Pleasanton settlement included Ohlone, Yokuts, and Plain Miwok individuals. The Plains Miwok were allied in language and culture, and probably marriage, with the Northern and Central Miwok. Gifford (1926:400) noted that the Pleasanton missionaries may have introduced the Ghost Dance to the people of the Sierra Nevada foothills while visiting their relatives there.

The condition with which many of the Indians were forced to convert to Christianity, and leave their traditional ways, was conducive to deprivation. Once within the mission structure, conditions became even worse. There are numerous accounts existing of the floggings, confinement, and other punishments committed upon the Indians by their "guardians" (Costo and Costo 1987).

INITIAL CONFRONTATION, INTERNMENT, AND ABANDONMENT

The initial confrontation between Native California and the invading EuroAmerican culture resulted in a drastic reduction in the Native population through the introduction of new diseases and acts of physical aggression. For the Indians of the San Francisco Bay Area, this period coincided with the arrival of the Spanish in 1769. For the Indians of the interior, the period coincided with the arrival of the Americans and other non-Indians attracted by the California Gold Rush of 1849.

Mission San Jose accepted converts from its founding in 1797, until secularization in 1834. Throughout its history, it, like all other California missions, had trouble with runaways. Mission records indicate that Mission San Jose had 15 neophytes escape in 1819, a number fairly small in comparison to the 280 fugitives from Mission San Francisco in 1795, and the 453 fugitives from Mission Santa Barbara in 1824 (Cook 1976:27). Fugitivism at Mission San Jose was punished by imprisonment and hard labor (Cook 1976:119). Sometimes, however, more lethal punishments were dealt out to runaways, as the following report indicates:

> Several days ago there came here an Indian from San Jose called Ildefonso with many mission Indians armed with bows, spears, and 2 guns, saying that they had come to hunt fugitives. They went to Ululatos and the Indian Ildefonso told them that they must come to San Jose and be made Christians, that Father Narcisco (Duran) was summoning them, and if they did not respond, the Father from San Francisco would come to get them, and they would suffer much because they would be severely chastised. The Ululatos,

Christians and gentiles, resisted, saying they did
not want to, whereupon they (the San Jose Indians)
held them (the Ululatos) up, robbed them, and
beat them. We (the Lybaitos) being afraid, ran
away and escaped. They then went to the
rancheria of the Chemocoytos, fought, killed five
men, and wounded one other. Afterward they
went to another rancheria, called Sucuntos, and
killed all the people. They carried off many
gentiles by force and shipped them away. They
went to another rancheria on an island called
Ompimes, and then we saw no more of them.
They were here three days and nights. Your
Christians, Ululatos, Suisanes, and the gentiles
unbound each other and set out for the Tulares,
for which reason they are here. All of us are
fatigued and dispersed (Cook 1976:77-78).

Within the missions, however, the Indians did struggle to
preserve some of their traditional ways. Kroeber (1908:25)
presents a description of a ceremony performed by the Mission
Indians residing at Mission Santa Cruz, and recorded by one of the
padres in 1811:

There are some among them, evil-minded old men,
who instill them with a panic fear towards the
demon whom they regard as the author of all evil.
That he might not trouble them, they make them
believe that they must place a little of the flour
which they eat, or of any other of their foods, on
this stone or in that log in such and such a place.
For the same purpose they sometimes hold secret
dances at night, always without the knowledge of
the fathers. It is known that at night the adult
men alone gather in a field or wood. In the middle
they place a tall stick crowned with a bundle of
tobacco leaves, or branches of trees or other plants.
At the foot of the stick they put their foods and
glass beads. They prepare for the dance,
tornandose their bodies and faces. When they are
all gathered, the old man whom they look up to as
their master or soothsayer goes out to give ear to
the commands of the devil. Returning after a
short time, he imparts to the poor innocents, not
what he op [sic] of the father of lies, but what his
own perversity and malice suggest to him.

Thereupon they proceed to their dance, which they
continue until day.

A ceremony very similar to the one performed at Mission
Santa Cruz was probably performed by the neophytes at Mission
San Jose. The following account is given for this area (the scene
of the performance being Walpert Ridge, which stops just north
of the Mission San Jose), and, although denied by the informant,
appears to have been practiced after missionization:

> They had a curious custom called "pooish," -
> throwing of prized bits of shell or cloth, or scraps
> of baskets upon piles of stone which were on the
> tops of the hills, and about which they danced at
> night to charm away the devil, which sometimes
> they drove out in the form of a great white bull, or
> a white snake. However, they believed the padres
> had driven out this devil, as it had never appeared
> since their advent (Anonymous 1965:53).

With the secularization of the missions, this way of life was
destroyed, forcing the Indians to once again redefine their cultural
gestalt. It was the emotional fatigue of this action, along with the
scars of missionization, that served to distinguish the Pleasanton
people from those Indians to whom they sent missionaries to
convert to the Ghost Dance doctrine. It is also this difference
which allowed for the zeal required of such missionary activities.

Under Governor Figueroa's Reglamento Provisional, the
Mission Indians were to receive approximately one half of the
mission land and equipment with which they were to continue
their daily affairs for the mission community. Each head of a
household, and every single person over twenty years of age, was
to receive, upon the secularization of the missions, a parcel of land
not to exceed 400 acres, nor to be less then 100 yards square.
They were to also receive one half of the missions' livestock.

In a few cases, mission land was actually distributed to the
Indians, but in most instances it never was. In the former cases,
the Indians were usually cheated out of their property soon after
receiving it. Most of the former neophytes drifted away from the
area, many settling in communities such as Pleasanton.

Following their abandonment by the mission system, the
life of the California Indians became, in many cases, a miserable
one. Although some were able to find jobs on ranches, or as sheep
herders, many more remained unemployed. Alcoholism, violence,
crime, and other forms of social decay manifested themselves in
the Indian groups set adrift. An example of this state is seen in

the following account of a Contra Costa County murder:

> In an affray at the village of Concord on Monday,
> May 2, 1869, a California Indian named Jose Vaca
> was killed by another called Fernando Feliz. The
> deceased had been well known in the vicinity for
> a long time as a drunken, brawling, besotted
> fellow, the other being also well known as a quiet
> inoffensive person, past the meridian of life and
> afflicted from an early age with an infirmity that
> made him a cripple. It appears that the deceased,
> who had been drinking to inebriation, approached
> the hut of Feliz with a bottle and wanted him to
> drink, an invitation he declined, saying: that "much
> whiskey is no good;" but told the other he would
> make a fire and give him something to eat. While
> making the fire Jose seized hold of him, saying:
> "Now, I have got you here I want you, and mean to
> kill you," thereupon striking him a heavy blow
> with the bottle and breaking it. Fernando
> struggling to defend himself, Jose in the
> meanwhile slashing and punching his face with the
> fragments of the bottle still held in his hand by the
> neck. In the scuffle that ensued they got outside
> of the shanty, where Fernando found an
> opportunity to seize a large knife with which he
> have his antagonist two or three lunges, one of
> which, as was found on the post mortem
> examination, passed entirely through the heart,
> severed the fourth rib, and killed him instantly. A
> judgment of justifiable homicide was returned
> (Slocum 1882:352-353).

The fate of the non-Mission Indians was not much better.
With the coming of the California Gold Rush, and the invasion of
miners, the relatively-sheltered Indians of the interior were
subjected to the same cruelty that their western neighbors had
been experiencing for years.

CONCLUSIONS

It is not surprising that the Ghost Dance doctrine was
accepted by the Indian community at Pleasanton in the early
1870s. It would have been more surprising if it had not been
accepted. The situation at Pleasanton was conducive to the

introduction and, as it happened, the redistribution of the messianic movement. Community leaders, elders, and, most importantly, shamans, were undoubtedly searching for a medium through which to express their collective reactions to the many stresses associated with the acculturation process. The medium for such revivalistic yearnings arrived in their community with the news of the Ghost Dance movement. The new doctrine was probably accepted by the Pleasanton community with great religious fervor. Given their conditions, they would have probably accepted any doctrine which promised a better life. Missionaries were sent out from the Pleasanton community to teach the Ghost Dance doctrine to their neighbors. In redistributing the Ghost Dance doctrine, the Pleasanton community modified it to reflect its own revivalistic tendency toward the Kuksu cult, a traditional ceremony practiced before conquest. In this regard, the *hiweyi* and *lole* dances, as well as the *kuksuyu*, were introduced as components of the Ghost Dance doctrine.

The traditional dances of the Chochenyo Ohlone, who were the original inhabitants of the eastern San Francisco Bay Area, included the *hiwey*, *loole* (i.e., *lole*), *kuksu*, and "coyote" dances (Levy 1978b:490; citing Harrington 1921). The *hiwey* and *loole* dances formed a pair, the men dancing the *hiwey*, and the women dancing the *loole*. Women dancing the *loole* wore a headdress of flicker feathers. The Chochenyo also had a *hiwey* doctor, who wore a flicker feather headdress, and a skirt of crow and raven feathers. The face of the *hiwey* doctor was painted, and he carried a snake wound around his forearm. He also wore down feathers that were sprinkled on his face. The doctor performed a ceremony in which he would sing and dance through the fire. He would embrace the trunk of a tree, and talk to the "devil", causing the earth to tremble. The *hiwey* doctor was able to cure all kinds of diseases.

The *kuksui*, *hiweyi*, and *lole* dances were performed at Pleasanton, according to an informant there in 1914 (Gifford 1927:230). The Central Miwok attributed their *uzumati* (grizzly bear) dance to having come from Pleasanton (Gifford 1926:399). It was in this dance that the participants carried the curved obsidian blades, in imitation of bear claws, which are known to archaeologists as "Stockton curves". The Rumsen Ohlone of the Monterey area performed a "bear" dance (Broadbent 1972:79), and it was probably known by the Ohlone of the eastern San Francisco Bay Area, as well.

The dances introduced into the Sierra Nevada foothills from Pleasanton were primarily concerned with curing, probably

a reflection of the ravages experienced by the Indians at the hands
of smallpox, epidemics of which spread throughout California in
the 19th century. The *hiweyi* and *tula* were still being practiced
by the Miwok in curing ceremonies early in this century:

> The dance manager Frank Powell, by virtue of his
> knowledge of tula and hiweyi ceremonies, mended
> a woman's supposedly broken arm at Ione. He
> affected the cure by assuring her repeatedly that
> the arm was not broken. He sang over her for four
> nights, causing eagle and owl feathers to "sprout"
> from the lower edge of her arm as he stroked it
> (Gifford 1926:402).

The Indian settlement at Pleasanton is no longer in
existence. The last tribal dance was held there in 1897 (Galvan
1968:12). As late as 1904, there were two communities of Native
Americans in that area. One was Alisal, located near the modern
town of Pleasanton, probably the community referred to as the
Pleasanton Indian settlement, and the other was El Molino, located
near Niles. There were approximately 50 people living in each of
these communities in 1904 (Anonymous 1965:53). The last
full-blooded Ohlone chief died in El Molino about 1901. At that
time, there were 11 houses and a sweat house located there (El
Molino was also called Verona Station, and is mentioned elsewhere
as occurring between Sunol end Pleasanton). On the death of the
chief, who was named Jose Maria Antonio, his wife, named
Havoca, ordered the sweat house torn down, in keeping with tribal
custom. Havoca and six other full-blooded Ohlones were living in
Alisal in 1904. Although earlier anthropologists thought the
Ohlone had become extinct (Kroeber 1925:464), there are over a
hundred descendants living today (Galvan 1968:12). Michael
Galvan, great grandson of Jose Maria Antonio, described his
people in an article he wrote while only seventeen years of age:

> And what of the Ohlone themselves, those who are
> living descendants? They are earnest,
> hardworking people, making their living in the
> best way they can. They are principally skilled or
> unskilled workers; some are in the professions. All
> are industrious, and there is not unemployment
> among them. They are a proud people. They have
> become accustomed to being ignored. No
> reservation has ever been set aside for them. No
> special emoluments, federal funds, or aid of any
> kind whatsoever has been given them at any time.

> They have still not been paid by the federal
> government for lands taken from them during the
> Gold Rush. They are still waiting for the justice
> due to them as the native people of this land, who
> owned the land and loved it and cared for it
> (Galvan 1968:12).

Like Galvan's present day relatives, those people living at Pleasanton a century ago were also a proud people. Through their acceptance of the Ghost Dance doctrine, and modification of it to facilitate the rebirth of the Kuksu cult, a unifying symbol of their cultural past, these people were reacting to the stresses forced upon them by the dominant culture in which they were engulfed.

In conclusion, it appears that there is ample evidence to be found in the Ghost Dance movement to substantiate Barber's thesis, which strives to show the correlation existing between the occurrence of widespread deprivation and the messianic movement. There can be no better reason found to explain the acceptance of the Ghost Dance doctrine at Pleasanton than that of the deprivation experienced by its inhabitants at the time.

NOTES ON THE WINTU SHAMANIC JARGON

Alice Shepherd

The religious practices of the Wintu and other native California groups centered around shamanism.[1] The shamans or "Indian doctors," as native speakers prefer to call them, were both priests and doctors, working with the supernatural, influencing and being influenced by good or evil spirits. They could predict the future, perceive unseen past or present events, change the weather, cure the sick, and kill enemies by supernatural means.[2] To accomplish these feats they had to be in a state of trance which was induced by self-hypnosis and drugs. Depending on the types of spirits they controlled they frequently spoke more than one language, one of them a more prestigious form of their native language.[3]

In the 1930s Dorothy Demetracopoulou Lee collected many myths, legends, and ethnographic texts from several Wintu speakers, and one of them, Sadie Marsh, recalled some of the shamanic language. Lee published a paper entitled "Some Indian texts dealing with the supernatural" (1941) where she discusses and presents in English a prayer, a shamanic prophecy, two accounts of doctoring, and a text in which a shaman recounts his initiation. I have found unpublished Wintu versions of all but the last text and would like to present here one complete text which is a particularly good example of Wintu shamanic speech, comparing it to the other accounts where useful.[4] Lee (1941: 407) assures us of Sadie Marsh's phenomenally accurate memory and we can assume that most of her rendition was identical to the shaman's speech.

THE DATA

Mrs. Marsh called her story "Charlie Klutchiehun łahi," "doctoring by Charlie Klutchie." The shaman's Indian name was *Qorit* and Lee's (ibid. p. 408) title is "Qorit doctors Mrs. Fan." I will now give this text collected by Lee, rewriting it in the orthography I use for Wintu and adding an interlinear morpheme-by-morpheme translation.[5] My free translation differs from that given by Lee (p. 408-11) in only a few details.

1. qor-i-t   Misus Fan-um wini·n-a ʔi-kila-k
grind-sd-p Mrs. Fan-obj doctor-sd do-con-com

tu-m tun-popil,   Harry-h t'erm-e-s-to·-t. 2. ʔuna·
eye-g ahead year   Harry-p interpret-sd-sd-dp-p   and

ken-wan-i   ʔuk-in łah-a·   ʔi-kila-k
down-get-sd(evening) then-loc doctor-sd do-con-com

ne-le-·n hen-e-t-'a.   3.ʔuna· pu-t wini·n-a
we-pl-gen arrive-sd-p-after   and she-obj doctor-sd

ʔi-kila-k pu-t   Misus Fan-um 4. ʔuna· k'eč-i
do-con-com she-obj Mrs. Fan-obj   and fern-sd

ni-s yur-a·   ʔi-kila-k. 5. ʔut ni win-e-har-a·
I-obj send after-sd do-con-com   and I see-sd-go-sd

ʔi-kila-k k'eč-i pu-r yum-u-s   ʔel-t'ub-e·-wer-e-s
do-con-com fern-sd he-pos saliva-sd-g in-spit-sd-rel-sd-g

ʔuni-buha ya·pay-tu·   doq-o-s-um. 6. ʔuna· lo·l
cot-and   evil spirit-being arrow-sd-g-obj   and tobacco

bih-e ʔi-kila-k, lo·l hisa-m-hon-da bih-e-buha
smoke-sd do-con-com tobacco some-g-long time-ts smoke-sd

tʰun-in dil-e   ʔi-kila-k.
and whole-loc fall-sd do con-com

7. ʔuna· po·-qa-t   č'a·w-a-buha ʔi-kila-k
and   now-as for-p sing-sd-and do-con-com

hon-da 8. pe-h-pe-h yup-a·-buha. 9. "ha·haq", ʔuni.
long time-ts thing-p-pl-p speak-sd-and   look! quot

10. "k'ay-i-s-koy-i-kuy-a-r   mi-s ho·la mi-s
     healthy-sd-g want-sd-want-sd-sub you-obj pipe

tʰil-a·-bih-e   ʔi-bi·-da, ʔoq-ti-t
you-obj eat with-sd-smoke-sd do impf-I same-at-p

k'ay-i-s-kuy-a   suk-en-so",   ʔuni t'erm-a-r.
healthy-sd-g-want-sd stand-I'll-before quot interpret-sd-sub

11. ʔu-he-t'an ʔel-ew   pe·-h   t'ip-n-a-min-a
    do-id-though exist-priv thing-p know-refl-sd-not

   ni pu-r łah-a·-r ti·n-he-t'an, ʔil-e·-s nom-ke·n-
exist-sd I he-pos doctor-sd-sub say-id-though be-sd-g west-

   su·-m łah-u-·t.
down- be-obj doctor-sd-p

12. ʔuna· pu-t   łah-a·   kerum-a-buha pu-r-kur-u-r
    and he-obj doctor-sd finish-sd-and he-pos-son-sd-pos

łes-um łah-a· ʔi-kila-k. 13.ʔuna· hisa·-m č'a·w-a
spirit-obj doctor-sd do-con-com   and some-g sing-sd

kerum-a-buha po·-qa-t   ʔuni, "me·m čal-i
finish-sd-and now-as for-p quot water good-sd

bol-o-s-ku-da   le·n-da   ne-le·n bol-o-s-to· sačaq-
drink-sd-sd-want-I ancient-ts we-pl-gen drink-sd-g-dp red

me·m." 14. ʔut łah-u-her-e-s-to·-t, "ne-t-o-me-n
rock-water   and doctor-sd-pas-sd-g-dp-p I-pos-al-one-gen

boh-e-h yo· x̣at-al-a-har-a·-be·   way-ti-q'ede,
big-sd-p emp weak-stat-sd-pro-sd-impf north-at-arm

no-ti-q'ede. 15. hesta-r pu-r naq-al-min-a ʔel-ew-a-r
south-at-arm   how-sub he-pos pity-stat-not-sd exist-priv-

ʔiy-e ʔi-biy-a-m?   16. te·d-i-me·m wer-e
sd-sub do-sd do-impf-sd-dub   red-sd-water come-sd

bol-en." 17. ʔuna· po·-qa-t   bul-a ʔi-kila-k. 18. ʔuna·
drink-I'll and now-as for-p drink-sd do-con-com   and

hi-we-hi č'a·w-a ʔi-kila-k hon-da. 19. ʔuna· pi-ʔuni ti·n,
id-sd-id sing-sd do-con-com long time-ts and that-cot say

"win-tʰu·-n-um pe·-h-um wi·n-le·-s-p'in-a·-da,
person-being-g-obj thing-p-obj see-can-g-can't-sd-I

ʔil-e·-s ni win-tʰu·-h ʔuwe-puk-i-t, ʔil-e·-s ʔila·-h ni
be-sd-g I person-being-p just-raw-sd-p be-sd-g baby-p I

ku·-t'e-t biy-a-r. 20. pe·-h po· ni t'ip-n-a-le·-s.
little-only-p be-sd-sub thing-p now I know-refl-sd-can-g

21. ʔuni-r ni win-tʰu·-n-un tʰo·s-in-pan-a-t
cot-sub I person-being-g-gen camp-loc-get-sd-p

hen-um-a· ni wi·n-le·-s-p'in-a·-ba·-k, ʔil-e·-s ni
how-dem-sd I see-can-g-can't sd-dur-com be-sd-g I

ʔila·-h q'o·t-ʔila-h. 22. ʔel-ew ʔi-se·-da ne-t
baby-p body dirt-dim-p exist-priv be-per-I I-pos

ʔuni-wer-e-s ni t'ip-n-a-min-a ma·qa ne-t ʔuni-wer-e-s
cot-rel-sd-g I know-refl-sd-not-sd hence I-pos cot-rel-sd-g

biy-a-kir-[r]e·-m.
be-sd-com-inf-dub

23. ʔut be·-di win-tʰu·-h, "ʔuk-in hadi
and be-don't person-being-p there-loc (exclamation)

tʰo·s-in-pan-a-r q'i'l-u-n-a·-kila mod-u-m-a-he-le-
camp-loc-get-sd-sub paint-sd-refl-sd-con heal-sd-g-sd-pas-

ba·-da", ʔuma· be·-di se-λ'am-ah-n-a-min-a,
can-dur-we thus be-don't around-think-sd-refl-sd-

ʔil-e·-s ne-t-o-me-n boh-e-h xat-al-a-har-a·
not exist-sd be-sd-g I-pos-al-one-gen big-sḋ-p weak-stat-sd-

ʔi-be, ʔol-k'ok-u-wil-[l]e·s-p'in-a· pe·-h-um.
pro-sd be-impf up-lift-sd-with-can-g-can't-sd one-p-obj

24. ʔol-k'ok-u-wil-i-s-to·-t ʔe-w-e-t-hi yaleq-t-a
up-lift-sd-with-sd-g-dp-p this-g-sd-p-id loose-p-sd

ʔi-suk ʔus-leˑn-da. 25.ʔut ne-t-o-me-n   boh-e-h
do-per last-ago-ts   and I-pos-al-one-gen big-sd-p

piy-o-ken hur-aˑ-r   hi pʰuˑr-u-m x̣at-a-wil-n-aˑ-
he-al-alone leave-sd-sub that heart-sd-obj weak-sd-with

-beˑ,   ʔol-pʰur-u-s   x̣at-al-a-har-aˑ-ntʰeˑ.
refl-sd-impf up-breath-sd-g weak-stat-sd-pro-sd-nvs

26. ne-t-o-me-n boh-e-m-um   ni ʔe-w-e-t   ʔel-bič-eˑ-
I-pos-al-one-gen big-sd-g-obj I this-g-sd-p in-exhort-sd-

baˑ-k, 'way-k'od-u-t nor-k'od-u-t beˑ-di war
dur-com north-get-sd-p south-get-sd-p be-don't imp

hi-da-boy saq-meˑm   bol-min-a' ʔuni-baˑ-k ni.
id-emp-much blood-water drink-not-sd quot-dur-com I

27. ʔu-he-t'an ne-t-o-me-n   boh-e-h ni-s
   do-id-though I-pos-al-one-gen big-sd-p I-obj

ʔel-eˑ-s-biy-a-k   q'omih-min-a. 28. ʔuni-r hi
exist-priv-g-impf-sd-com understand-not-sd cot-sub emp

ʔus-leˑn-da ʔe-h po·m-way-t'ir-a   ʔi-suk čok-i-ʔila-y.
last-ago-ts this-p ground-north-get-sd do-per near-sd-dim-g

29. pu-t ʔel-ti-win-tʰu-n-um   kalay-ʔił-n-aˑ   hi,
   he-p in-at-person-being-g-obj among-get-refl-sd   emp

saq-meˑm   ʔel-bul-a-ʔilay-a kir-ke-ntʰeˑ-m, pu-be
blood-water in-drink-sd-dim-sd com-pot-nvs-dub there-be

ʔuni-r x̣at-al-a-har-aˑ,   ʔol-pʰur-u-s woroˑt-a-har-aˑ.
cot-sub weak-stat-sd-pro-sd up-breath-sd-g short-sd-pro-sd

      30. "e-h   ne-t nom-tay-ʔilay-i xun-p'onor-t-a ne-t
          here-p I-pos west-loc-dim-sd here-run-p-sd I-pos

wer-e-s-in   ʔe-w-in pe·-t ni-s way-ti ʔel-halap-
come-sd-sd-loc this-g-loc thing-g I-obj north-at in-whisper-

t-a-ntʰeˑ. 31. pe·-h ni-s ma·n leweq-a-r ʔiy-e-ʔel.
p-sd-nvs   thing-p I-obj now tell-sd-sub be-sd-exp

32. ʔut čiri·k-a-da. 33. ni-qa-t-i   pe·-h ma-le-·t
and frightened-sd-I   I-as for-p-sd thing-p you-pl-obj

leweq-a-le·-s p'in-a·-da ʔil-e·-s ʔuwe-puk-i win-tʰu·-h,
tell-sd-can-p can't-sd-I be-sd-g just-raw-sd person-being-p

ʔila·-h po· ni ʔil-e·-s. 34. ʔel-ew-qa-t   kila-ʔel
baby-p still I be-sd-g   exist-priv-as for-p con-exp

ʔila-wi hi-da-ko·-m t'ip-n-a-suk-min-a. 35. ʔuni-r ni
baby-pl id-emp-all-g know-refl-sd-per-not-sd cot-sub I

ma·n pe·-h   mal-n-a·-wir-a   ʔi-be-wi·ʼ, ʔuni
now thing-p make-refl-sd-rel-sd do-impf-int quot

ʔi-kila-k č'a·w-a kerum-a-buha.
do-con-com sing-sd finish-sd-and

      36. ʔuta po·-qa-t   Misus Fan dollar-and-a-half
         and now-as for-p Mrs. Fan

mutm-a ʔi-kila-k. 37."ʔe-be mi-s   ʔe-w-i·n
pay-sd do-con-com   this-be you-obj this-g-with

se-q'i·l-u-n-a·-s-kuy-a-r   ʔiy-e ʔi-bi·-da
around-paint-sd-refl-sd-g-want-sd-sub do-sd- do-impf-I

tu-m kuy-a-r, pe·-h win-le·-s-p'in-a· ʔi-bi·-da.
eye-g hurt-sd-sub thing-p see can-g-can't-sd do-impf-I

38. pe·-h-un   ni ma·n λ'o·m-u-t λ'itiq-n-a· ʔiy-e
    thing-p-gen I now kill-sd-p do-refl-sd do-sd

biy-a-ʔel. 39. ʔuni-r mod-i-kuy-a-r   mi-s
be-sd-exp   cot-sub heal-sd-want-sd-sub you-obj

wini·n-u-n-a·-r   ʔiy-e-bi·-da. 40. hi-baqi ni ɬah-
doctor-sd-refl-sd-sub do-sd-impf-I   id-or I doctor

-i-n keneh-a λ'o·m-u-t ʔiy-e biy-a-ʔel. 41. ʔuni-r mi
sd-gen maybe-sd kill-sd-p do-sd be-sd-exp   cot-sub you

ni-s hen-ʔu-le·-s xan-pʰuɬ-u-min-a hi-baqi pu-t ni-s
I-obj how-do-can-g off-blow-sd-not-sd id-or he-obj I-obj

λ'o·m-i-to·-n-um neq-u-wil-kila war pu-t-am yi·-l-a",
kill-sd-dp-g-obj find-sd-with-con imp he-obj-obj send-sd

ʔuni-ki-nt^hi-k.
quot-com-nvs-com

42. ʔuta pu-t, "daw-in ʔe-w-in ken-ł-a·",
and she-obj front-loc this-g-loc down-sit-sd

ʔuni ʔi-kila-k. 43. ʔuni-buha po·-qa-t p^hoyoq čin-e·-buha
quot do-con-com cot-and now-as for-p head take-sd-and

pu-t hay-a·-buha ʔi-kila-k hon-da. 44. hay-a·-buha-r-
she-obj look-sd-and do-con-com long time-ts look-sd-and

kel-t'an pu-t, "ho·", ʔuni ʔi-kila-k.
sub-long-though she-obj yes quot do-con-com

45. "ma-t-a ma·n po·-loyme-s-a-r ba·-s-biy-a-nt^he·;
you-pos-sd now young-girl-g-sd-sub eat-g-impf-sd-nvs

hi-baqi ma-t ʔila-·m se-tep-č-u-n-a·-biy-a-r
id-or you-pos baby-obj around-come to life-mp-sd-refl-sd-

ba·-s. 46. ʔel-ew-qa-t kila-ʔel
impf-sd-sub eat-g exist-priv-as for-p con-exp

len-da-da ʔuma· λitiq-n-a-min-a win-t^hu·-h loyme-
ancient-ts-emp thus do-refl-sd-not-sd person-being-p girl-

s-a-be·-t'an, hi-baqi ʔila-·m
g-sd-be-though id-or baby-obj

se-tep-č-u-n-a·-biy-a-r", ʔuni.
around-come to life-mp-sd-refl-sd-impf-sd-sub quot

47. "ma-t-a ʔe-w ba·-s q'omih-n-a·-s koy-i-biy-a-nt^he·.
you-pos-sd this-g eat-g full-refl-sd-g want-sd-impf-sd-nvs

48. tu·n-ʔila-·n ni ma-t t^ho·s-in-pan-a-paq-a-t hen-ʔu-
first-dim-loc I you-pos camp-loc-get-sd-or-sd-p how-do-

le·-s. 49. po·-qa-t mi hi-da kuy-a-wenem-dil-m-a-
can-g now-as for-p you id-emp sick-sd-mid-fall-g-sd-

be·-sken. 50. ʔel-ew-qa-t-kila ʔeh le·n-da
impf-you exist-priv-as for-p-con this-p ancient-ts

łah-a·-r win-tʰu·-h, 'hi-da mod-u-m-ah-le-
doctor-sd-sub person-being-p id-emp heal-sd-caus-sd

ba·-da ʔume·na', "uni-r ma·n mi-s ʔel-wan-u-we-n."
can-dur-I like that cot-sub now you-obj in-get-sd-rel-I'll

51. ʔuni-buha po·-qa-t pu-t čin-e·-buha tu-m-to·
cot-and now-as for-p she-obj take-sd-and eye-g-dp

xun-č'u·y-a ʔi-kila-k. 52. ʔuna· pu-t "he·s-in
toward-himself-suck-sd do-con-com and she-obj ever-loc

ma-t tu-win-her-e-s-top-i-m tu-win-min-a
you-pos ahead-see-pas-sd-g-with-sd-obj ahead-see-not-sd

53. tu-h bi-ke· ʔe-w wini·n-u-he-le·-s-p'e.
eye-p be-hearsay this-g doctor-sd-pas-can-g-without

54. pe·-h tu-m-pan-ti tu-kur-a-m-a ʔule·s ʔuni-
thing-p eye-g-top-at ahead-grow-sd-caus-sd just like cot-

bi-ntʰe·." 55. ʔuna· pu-t hisa-m-pom xun-č'u·y-a-ʔa
be-nvs and she-obj some-g-time toward himself-suck-

kerum-a ʔi-kila-k.
sd-having finish-sd do-con-com

56. ʔuna· ʔuk-in-a xaydan-i pi qor-i-t min-el.
and then-loc-sd fall-sd he grind-sd-p die-stat

FREE TRANSLATION

1. Qorit doctored Mrs. Fan's eyes last year; Harry was the interpreter. 2. And he doctored in the evening after we had arrived. 3. And so he worked on her; he doctored Mrs. Fan. 4. Then he sent me after fern. 5. And so I went to get the fern into which he was going to spit his spittle and the supernatural arrows. 6. And he smoked tobacco; he smoked tobacco for quite a while and fell into a trance.

7. So now he was singing for a while. 8. He spoke prophetically. 9. "Look upon me," he said. 10. "I smoke a pipe in your company because I want you to be healthy, so that I can be

healthy in the same way." Thus the interpreter. 11. But I did not understand any of his doctoring as he spoke in the language of the northwesterners.

12. Then he finished commanding this spirit and addressed the spirit of his son. 13. Having finished singing a little he now said, "I want to drink the good water, our drink of red-rock water from long ago." 14. Then he who was in the shaman's command said: "My father's arms are getting weak. 15. Why don't you show pity for him? 16. Get red water so that I may drink." 17. And now he drank. 18. And again he sang for a long time. 19. And the same spirit spoke: "I am unable to help anyone as I am a person who has not been perfected, a little baby. 20. What can I know now? 21. Thus when I come to people's camps, how can I attend to them, as I am a baby, a little body-dirt baby. 22. I never thought that this would be my destination; for this, I gather, has been my destination.

23. "So, you people, say not in your thoughts 'when we go to his camp and he rubs us with spittle, we shall be healed'; for my father is getting weak and can give no support to anyone. 24. She who was his supporter has recently relinquished her hold. 25. And so my father, left alone, is weak of heart and his breath is getting weak. 26. I have been exhorting my father, saying 'when you go north and when you go south, do not drink so much liquor', I have been telling him. 27. But my father does not understand me. 28. Thus only recently he went a short distance to the north. 29. He mingled with the white people, drank quite a bit, and so now he is getting weak and his breath is getting short.

30. "When I was running, coming here a short distance from the west, I heard something whisper into my northward ear. 31. It told me something. 32. And I was frightened. 33. As for myself, I cannot tell you anything since I am an unperfected person, being still a baby. 34. Children do not know everything. 35. Thus what am I to achieve?" Thus he spoke after he had finished singing.

36. And now Mrs. Fan gave him a dollar and a half. 37. She said: "Here, by means of this I want to be rubbed with spittle, as I ail in my eyes; I cannot see anything. 38. I am being done to death by someone, I think. 39. So, wishing to be healed, I come to you to be doctored. 40. I consider that perhaps it is a shaman who is killing me. 41. If so, can you blow the evil force away from me; or, if you find what is killing me, send it back to the one who sent it?" I heard her say.

42. And so he said to her: "Sit here in front of me." 43. And now he took her head in his hands and looked at her for a long time. 44. After looking at her he said, "Yes," he said to her. 45. "It is your own doing. I know that when you were pubescent,

you kept eating; furthermore, when you brought your child to life, you were eating. 46. In the old days, people did not behave like that when they reached puberty or when they brought children into being." he said. 47. "This disease is your own doing, your desire to eat yourself full of food. 48. If I had come to your camp earlier, I might have done something. 49. Now you have fallen too deep into illness. 50. Neither did the doctoring people in the old days say, 'I promise a complete cure'; on this understanding let me doctor you."

51. And now he took hold of her and sucked her eyes. 52. Then he said to her: "You will never see again with your eyes. 53. It is said that eyes cannot be doctored. 54. There is something like a thin cover growing on top of them." 55. And after he had sucked her for some time he was finished.

56. And that fall Qorit died.

SPEAKING IN TONGUES

The first point to note is that sentence 10 is the interpreter's translation of a sentence spoken by Qorit in a language other than Wintu. Shamans always had interpreters with them to translate those parts of the speech for monolinguals in the audience. The interpreter traveled with the shaman to other tribes and thus learned the languages the shaman learned (Du Bois 1935: 107). The first spirit speaking through Qorit only says one sentence; as we learn later, Qorit is not well and is losing his power to command spirits. Shamans would let the evil spirit speak through them to discover what it did to the sick person, hoping to find a cure knowing the cause and location of the disease.[6] This spirit speaks in the language of the *nomke'nsu's* which is another name for the *nomyoh*. The *nomyoh* are particularly powerful spirits (Lee 1941: 408) and apparently Qorit loses control of the first spirit before he can tell him anything. He is not able to cure the patient in the end, perhaps because of this weakness. This first spirit may have been the evil spirit that made Mrs. Fan ill. In another text only available in English (Lee 1941:408) Qorit says that his "yoh" spirit power is killing him. Lee explains (ibid., p. 408, footnote 14): "The *yoh*, or, as they are commonly called, *nomyoh* (*yoh* of the west) are the potent spirits of the Indians of the northwest coast of California, who turned themselves at will into beasts. Children were warned: 'Never say *nomyoh* at night: say *west-coast-beings* instead.' *yoh*-old-man was the term applied to a great doctor."

Grace McKibbin, a native speaker I worked with,

identified the nomyoh as Hupa Indians who have turned into beasts and poison doctors by spending a lot of time out in the woods. Her "Hupa" does not necessarily refer to the Hupa tribe. The Wintu identified most tribes by the direction in which they lived as seen from Wintu territory and often applied the same name to several groups all of whom were in the same general direction. The name is translated into an English tribal name which then also comes to refer to more than one tribe. Qorit could have been speaking in the language of any group west or northwest of Wintu territory. Sadie Marsh told Du Bois (1935: 95) that when Qorit was "half-crazy" mourning his son's death he was helped by a nomke˙nsu˙s doctor at Fort Jones and that for that reason he sometimes talks nomke˙su˙s when he doctors. Du Bois thinks that this doctor was "probably a Shasta Indian."

Other shamans used other languages, whichever they happened to know. Du Bois (ibid., p. 91) tells us that the shaman Albert Thomas, when in trance, spoke Achomawi or "the language of any western group," or English when being helped by a white man's spirit. It is possible that especially evil spirits always spoke through the shaman in a language other than Wintu. The Wintu language was a symbol of tribal identity and pride and as such could not be spoken by evil spirits. Evil came from outsiders.

WINTU SHAMANIC REGISTER[7]

The second spirit Qorit addresses is that of his dead son. According to Du Bois, the Wintu could become shamans in two ways: through initiation and formal instruction in the sweathouse (ibid., p. 88-90) and through grieving over a dead relative. Qorit became a shaman in the second way when his son died at the age of ten or eleven and so uses the son's spirit as a familiar and helper. As pointed out by Lee (p. 409, footnote 17) Sadie Marsh was able to tell that Qorit was addressing his son's spirit because he switched from the nomyoh language to Wintu. The son's spirit speaks through Qorit, that is, Qorit speaks as if his and his son's personalities had merged into one.[8]

How does the shaman's language differ from colloquial Wintu? The body of data is so small that whatever we can discover must remain speculative, but I believe that it can give us a few general ideas which point in the right direction.

First of all, Qorit obviously avoids the direct mention of taboo concepts such as bodily functions and death. In sentence 24 *yaleqta* 'to let go' is used instead of *minel* 'to die'. In sentence 45 *po˙-loymesa* 'to be a young girl' and in 46 *loymesa* 'to be a girl' replace *bała* 'to be pubescent, menstruate for the first time'. In the same two sentences *ʔilaˑm se-tepčunaˑ* 'to bring a baby to life' is used as a substitute for *kuˑra* 'to give birth'. In 47 *baˑs q'omihnaˑ* 'to fill oneself with food' is probably more formal than *baˑs baˑ* 'to eat food'.

Further, he uses paraphrases for two kinship terms, as already noted by Lee. In sentence 14 we find *netomen boheh* 'my alienable particular big one' for *nettaˑn* 'my father'. The reason for the use of the alienable possessive pronoun may be that the son is dead, but *boheh* is not the usual way of referring to one's father. The second kinship reference is in sentence 24: *ʔol-k'okuwilistoˑt*, literally 'one who lifts someone up', i.e., 'supporter', instead of *p'uqat* 'wife'.

Other "idioms" or "ceremonial phrasings," as Lee calls them, are *haˑhaq* 'look upon me!' (sentence 9), an exclamation used only by shamans and not related to the word for 'to see, look'; and *sačaqmeˑm* 'red-rock water' in sentence 13. *teˑdimeˑm* 'red water' in sentence 16 may refer to the same thing, but I am uncertain about its meaning. Native speaker Renee Coleman used it for 'alcohol' but I do not believe that was its original meaning. She said *sačaq* refers to rocks used to heat liquid in cooking, so the 'red' might be that of the glowing hot rocks. Another kind of red rock is iron oxide clay which colors spring water. Du Bois (ibid., p. 116) reports the existence of red-clay water "used in burials and to propitiate souls which manifest themselves in swirls of dust." She also mentions (p. 117) "red-rock water" as part of the regalia of a shaman but does not give the Wintu term. According to Du Bois (p. 104) the shaman used red-rock water to moisten his lips for sucking out pains; perhaps it also served to facilitate trance.

Other expressions in the register of shamanism are *tʰoˑsin-pana* 'to get to someone's bed or camp' (sentence 21) and *maˑqa* 'hence, it follows' (sentence 22) which is now obsolete and was rare at Lee's time. Sadie Marsh explained its meaning by telling Lee a story she heard from her mother. Lee comments on *ʔuniweres* (sentence 22): "The term *destination* here is not to be taken as the equivalent of *fate*. The *-weres* of personal intention is used, not the *-les* of impersonal necessity, or the inescapable future. Perhaps he implies that his father, through his excessive mourning, deliberately made him into a spirit power."

In sentence 26 *saqmeˑm* means 'alcohol, intoxicating liquor'. *meˑm* is 'water', *saq* must be an archaic word for 'blood', perhaps related to the above-mentioned *sačaq* 'red rock'. Grace McKibbin was unfamiliar with *saq* but knew that the male proper name *saˑqa* once meant something like 'blood stain' or 'color of blood'.

In sentence 52 eyes are called *tu-winherestopi*, literally 'used for that which is seen ahead', i.e., 'those with which you see what is ahead'. In 49 *ʔel-wana* 'to get in, enter' is used instead of *ɬaha·* or *wini·na* 'to doctor'.

Lee also points out *wi·nle·sp'ina·* 'not be able to see' (sentence 19) instead of 'not be able to help', noting that the form of the verb is obsolete. I am not quite sure which part of the verb she refers to but I believe it is *p'ina·* 'to lack, not to be, be without' which is used frequently in this text in favor of the negative *ʔelew . . . -mina*. It is also used by narrators who are not shamans in Lee's texts, but native speakers I have worked with did not use it. I conclude that obsolescent expressions survive longer in shamanic speech.

A third class of characteristic features of shamanic register involve understatement; "ceremonial speech is given to self-belittling and understatement" (Lee ibid., p. 409, footnote 25). Qorit's son speaking through Qorit refers to himself as *ʔila·h*. Lee translates this as 'child', but my native speakers said it means 'baby'. 'Child' would have been the truth--Qorit's son was about ten years old when he died--'baby' is an understatement. He continues to emphasize how little he knows while it is clear that he knows more than his father, advising him not to mix with white people and not to drink.[9] He also calls himself *q'o·t'ʔilah* (21) 'little body dirt', perhaps a reference to the way babies leave the mother's body.

When Qorit's son calls himself *ʔuwe-pukit* 'just a raw one' (19, 33) he is also speaking for Qorit who was one of the "raw" doctors (Du Bois ibid., p. 98, 103) because he did not go through the sweathouse initiation and instruction but became a doctor by grieving. However, Qorit was considered the greatest doctor of his time and *ʔuwe-pukit* remains self-belittling.

Lee (p. 410) further notes *ʔel-bulaʔilaya* 'to drink in a little', in sentence 29, meaning 'drink a lot'. Another special expression is *waytiq'ede notiq'ede* 'northern arm, southern arm' in sentence 14. The son's spirit says that his father's arms are getting weak which may be true but has nothing to do with shamanic powers. What matters is that Qorit's mind and concentration are weakening making it difficult for him to cure people. His health is so poor that he has less power than his son. Qorit feels like a powerless baby which may be why he chose to address the spirit of his son. On the other hand, the idiom concerning weakening arms may have been a metaphor in general use.

The list of special vocabulary used by shamans can be expanded with expressions found in other texts. In Ida Fan's prophetic speech (Lee, p. 411) we find *wayk'oho·la nok'oho·la* 'wandering to the north, wandering to the south'. Lee notes (p. 411, footnote 36) that *k'oho·la* is obsolete and only used by shamans. The same is true for *wayhami·la nohami·la* 'drifting to the north, drifting to the south'.

In "Doctoring" (Lee, p. 411) , it is *tu-k'udawirabint^he·* 'she will go onward, I sense' meaning 'she will die' and *putun lesto·t yelta·nk'uda sukebint^he·* 'her spirit stands a short distance behind her, I sense', meaning 'she is close to death'. From the last two examples we can infer that the shaman was free to choose among several possible variants when using circumlocutions.

Only a few of the ceremonial phrasings replace direct words for taboo concepts such as death while others must simply be part of the special register of shamanism. This aspect of the register was artistic, approaching poetic style.[10] As, for example, Emeneau showed for the Todas (1964, especially pp. 336-40), poetry is universally characterized by the enigmatic and allusive, marked by suggestions and implications. Perhaps the closest parallel to the metaphors used by the Wintu shaman is found in the "kennings" of Anglo-Saxon and especially Norse skaldic poetry. Gordon (1957: xxxvi-xlii) explains that the kennings are logically metaphors but do not represent the emotional or highly imaginative perception frowned on in English as "poetic diction." Rather they are devices for introducing descriptive color and for suggesting associations without distracting from the essential statement. The kenning has the meaning of a subordinate clause but expresses it in a briefer space and with less emphasis. The Wintu were able to do just that because of the synthetic structure of their language. What would be a clause in a language with little morphology and much syntax (e.g., "used for that which is seen ahead" or "one who lifts someone up") can be a single word in Wintu (*tu-winherestopi* or *ʔol-k'okuwilisto·t*).

A parallel to this allusive character of the jargon's lexical material is found in Wintu myths: the main protagonist often remains unnamed and is referred to only by descriptive formations (e.g., *č'arawah* 'one who is in the fields' replaces *sedet* 'Coyote').

Another characteristic of shamanic register is repetition. In the text given above we find *k'ayiskoyikuyar . . . k'ayiskuya* (sentence 10); *boloskuda . . . bolosto·* (13); *ʔile·s . . . ʔile·s* (19); *wi· nle·sp'ina·da* (19) . . . *wi·nle·sp'ina·ba·k* (21); *ʔile·s ʔila·h ni* (19) . . . *ʔile·s ni ʔila·h* (21); *ʔuniweres . . . ʔuniweres* (22); *ʔol-k'okuwile·sp'ina·* (23) . . . *ʔol-k'okuwilisto·t* (24); *netomen boheh* (14, 23, 25, 26, 27); *xatawilna·be· . . . xatalahara·nt^he·* (25); *way-k'odut . . . nor-k'odut* (26); *waytiq'ede . . . notiq'ede* (29); *ʔila·m se-tepčuna·biyar* (45, 46); *po·loymesar*

(45) . . . *loymesabe·t'an* (46); *tu-winherestopim tu-winmina* (52).
In the text of Ida Fan's prophetic speech (Lee ibid., p. 411) there
is *wayk'oho·la nok'oho·la* and *wayhami·la nohami·la* (see
above). While we usually avoid repetition in elevated styles of
English, Wintu shamanic register favored it. One reason was
certainly emphasis; perhaps repetition was also part of the Wintu
concept of euphony.

In the construction of the repeated phrases alliteration and
assonance may play a role. For example, *netomen boheh* favors
bilabials, nasals, and the vowels o and e; *ʔile·s (ni) ʔila·h
(q'o·t'ʔilah)* repeats *ʔil-*; *wintʰu·h ʔuwe-pukit* has the vowels i and
u and the consonants w - w - p; *ʔol-k'okuwile·sp'ina·* or *ʔol-
k'okuwilisto·t* has two l's, two k's, and two or three o's. There
may be other examples but they are not as convincing. Especially
assonance is difficult to distinguish from words in which ablaut
has caused certain vowels to co-occur.

An alternative interpretation is echoism which
characterizes glossolalia (Samarin 1973: 79). Observe the vowels
in the following expressions: *netomen boheh*, *ʔol-k'okuwilisto·t*,
xatalahara·, *waytiq'ede*, *notiq'ede*, *wintʰu·h ʔuwe-pukit*, and
many others. Echoic devices, as noted by Samarin (ibid., p. 81)
figure also in poetic discourse.

A second phonological characteristic of Qorit's speech--
more obvious than alliteration and assonance--is the favoring of
certain vowels and consonants. A calculation of the frequency of
vowels shows a to be the most often used by both Sadie Marsh and
Qorit; i follows at about the same distance for both. The next
most frequently used vowel is u for Sadie, occurring almost as
often as i, but e for Qorit, used almost as often as i; Sadie uses e
only about half as often as i while Qorit uses u about half as often
as i. Thus the ratios of e and u per total number of vowels used
are reversed. O is the least frequently used vowel for both, but its
frequency is 1/3 of that of a for Qorit, 1/4 of that of a for Sadie.
In short, the shaman's speech is characterized by greater frequency
of the vowels e and o.

Two interpretations of the increase of e and o are possible.
One goes as follows. Many Wintu i and u are derived historically
from *e and *o. Patwin, the only extant cognate language, has e
and o where Wintu has the morphophonemic alternation i~e and
u~o. The Wintu innovation may have been quite recent, at any
rate later than the split from Proto-Wintun. Perhaps shamanic
tradition dictated the use of many words with e and o which gives
the register an archaic "flavor" reminiscent of a time when e and
o were the most frequent Wintu vowels together with a. (If vowels
were used for emphasis one would expect a preference for i - a -

u, the extremes of the vowel system.)

A second explanation for Qorit's favoring of e and o is based on the argument made earlier that shamanic speech in Wintu is an art form. The Wintu also prefer e and o in the linguistically meaningless syllables of many songs. As Hinton (1976: 67ff) pointed out, the high aesthetic value placed on low vowels is an almost universal phenomenon in singing. Havasupai songs show an increase of low vowels as part of the preference for the "maximization of resonance" (Hinton ibid., p. 76) but this language achieves the increase by phonological rules, such as vowel lowering and insertion, while the Wintu produce the same effect by the selection of lexical items, or meaningless syllables in songs, which contain the desired vowels.[11]

In contrast to the characteristics of the vocalic inventory, a calculation of the frequencies of consonants brings us to a major difference between the jargon and glossolalia.[12] In producing glossolalia, the speaker maximizes what is already common in his primary language (Samarin 1972: 84) A comparison of the frequencies of stops and fricatives for English and glossolalia shows a decrease in the number of fricatives for glossolalia while the number of stops increases. There is no evidence for any such trend in the shamanic register. Instead we find an increase in the number of voiced consonants (m and w increase by 4% d, l, and n by 2%; y and b by 1%) and a 3% increase for s, 1.8% for t^h, 0.5% for x, 0.3% for λ', while the frequency of the other voiceless consonants decreases (k by 9%, p by 5%, ʔ and h by 3%, ł by 1.7%, t by 1.1%, č' and q by 1%, x̣ by 0.4%, č by 0.1%). The shaman favors the greater "resonance" (following Hinton 1976) of voiced consonants, just as he prefers e, a, and o, and the high frequency components of s, x [x̣], t^h, and λ'.[13]

There are other aspects of Wintu shamanic register which can be compared and contrasted with glossolalia. Samarin (1972: 122) defines glossolalia as "unintelligible extemporaneous post-babbling speech that exhibits superficial phonologic similarity to language without having consistent syntagmatic structure and that is not systematically derived from or related to known languages." Wintu shamanic jargon certainly does not fit this definition. However, the jargon has several elements in common with glossolalia as described in detail by Samarin 1972, 1973, and since Samarin argues that glossolalia is continuous with other marginal linguistic phenomena, "anomalous speech," I would like to suggest that shamanic jargon is part of the same continuum and not too far removed from glossolalia.

Samarin (1973: 79) notes that glossolalia is not "meaningless" or "gibberish." Although it is unintelligible, the speaker or an interpreter can translate it into normal languages.

The same is true for the shaman's speech when he uses languages other than Wintu.

Another feature the jargon shares with glossolalia is that a state of trance is not necessary for its production. As Samarin (1973: 85) notes, a person can use glossolalia in a fully conscious, normal state if he wants to. A speaker of Wintu can use a register similar to the shaman's for different purposes, such as praying (see below).

Glossolalia is learned behavior (Samarin 1969b, 1973: 87). The speaker learns that he must produce some form of it to be accepted as a member of the Pentecostal Society. He learns favored phonological and paralinguistic features; and he learns to use certain sequences of syllables he hears from other glossolalists. The same three things must be learned by the shaman.

From a sociolinguistic point of view, glossolalia is just another "language" in the Pentecostalists' linguistic repertoire (Samarin 1972: 121, 124). The glossolalist selects from his repertoire according to his needs in the same way as a bilingual switches codes depending on the subject under discussion. On the one hand, shamanic jargon is one of the shaman's registers; on the other hand, it is a point in the Wintu stylistic continuum sharing many features with other registers.

Samarin rejects trance as causation of glossolalia and favors defining it as regressive speech: "the speaker returns to processes that characterized his language learning in early childhood, at a time when he was first learning the part of language most obvious to a child--its phonetic representation (1973: 85). At this point the jargon has nothing in common with glossolalia. Even though the shaman is in trance when using his jargon while the Christian using glossolalia is rarely in a state of trance (Samarin 1972: 123), he does not return to a more primitive stage of his language. Rather, the jargon represents an elevated style of Wintu. It comes close to poetry in its use of metaphors and echoic devices. It seems ironic that in a "primitive" culture the religious register is the most elevated style while in "advanced" civilizations religious glossolalia returns to the primitive "post-babbling" stage. According to Chadwick (1942: 57), " . . . it may be safely said that the inspired prophet and seer is the leading intellectual and artistic influence in primitive and backward society."

There are differences between shamanic Wintu and colloquial Wintu beyond the use of special vocabulary. An obvious one is that in the above text almost every single sentence spoken by Sadie Marsh when she is not speaking as Qorit begins with the connective ʔuna· 'and, and then'. A few begin with ʔut which has the same translation but implies change of subject. When she is speaking for the shaman, she uses ʔut three times (23,

25, 32), *ʔuna·* never; other connectives used by Qorit are *ʔunir* 'thus' (21, 28, 35) and *ʔuhet'an* 'however, but, although' (27). *ʔuna·* is the unmarked connective having no meaning other than 'connective' while *ʔut*, *ʔuhet'an*, and *ʔunir* have added meanings. Thus the main function of *ʔuna·* is to give the speaker an extra second to think of what to say next while keeping the floor. Sadie Marsh uses it when telling her own experience at the curing ceremony as long as it is up to her to decide what to mention and what to leave out, or to try to remember as much as possible. The shaman's speech she reports is fixed. She remembers it literally or as she heard it and understood it and is not free to choose what to say. *ʔuna·* is used only as an aid in the reconstruction of a sequence of events (cf. Chafe 1973: 269) and, of course, is not used within a quote unless the speaker being quoted used it.

If one function of *ʔuna·* is to signify to the audience that one is not yet ready to give up the floor, a shaman need not use it since no one would interrupt him. Other reasons why Qorit did not use *ʔuna·* will become clear below.

Another feature of shamanic speech as exemplified in our text is the greater length of some of the sentences. I counted the number of words per sentence for Sadie Marsh's own speech (sentences 1-8, 11, 12, 17, 18, 36, 43, 51, 55, 56) and for Qorit's speech (sentences 13-16, 19-35, 45-47, 50, 52-54) excluding of course the parts of those sentences spoken by Sadie Marsh introducing the quotations. I did not count the interpreter's or Mrs. Fan's sentences. The ratio of words per sentence for Sadie Marsh is 6.9 (and that includes the repetitive *ʔuna·*), the ratio for Qorit is 7.6. For the same sentences, I counted the number of morphemes per word: Sadie Marsh's ratio is 2.4, Qorit's ratio is 3.1.[14]

This indicates that the relation of shamanic Wintu to conversational Wintu is somewhat similar to that of written to spoken language in other cultures and so we can attempt further comparisons in that vein. We know, for example, that in spoken English coordination and right-branching subordination prevail while subordination and left-branching are more common in written language (Pawley and Syder 1976). When Sadie Marsh is speaking for herself she uses right-branching subordination[15] in sentence 2 (*nele·n henet'a* 'after we had arrived'); in sentence 5 (*pur yumus ʔel-t'ube·weres . . .* 'into which he was going to spit his spittle . . .'); in 11 (*ʔile·s nomke·nsu·rı łahu·t* 'doctoring in the nomke·n-esu·s language'). Left-branching subordination is used twice, in sentence 44 (*haya·buharkelt'an* 'having looked for a long time') and in 55 (*xun-č'u·yaʔa* 'after he had sucked'). In both cases the left, subordinate verb describes an event which is temporally anterior to that of the right, superordinate verb. Qorit uses right-branching subordination in sentence 19 (*?ile's ni wint^{h}u'h ?uwe-pukit* 'as I am just a raw person' and *?ile's ?ila'h ni ku't'et biyar* 'as I am a small baby'); in 21 (*?ile's ni ?ila'h q'o't- ?ilah* 'as I am a little body-dirt baby); in 23 (*?ile's netomen boheh xatalahara˙ ?ibe* 'as my father is getting weak'); in 33 (*?ile's ˙. . .*); and in 46 (*loymesabe't'an . . .* and *se-tepčuna'biyar . . .*). He uses left-branching subordination in 21 (*wint^{h}u'nun t^{h}o'sinpanat* 'approaching people's camps'); in 23 (*t^{h}o'sinpanar q'i'luna'kila* 'getting to his camp when he rubs us with spittle'); in 25 (*netomen boheh piyoken hura'r* 'my father being left alone'); in 26 (*way-k'odut nor-k'odut* 'going to the north, going to the south'); in 30 (*net weresin* 'when I was coming'); and in 45 (*po'-loymesar . . . se-tepčuna'biyar* 'being a girl . . . bringing to life').

Apparently Qorit uses more subordination and left-branching than Sadie Marsh, but the difference is not statistically significant because she speaks as herself much less than as Qorit. When her own sentences consist of more than one clause, she prefers conjoining by the suffix *-buha* 'and' to subordination (sentences 6, 7, 12, 13, 35, 43, 44, 51); as Qorit she never uses *-buha*.

OTHER TYPES OF SPEECH

Before drawing final conclusions about shamanic Wintu, let me digress briefly to look at other special registers of this language.

Aside from the work of the shaman, the Wintu had little division of labor: there were people whose job it was to spank children, a man for the boys, a woman for the girls; only authorized individuals were allowed to make headdresses out of eagle feathers; and only certain middle-aged women were assigned the job of splitting elderberry sticks to make rattles. No special registers are reported for these professions. However, Du Bois (ibid., p. 11) mentions "circumlocutions" characteristic of bear hunts such as "let us visit our friends" meaning 'let us hunt bear', and "here is one of my people" or "I see that my friend has been here" meaning 'I see tracks of a bear'. (She does not give the Wintu equivalents.) The same type of hunting taboo is responsible for our word *bear* which is derived from an expression originally denoting 'brown one' which replaced the Indoeuropean word for 'bear'.

There may have been similar expressions for deer hunting, gathering, war, and other activities, but they have, to my knowledge, not been preserved. The only one I was able to collect from Grace McKibbin is a poem her grandmother used to say when showing her wild potatoes (of a species called *ko·nat*) she had dug:

> ʔoltepum xi·, ʔel yo· siktut.
> pomisim xi·, xan yo· siktut.
> 'Spring sleep, sweep in for me (meaning 'let me sleep well').
> Winter sleep, sweep away from me.'

Another register was that used in prayer. There were probably no formalized prayers, according to Du Bois (ibid., p. 73), but qo·l čulu·li's prayer (Lee, ibid., p. 407) shows that praying was not identical with colloquial Wintu. It seems to represent a register intermediate between ordinary and shamanic Wintu. Sadie Marsh explains (Lee ibid.) that her grandfather, qo·l čulu·li (literally 'mouth black'), used to get up early in the morning, wash his face and pray. It is not clear whether he said the same prayer every morning or made up a new one each time, so we cannot be sure to what extent his prayer was memorized and formalized. He uses a few circumlocutions similar to those of shamanic speech: *mi baheresas sukeʔel* 'you whose nature it is to be eaten' instead of mi *no·p* 'you deer' when addressing deer, but he uses the usual terms when addressing other animals. He also speaks of *waytiqʔede notiqʔede* 'north arm south arm' like Qorit above to describe himself as getting weak. Further, *neto λʔoli·n ni ma·n ken-diler ʔiye ʔibiyaʔel* 'I am falling back into my cradle (basket)' is used to mean 'I am dying', and *neto qomosto·t ho·n tu-kʔodito·t* 'my ancestors who have already gone ahead' for 'who have already died'. He also employs the obsolescent *p'ina·* found in Qorit's speech. His average number of words per sentence is 7.4; that of morphemes per word is 3.04; both are intermediate between Qorit's and Sadie Marsh's figures. Left-branching is favored over right-branching. Coordination is without the use of conjunctions. The most characteristic feature of the prayer is frequent repetition of certain clauses, especially the repetition of frames for clauses with the substitution of single words for one another. For example: If you are rock, look at me; I am advancing in old age. If you are tree, look at me; I am advancing in old age. If you are water, . . .

Another example of speech intermediate between Sadie Marsh's conversational Wintu and Qorit's shamanic register is found in a prophetic speech by the shaman Ida Fan in a trance; she is speaking for the spirits of dead Wintu (Lee ibid., p. 411). The text is very short (eleven sentences) and we cannot determine anything about it with certainty. Her special vocabulary has been mentioned above. The average ratios of words per sentence and morphemes per word are 7 and 3.12, respectively. The latter is almost identical with Qorit's, but Ida Fan's sentences are somewhat shorter than his. Left and right-branching subordination are used with equal frequency.

Wintu who were not shamans could, of course, switch register depending on the topic they were discussing. Du Bois (ibid., p. 75) reports that Kate Luckie once paid two shamans to speak about the end of the world and, in repeating their prophesies, she switched to a high poetic style. (The prophesy is given in English only.)

Another type of specialized speech consists of a set of formulas spoken at the end of an evening of myth-telling.[16] My native speakers did not use these but Lee was able to collect the following:

1. *pomisimyus pat-hubu!*	'Winter mosquitoes swarm out!
po·pilyus ?el-hubu!	Summer mosquitoes swarm in!
witil ?ol-t'ipt'ipa war!	Be spring soon!'
2. *witil ?ol-t'ipa war!*	'Be spring soon!
witil saniha war!	Be daylight soon!
witil bohema· war!	Grow up quickly!'

Both of these are wishes that winter may be over soon--myths were told only in the winter. I am not sure what the last part of the second formula refers to. Perhaps it was addressed to children listening to the myths. A third formula must have had a similar significance but its exact meaning was unknown even at the time of Demetracopoulou [Lee] and Du Bois' *Study of Wintu Mythology* (1932).

3. *huh ?una· xanpumpu·mču*   ('Blow it away!'?)

Another form of speech different from colloquial Wintu must have been that used by chiefs when making speeches. There is a special term for that activity, *se-tina* 'to talk in all directions'. Examples of this style are insufficient for discussion. Two other styles are the one used in songs whose discussion merits a separate paper, and a form of Wintu used in telling myths which has already been discussed by Demetracopoulou [Lee] and Du Bois 1932.

CONCLUSION

I have shown that Wintu shamans used more than one language when in trance, depending on the spirit they controlled. They were not interested in concealment and thus did not use unintelligible glossolalia. When they spoke in a language other than Wintu, interpreters were present to translate for monolinguals in the audience. The other languages functioned to make the switch from one spirit to another explicit, to represent evil spirits, and perhaps to impress with one's knowledge and number of spirit helpers and languages.

The shaman's special register of Wintu represents a point in two different continua. One is the continuum extending from normal to abnormal speech, on which the jargon shares features with glossolalia but shows some important differences. The other is the Wintu stylistic continuum extending from ordinary speech used in everyday conversation to fixed formulas. Shamanic register differs from the former by special idioms and metaphors, more "polite" words for concepts considered taboo, understatement, archaisms, repetition, a preference for certain vowels and consonants, perhaps alliteration and assonance, the lack of the hesitation-type connective ʔuna·, longer words and sentences, and more subordination and left-branching.

Each of these differences derives from a unique cause. The shaman learned special lexical items from older practitioners as part of the sweathouse initiation or, if he was an uninitiated "raw" shaman, he may have heard them used by other shamans. These lexical items and the preference for words with low vowels and voiced and high frequency consonants are simply the speech of shamans, just as today many professions have their own register.

ʔuna· is absent because a shamanic ceremony is not a type of conversation. Except when the shaman speaks another language at which time the interpreter may ask questions, the ceremony is a monologue and the speaker need not struggle to keep the floor.

The greater length of sentences and words, the increase of subordination and left-branching, elsewhere characteristic of written language, have their origin in the nature of the trance. When we write we have time to think, nobody is interrupting us, we are concentrating on what we are doing and on the subject we are writing about, and we can go back and look at what we have already written to change it or refresh our memory. The shaman is in a similar situation: he is not being interrupted, he can speak as slowly as he wishes, and he is completely concentrated on his work.

The state of trance is adduced by singing, concentrating,

and smoking, especially by "swallowing" rather than inhaling the smoke of the potent Indian tobacco (Nicotiana; Du Bois ibid., p. 108).[17] The degree of dissociation and the nature of the trance appear to differ widely in different parts of the world (Chadwick 1942) and I would like to suggest that the Wintu shaman's trance was very similar to hypnosis and by no means involved a loss of control. Hypnotized people are often able to recall things they cannot otherwise remember. The shaman can speak other languages well when in trance although he may never have actively learned to speak them; just hearing them spoken, understanding what is being said, may be sufficient for storage in those parts of the memory activated by hypnosis.[18] The shaman Fanny Brown told Du Bois (ibid., p. 94): "I don't know how or when I learned doctor's language. It is just my spirit talking to my heart." Being in a trance is different from dreaming in that the mind's output in dreams usually makes no sense because we are unable to monitor it while asleep. The shaman's output makes sense and the input consists of knowledge acquired in the initiation or the memories and feelings of grief about the dead relatives whose spirits he controls; his knowledge of what is expected of him as part of his work; and everything else stored in his mind: experiences, memories, knowledge, wishes, hopes, fears. The concentration on a particular kind of spirit he knows to be in his power influences the shaman's voice quality, language, and behavior--he can behave like an animal when contacting an animal spirit. Possibly the shaman also has more extrasensory perception in his condition of hypnosis, a type of knowledge not functioning well and usually ignored as nonsensical in a fully conscious state. He may be able to "read the mind" of the patient and get clues as to the cause of the disease. This is similar to the merging of minds of shaman and spirit as when Qorit speaks as if he and his son were one person. What he said about his own illness when influenced by his son's spirit may have helped him to diagnose Mrs. Fan's illness. Qorit knows in his trance that he is drinking too much and losing his powers; Mrs. Fan is ill because she failed to observe Wintu taboos and ate too much at the wrong time. Both are suffering from the ways of the white man.

ENDNOTES

[1]An earlier version of this paper was published in
Report No. 1, Survey of California and Other Indian Languages
(1981). For many valuable comments on versions preceding the
original publication I am grateful to Wallace Chafe, Leanne
Hinton, Carol Justus, Kathryn Klar, Robert Oswalt, and others
who attended the meeting of the Berkeley Group in American
Indian Languages on November 4, 1980.

[2]There was no division of labor among shamans as in
some other areas of North America. The same shaman could
perform all these tasks if he wished.
      Du Bois 1935 provides a detailed account of Wintu
shamanism (especially pp. 88-117) and I will not paraphrase her
findings but rather examine the linguistic aspects of shamanism.

[3]A special shamanic language, usually called "high
language" by native speakers, has been reported for other tribes
of the area, e.g., by Buckley (1984) for Yurok and by
Elmendorf 1980 for Wappo (p. 4) and Yuki (pp. 7, 8, 13).
Elmendorf points out that in a situation of language
obsolescence stylistic variation is always one of the first things
to disappear.

[4]The Wintu versions of the texts published in English by
Lee are on microfilm in the possession of the Survey of
California and Other Indian Languages, Department of
Linguistics, University of California, Berkeley.
      Lee has already made some of the observations about
vocabulary differences, but since she was mostly concerned
with the expression of supernatural ideas, much remains to be
said.

[5]Abbreviations used in the interlinear translation are:
al(ienable), com(pletive aspect suffix or auxiliary), con(ditional
aspect auxiliary), cot connective, dem(onstrative), dim(inutive),
dp disjunctive postclitic, dub(itative), dur(ative), emp(hatic),
exp(eriential evidential), g(eneric aspect), gen(itive case), id
interrogative-demonstrative root, imp(erative), impf
imperfective aspect, inf(erential evidential), int(errogative),
loc(ative), mp medio-passive, nvs nonvisual sensorial evidential,
obj(ect case), p(articular aspect), pas(sive), per(fective aspect),
pl(ural), pos(sessive case), pot(ential), priv(ative), pro(gressive
aspect), quot(ative), refl(exive), rel(ational aspect auxiliary), sd

stem-deriving suffix, stat(ive), sub(ordinating suffix), ts
temporal-locative suffix.
    The grammatical analysis relies largely on Pitkin 1984.

    [6]In a story told by Grace McKibbin of Hayfork, a
werewolf speaks through a shaman allowing him to decide that
the disease it gave to the patient is incurable (Shepherd 1989, p.
374).

    [7]I am using *jargon* for the shaman's speech including
other languages he uses, while *register* refers to his variety of
Wintu; I am reserving *style* for written language except when
quoting other writers.

    [8]Some Wintu shamans had animal spirit helpers and
when in trance would impersonate the animal in their control.
The impersonation of the dead or of animals has a parallel in
Uganda, as Chadwick (1942: 32-3) reports.
    The dead are universally the most common source of
inspiration (Chadwick ibid., p. 50).

    [9]Du Bois (ibid.) reports that shamans cannot cure white
men's diseases (p. 93) and that alcohol makes them lose their
powers (p. 115).

    [10]The close relationship of poetry and manticism has
been described in detail by Chadwick 1942. "Poetry and
Prophecy are the expression of human thought at its most
intense and concentrated moments, stimulated by excitement,
and expressed in artistic form." (p. xi). "Over a wide area of the
earth poetry and prophecy are the two essential elements in the
coordination and synthesis of thought and its transmission" (p.
xiii).

    [11]However, in Havasupai it is most often "grammatical"
lexical items, not "content" words which undergo lowering
(Hinton ibid., p. 79).

    [12]The percentage of consonants per total number of
consonants are as follows. For Sadie Marsh: p 9%, p^h 0.2%, p' 0,
b 5%, t 8%, t^h 0.2%, t' 2%, d 2%, ł 9%, ł 2%, λ' 0%, m 6%, n
16%, w 3%, y 3%, s 4%, k 13%, k' 0.5%, q 3%, q' 0, r 5%, x
0.5%, x̣ 0.2%, ʔ 14%, h 11%, č and č' 1%.
    For Qorit: p 4%, p^h 0.4%, p' 0.9%, b 6%, t 8%, t^h 0.9%, d
4%, l 11%, ł 0.3%, λ' 0.3%, m 10%, n 18%, w 7%, y 4%, s 7%, k

4%, k' 0.5%, q 2%, q' 0.9%, r 5%, x 0.1%, x̣ 0.7%, ʔ 11%, h 8%, č 0.9%, č' 0.

[13]I have no explanation for an increase in the shaman's speech of p by 0.9%, q' by 0.9%, p^h by 0.2%. It may be the result of the repetition of favored words. The frequencies of t, k', and r remain the same.

[14]From these figures I would expect an increase for Qorit in the number of different morphemes used and I have no explanation for the opposite result. The percentage of different morphemes per total number of morphemes used is 19% for Qorit, 27% for Sadie.

I realize that distortions are possible because Sadie Marsh had to dictate the text to Lee. If the text had been tape-recorded, we could also check for differences in the length of pauses, the nature of hesitations, voice quality, etc. Further, Wintu shamans appear not to have chanted, but only a tape-recording could tell us whether Qorit was employing a normal speaking voice, assuming that Sadie Marsh would have imitated him. She mentioned that Qorit sang but gives no details.

[15]Verbs subordinated to their auxiliaries do not count as subordination.

[16]These formulas are not to be confused with phrases used to indicate that one has finished telling a particular story.

[17]The first hypnosis happens during the initiation in the sweathouse (Du Bois ibid., p. 89). Indians who are unable to fall into trance at that time drop out and give up their plans to become doctors. Thus only those easily hypnotized become shamans.

The external conditions helpful to adducing trance in the Wintu shaman are universal. As Chadwick reports (1942, p. 59), ecstacy is usually stimulated by intoxicating food, drink, or fumes, and the first prerequisite for purposes of concentration is solitude and quiet.

[18]The use of other languages by the Wintu shaman is not unusual. Chadwick (1942: 18) reports that shamans in northern Siberia speak *khorro* 'shaman's language'. "Khorro is generally the language of a neighboring people which the shaman does not himself understand. A Tungus shaman will sometimes speak, during his fit of inspiration, in Koryak, though he is said to be normally quite ignorant of the language."

WINTU SACRED GEOGRAPHY

Dorothea J Theodoratus and Frank LaPena

The world is a gift from our old ones. This sacred gift was created through love and respect by those elders who understood the beauty of their surroundings . . . The evidence for the representation of the earth as a mystical and magical place was given embodiment through the experiences of those who made visits to sacred places . . . We respect those thoughts and teachings; when we are forgetful and need reminding of those teachings they are given back to us in our dreams (LaPena 1987:n.p.).

INTRODUCTION

This paper is about Wintu sacred geography: specifically those topographical features that give meaning and distinction to people and place and are apart from villages and daily home life. It is about topographical features that are the embodiment of Wintu expression of an ordinary and nonordinary world. It is about a concept of land and interpretations of that natural universe that translate into a coherent world. I am concerned here with a physical geography--an ethnogeography that, as a whole, forms a complex unit of sacred domain.

The data used here come from a "cultural inventory" of religious places on federal lands that were compiled to meet the requirements of the American Indian Religious Freedom Act (PL.95-341, 1978) (Theodoratus 1984). The approach was to review past anthropological and historical data and to consult with Wintu traditionalists. I conducted the field research in 1983 with native anthropologist, scholar, poet, artist, and Wintu traditionalist

Frank LaPena.

The study resulted in a recording of places and regions of "religious significance" to the Wintu. These places and regions were seen to be a major aspect of Wintu identity. As the study progressed it became clear that topography is essential for Wintu identity-maintenance and cultural continuity. Cultural and personal loss occurs when "locales" are altered, destroyed, or placed off limits. It is clear that significant alterations have taken place in the Wintu domain due to non-Indian development of artificial lakes, railroads, highways, and habitation areas, and through economic ventures such as mining, ranching, deforestation, and recreation. The 1983 federal study aimed at translating Indian realities into concepts understandable and useful to government officials in designing meaningful accommodations for site protection.

Federal land management policies and their burdensome, often ethnocentric, interpretations and distortions sometimes serve to polarize the assessment of Indian claims as unusual and illogical. In other words, the qualities of a place or a region that make them sacred--as well as the concomitant reverence and spiritual activities of the native practitioners--are profoundly different from mainstream perceptions of these places, attitudes, and actions. This is, of course, the problem in converting Native American site realities into "understandable" non-Indian categories. The intent here is to present a perception of some of the structures and characteristics of the Wintu universe that will provide a clearer conception of Wintu ethnogeography and prompt us to devote greater effort toward developing a methodology for examining sacred geography (see Nabokov 1986:486 for discussion of requirements for a sacred geography methodology).

POWER OF PLACE

As the secrets of an esoteric world became known
to seekers of knowledge and told to the people,
never again was it possible to take for granted or
approach the earth in a thoughtless fashion . . . .
The earth is alive and exists as a series of
interconnected systems where contradictions as
well as confirmations are valid expressions of
wholeness . . . (LaPena 1987:n.p.).

Religious cosmology, often related through myth, defines power and directs human action and interaction so that dangers may be minimized and success maximized. At the center of the

Figure 16. Mountain Travelling. Painting by Frank LaPena (1989).

Figure 17. East. As a Wintu travels he/she starts from the east. Painting east is about the sun and the beginning of a new day. Birds sing before sunrise. Then it is quiet while the sun comes up. Then they sing again. Painting by Frank LaPena.

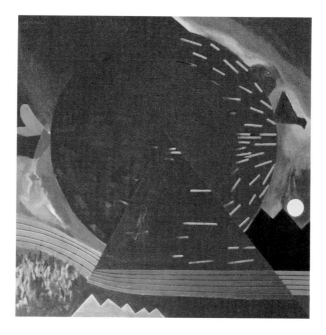

Figure 18. South. The south gives reference to life. The red is the travelling sun. South is about badger, the obsidian keeper who went south and set the world on fire. The green road is the milky way--the "spirit road." Painting by Frank LaPena.

Figure 19. West. West is oriented toward the jagged edge of the world. You can see it in the evening when the sun goes down--as presented here in the sky. Part of west's orientation is the spirit of moving up and facing west. Painting by Frank LaPena.

Figure 20. North. North is the "main one" and the orientation of Bohem Puiyuk (Mount Shasta). LaPena's auntie is in direct association because she lived as close as you can get. Painting by Frank LaPena.

Figure 21. Olelbis is a spiritual force. Olelbis is neutral and not static. It is responsible for the creation of all life. Painting by Frank LaPena.

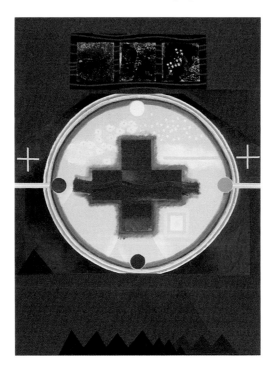

Figure 22. "House of Six Directions." In this we see the green spiritual road. In the blue above world we see the stars. At the bottom of the earth is green, and the red has mountains. Painting by Frank LaPena.

Native American religious system is the affirmation that spiritual power is infused throughout the environment in general, as well as at interconnected special places, and that knowledgeable persons are participants in that power. Thus some special locations are imbued with benevolent sacred qualities that assist people, for example, in having good health, good luck, and good energy. Other localities are imbued with malevolent forces capable of aiding in injurious acts. LaPena reminds us in *The World Is a Gift* (1987:n.p.) that such "poison places" are warnings

> . . . that caution and preparation must be used in order to maintain a proper respect for life and the unexpected. With things of power and life everything is possible. Our actions determine both good and bad. There are new things to learn, which can enlighten us or confuse us by their challenge . . . .

Specific types of features, such as mountains, rock outcroppings, caves and pools, possess qualities important for Wintu spiritual experience or veneration. These form the sacred domain that is integral to the maintenance of Wintu cultural tradition. Humans relate to topographical features (i.e., sacred sites), and these features, in turn, give expression to conceptual life and cultural identity. The landscape provides images whose meaning has influence on daily activities, spiritual life, and ethical considerations. This is perhaps what Nabokov means when he discusses the "innerlandscape," which he defines as the "soul behind the surface that our eyes pick up" (Nabokov 1981), or what Bean describes as "empowered places" (Bean 1990:personal communication). For the Wintu, these localities are not discrete elements or cultural shards. They are combined and bonded into cultural domains and sacred realms that provide essential meaning to life. As a Wintu travels through the countryside, he/she is aware of this sacred dimension that is "power òf place," and of its interconnectedness in Wintu sacred cosmology (note especially, Towendolly's stories of travel in Wintu country [Masson:1966]).

THE WINTU

The Wintu or Northern Wintun were (and remain) a comparatively large and widespread Native American (California) group occupying the present day Shasta and Trinity counties, and parts of Tehama and Siskiyou counties. Wintu territory includes an extensive range of environmental topography, ranging from a relatively flat terrain to rugged canyons and mountains, all of which provided a diverse subsistence base for the benefit and maximization of the Wintu lifestyle. The Wintu held portions of the Trinity, Sacramento, and McCloud rivers, as well as a network or creeks. Within this domain, they recognized a number of geographically based population divisions, but the exact social boundaries are not precisely known today. Currently, there are several Wintu organizations or groups, but no single one is representative of all the Wintu. After contact, the Wintu suffered substantial destruction of their habitat and native economy as non-Indians expanded into their territory, destroying traditional economic conditions and developing a new, non-Indian land base (mining, logging, transportation routes, towns).

Wintu mythology provides an insight into their concept of the universe and a cultural map for their relationship with the environment (DuBois and Dematracopoulou 1931; Masson 1966). Myths often explain natural phenomena and set models for behavior within the context of the geography, and all have meaning as part of Wintu cosmology. Mythology helps keep the balance of spirit and body, and gives direction to Wintu life. It paints a philosophical portrait for those beings--human, animal, and spiritual--which inhabit the earth, providing an ongoing process and meaning to life (LaPena 1987:n.p.). Mythology, then, is intricately entwined with the environment. Features of nature are imbued with various powers and levels of sacred importance. Wintu people understand their own humanity in relation to the perception of this universe. Wintu poet Tauhindauli (1979:13) writes,

> I am related
> in a universe
> bigger than
> my mind . . .
> . . .
> I travel
> both earth and heaven
> trails
>
> lost in reference
> to other lives
>
> to other stars
> and songs
> of other constellations.

Familiarity with the way the environment "should be" is related to the Wintu sense of "well-being," and thus "reality." LaPena (1987:n.p.) sees the "subjective spirit world" and the "objective physical world" as giving vision and meaning to life, and thus, in a conceptual sense, as both real and symbolic. Myth and its embodiment in geographical reflections enhance the Wintu sense of consciousness. Geographical formations remind the Wintu that a great range of possibilities exist, and that a person must be open to reality if he/she is to be enlightened about the world. LaPena reminds us that the essence of the living Wintu world is meaningful and not to be taken for granted (LaPena 1987).

GEOGRAPHICAL FEATURES

Localities of unusual configuration, such as distinctive rock outcrops (often in human or animal shapes), caves, knolls, whirlpools in a river, and seepage holes, often housed or were dwellings of spirits--especially those of Coyote, Deer and Sucker. The spirit often made its presence known through an audible buzzing. Such places were visited chiefly by men--often shamans--who sought transcendence in order to achieve another level of jurisdiction over a domain more potent and supreme in its influence than that found in the everyday world. Such locales were generally avoided by women, and they were especially dangerous to unmarried or menstruant women. Only places inhabited by the coyote spirit were used by women (DuBois 1935:79-81). A person in quest at these locations might travel from one sacred locality to another in search of dreams and spiritual influence. Different locales possessed different degrees of sanctity; some were sources for shamanistic power while others were primarily used for special skills such as gambling or hunting, or, in the case of women, for basketmaking. Many such places were recognized by Wintu people (DuBois 1935:81; TCR Field Data).

Shamans sought sacred energy at locations where they could acquire the skills necessary to serve as practitioners in the medical and religious aspects of Wintu life. A candidate would visit a sacred place and invoke the spirits associated with that esoteric domicile. The Wintu revere a creator or omnipotent spirit, *Olelbis*, who plays an integral role in the mythology, and to whom prayers are addressed. Prayers are a part of daily life, associated with sojourns in sacred places. Topographical features such as caves, springs, and rock outcroppings serve as settings for these functions. Tauhindauli (1979:24) tells us about caves in the poem "Power Waits,"

The cave has power
whirlwind dances
on the valley floor

sometimes people
come to watch
not all of them can see

Caves were used for gaining skills or for success in secular
endeavors, and some offered enrichment in a full range of
activities. These could be used by any person who sought the ends
for which the cave was known. Some caves, known as *sauwel*, had
to be approached in a specific manner. A *sauwel* has been
specified by Wintu consultants as a place for religious people to
acquire special power and spiritual guidance (see Samwell Cave).
      Springs possessed importance in numerous ways. They
often formed a component in healing practices, and as such were
related to activities such as mud bathing, herbal treatment, or use
of water in some other physical manner. The healing properties
of some water was such that in some springs it was used directly
for healing physical ailments and treating open wounds, as well as
in cleansing and purifying the body of poisons. Other springs
offered spiritual energy, where prayer could be made to attain the
guidance of the specific spirit-beings found in such places. Of
particular importance were springs found inside caves, especially
sauwel. These springs were instrumental in acquiring spiritual
prowess and other favors. Springs were also used for bathing and
swimming.
      Springs might also be created for specific purposes. For
example, I was shown a basin or spring of water in a basaltic
formation. It was created by a shaman to supply water to a group
of Wintu who were hiding out from vigilantes and American
troops (TCR Field Data). Vernal pools or seasonal rain ponds
might also have significance. One seasonal rain pond used by
doctors as a source for power took on the "look of blood" when
filled (TCR Field Data).
      Indwelling spirits are attributed to rock features of unusual
configuration. Numerous places, considered sacred, are mentioned
in the literature, particularly in the mythology, and are said to
resemble a spirit, a heart, or a salmon. Present-day consultants
discussed the importance of these formations to modern Wintu
(TCR Field Data). Tauhindali writes in "A Rock, A Stone,"

Figure 23. Bag of Bones. Photo by Frank LaPena.

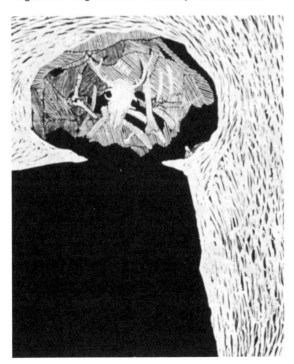

Figure 24. Bag of Bones. Drawing by Frank LaPena.

I can't pass a rock
like you
without being mystified
or hypnotized

I have heard stories
of rocks
and have known some
rocks personally

They represent the
world by their presence
wisdom has no
relationship to size
. . .
One time, perhaps many times
a man became a rock
thinking that a fine way
to gain immortality

A "guide rock" was one particular kind of formation used to show directions to particular places, some of which were sacred. One type of guide rock, for example, a split rock on the side of a hill, was visible from a distance, and was used to direct travelers to both ordinary and non-ordinary places. Many guide rocks were pointed out by a Wintu consultant who had traveled extensively by foot through a Wintu area (TCR Field Data). The guide rocks were interconnected, and a traveler would understand the direction to proceed to the next guidance point.

Streams and rivers often were used to determine cardinal orientations, thus being part of a configuration of the Wintu world view. Rivers were sometimes named in a manner which included directions of flow. Pools or holes which formed along a watercourse were frequently assigned spiritual significance. Other topographic features--such as special rock formations, natural bridges, and caves associated with watercourses were thought to contain spiritual beings within their confines. Wintu myths often detail the creation of streams, and numerous references to streams in the mythology reveal them as significant elements of Wintu life. Streams were generally avoided by menstruating women; however, some streams presented such spiritual danger that women avoided them at all times.

Mountains housed supernatural animal beings (such as werebeasts, mountain lions, mountain boys, bush boys) that could transform themselves into human form. Werebeasts were associated with evil or malevolent influences, so areas inhabited by these creatures were avoided (DuBois 1935:84-85). Mountains also possessed benevolent spiritual power, and a number of such peaks were named by consultants--Mount Shasta being the "main one" (TCR Field Data). LaPena reminds us that mountains (along with rocks) have slow, deliberate ways about them (1987:n.p.). *Sanchaluli*, a sacred place, is described as "constant and patient in its teaching" (LaPena 1987:n.p.). Tauhindauli (1979:22) tells us about a mountain in "Bird Healer":

> Yolla Bolli
> holds the imprints
> of mud tracks
> showing mother
> father
> and the children . . .
>
> One of each
> covered with
> feathers and wings
> suitable for
> this mountain
>
> Suitable for
> a spirit responsible
> for the beginning
> of the world

Spirits of the living and the dead could also be manifest in the environment. The spirits of the dead might manifest themselves in whirlwinds of dust, or as ghosts. The soul of the newly deceased could linger a few days before traveling northward, where it would go to Mount Shasta or to a spring known only to souls. It would then rise to the Milky Way where it would travel south to a fork in the spirit trail, and then east to a grassy plain where Indians "are always having a big time" (DuBois 1935:79; TCR Field Data). Generally, at death, the body would be oriented toward the north, the direction the ghost must travel to drink from the spring of life before starting the journey to the next world (DuBois 1935:65). Different soul-travel orientations might be used for a person buried outside the Wintu area. Then, the spirit would be released in the direction of Mt. Shasta, but funeral oratory would always direct the soul on its celestial journey.

Many Wintu today are particularly synchronized with, engaged in, and committed to their landscape. One consultant told me that in order to record the Bald Hills area properly I would

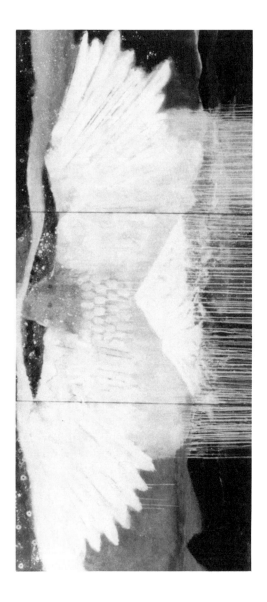

Figure 25. North Mountain (Bohem Puiyuk). Painting by Frank LaPena.

have to be content to cover less than a mile each day. Other Wintu
have similar knowledge of the network in their landscape, showing
intense regard for their physical environment even though the
order of the Wintu world has been broken by development and
western disorder. For many, there has been a perpetuation of the
meaning of landscape--that is, the relation of geographical
features to life in general. LaPena reminds us, in *The World Is a
Gift* (1987), that "we are all connected because time has no
boundary and space is of one continuity" (LaPena 1987). Clearly,
the Wintu perceive the sacredness of features and the power of
place in their environment, but also resplendent in this wide-angle
vision is the interconnectedness of these features into a broader
cosmology, or a complex sacred geography.

Again, according to Tauhindauli, in his poem, "I Am
Related,"

> I am related
> in the universe
> bigger than
> my mind
>
> I am connected
> to the stars
>
> and sing to
> chosen star groups
> . . .
> I travel
> both earth and heaven
> trails
> . . .
> to other stars
> and songs
> of other constellations

RIDGE WALKERS OF NORTHWESTERN CALIFORNIA: PATHS TOWARD SPIRITUAL BALANCE

Jack Norton

In the 1860s soldiers stationed in Northern California were often astonished to see the same Indian men that they had left, now silently watching them arrive at their new destination. If the soldiers, for example, had left Fort Gaston, in the Hoopa Valley and had hurried along the Trinity and the Klamath Rivers to answer a call for assistance from the community at Orleans, they were often met with a wry smile from the warriors of the Hupa Village of *Tswelnaldin*. The soldiers riding briskly had covered the distance in about a day and a half while carrying food and other provisions for a week's maneuvers. *Tswelnaldin* John's warriors however, had run the ridge tops with a small pouch of dried meat and their weapons in hand.

In Northwestern California there are hundreds of ridges that define small beautiful pocket valleys or that criss-cross to confuse the uninitiated and the unwelcomed. To walk these ridges is much more than to merely traverse them. They often narrow from several hundred yards to a few feet with spur ridges radiating from the main trail. To follow one of these may lead into steep and dangerous terrain that can drop off into chasms hundreds of feet above creeks or lead to other ridges that carry one in the opposite direction. There are numerous stories of men that have not returned from hunting or tales that imply that someone had been lost because, "they did not belong there."

Therefore to say that the ridgetops are merely trails limits and demeans their presence not only to socio-geo-politico terms but also tends to restrict them cosmologically. Although the network of trade routes among the tribes of Northwestern California follow some ridge-tops, not all ridge top trails were used for trade and communication. There were some for only the Indian Doctors or their trainees. These were the spiritual paths of the Ridge-Walkers, the men and women who assumed the responsibility to contend against evil. Through their efforts the Creator's plan to destroy evil in this earthly battleground was waged; however, the outcome of the warfare was never determined and either side could win at any given moment. Therefore the awesome responsibility of these Indian Doctors were recognized by all and given the respect they deserved.

The paths along the ridge tops become a physical manifestation of a cosmological principal of walking between the dimensions of good and evil. Balance was the strength of position and to be successful in the warfare was not only to fulfill Creator's desire, but also to be able to heal the family of creation and community members.

Invariably the trails began from the sweathouses of the villages and converged to a main path, often above the area considered to be the center-of-the world. In the example of the Hupa, above the Village of *Takimildin* the trail travels Eastward to the high-country and the spiritual training grounds. In recent studies, in an attempt to protect it from Forest Service timber harvest plans, this spiritual path has been identified as the "Trail of the Blue Sun". Whether it will be safe from attack or not is a dilemma that many Indian people face today. Do we speak or write of these spiritual things, for example, in order to inform others so that they may understand and reciprocate a respect for differing belief systems, or will we be further exploited and disregarded in schemes of modernity? It is to the hope within the former question that this paper is presented. Respect coming not from a naive ubiquitous statement of the virtues of a democratized and propagandized citizenry, but from the hope that in the few remaining years of the 20th century some people have truly embraced a cosmology that perceives that diversity, uniqueness and spatial relatedness is absolutely vital for life upon this planet. This view would at least include a commitment to the idea that all things have integrity unto themselves in relationship to their time and space, and that humans are of this Order. However, it must be realized that humans have the most difficult task of all--they must choose between sustaining the beingness-of-things or continuing to rearrange this Orderliness in a projected plan of anthropocentric exploitation and convenience.

Although today many have begun an exploration of sustaining relationships within the patterns of life, there are others who have often arbitrarily grabbed bits and pieces of ritual, colorful paraphernalia and popular psychic pap, in a "New Age" of understanding. Their experimentation and eclecticism often feeds their egoic needs without the balancing forces of tradition arising from the community and its related space. Therefore, Indian tribes are cognizant of the potential trivialization and diminution of their belief systems that define them as a people. As well-intentioned as most "New Age" advocates proclaim to be, there are still areas that tend to exacerbate misunderstandings, and these often range from naive and unconscious disrespect, to arrogant and sanctimonious religiosity. Recently the front page of the *Santa Rosa Press Democratic* depicted the confrontation between a group of Indian people and a religious celebration of "environmental protectionism," led by "Shamanic Counselors". The Indians were pictured carrying signs that proclaimed "Do Not Support Spiritual Genocide" or "What About Me? My Heritage is Being Destroyed by New Age Shamanism." Certainly the frustration of the Indians born of the long bleak record of broken treaties, congressional inequalities and intermitted remorse can be recognized, but more specifically the irony for survival of Native religions loomed large. Perhaps few of the participates who came to deepen their "cosmic awareness" and show respect for Indian's belief systems knew of the ten thousand Indian baskets in Sacramento warehouses, or the arsenic impregnated religious regalia stored in the Lowie Museum, or the thousands of religious items locked away upstairs at the Smithsonian. These are truly stolen items and they bear witness to religious persecution. In addition, today there are serious attacks by governmental agencies on Indian religious sites and freedoms of expression. Decisions with regard to the Gasquet-Orleans Road in Northwestern California, to the Black Hills in South Dakota, and the recent one affecting the Native American church, are but a few examples. The question of whether someone can steal or destroy a religion is much more complex and ontological. History is replete with conquests of religious sites and deicidal activities. For example, in 1887 the Kiowas had to substitute a cow's skull for the sacred buffalo that was central to their Sun Dance religion, and in 1890 the soldiers of Fort Sill, Oklahoma rode out and forbade the Kiowas the Sun Dance altogether. N. Scott Momaday writes of his grandmother:

> She was about seven when the last Kiowa Sun Dance was held in 1887 on the Washita River above Rainy Mountain Creek. The buffalo were gone. In order to consummate the ancient sacrifice--to impale the head of a buffalo bull upon the medicine tree--a delegation of old men journeyed into Texas, there to beg and barter for an animal from the Goodnight herd. She was ten when the Kiowas came together for the last time as a living Sun Dance culture. They could find no buffalo;

they had to hang an old hide from the sacred tree.
Before the dance could begin, a company of
soldiers rode out from Fort Sill under orders to
disperse the tribe. Forbidden without cause the
essential act of their faith, having seen the wild
herds slaughtered and left to rot upon the ground,
the Kiowas backed away forever from the medicine tree. That was July 20, 1890, at the great
bend of the Washita. My grandmother was there.
Without bitterness, and for as long as she lived, she
bore a vision of deicide (Momaday 1969:8-10).

Ironically or perhaps, more accurately, with poetic justice,
it may be noted that if there has been any particular person, living
today, that has articulated beautifully and consistently the
relationship between land and people, it is N. Scott Momaday, a
seven-eights Kiowa Indian. In the *Way to Rainy Mountain*, he
wrote:

Once in his life a man ought to concentrate
his mind upon the remembered earth, I believe.
He ought to give himself upon to a particular
landscape in his experience, to look at it from as
many angles as he can, to wonder about it, to dwell
upon it. He ought to imagine that he touches it
with his hands at every season and listens to the
sounds that are made upon it. He ought to imagine
the creatures there and all the faintest motions of
the wind. He ought to recollect the glare of noon
and all the colors of the dawn and dusk (Momaday
1969:83).

Momaday, perhaps, provides a meeting ground for
religious integrity and a meaningful cosmology in today's world.
"One's idea of the self," he writes, "involves the environment, you
don't really know who you are until you know where you are in a
physical sense (Schubnell 1985:149)." Perhaps most Indian people
have an intuitive suspicion that many "New Age Shamanistic"
movements have not secured themselves to place, and therefore,
their experimentation seldom has cultural consensus or a feeling
of rootedness. Religiously and philosophically western societies,
at least from the 17th Century on, have allowed the individual to
determine socio-economic patterns at the expense of village
customs and mores. Thus, individuals often assumed interpretations of their worth without regard to the group or the environment. In addition, some have observed that their sense of self may

tend more towards ego inflation and exhibitionism rather than to the larger or higher transcendent Self. By contrast, most Indian societies enhanced the unique qualities and attributes of the individual by close guidance through traditional ontological parameters that recognized the factors of good and evil. That is, the individual visionary experience was evaluated within cultural convention that addressed the dark side of humanity, the shadow of selfish arrogance, as well as the positive forces of oneness and wholeness. Although these observations may be accurate in various settings, there is growing evidence that a genuine concern for all life is present.

Recently a young woman wrote:

> One day soon, the native fad will wear off, and the true people--those who believe in living simply, living off the land, respecting the land, plants, animals--consisting of Indian, non-Indian, and people of many backgrounds--will emerge and be shining examples to others. With an equal understanding of how we all live and how many of us would like to live, we can start to build a solid bridge of open communication, respect, support, and trust. Then we will be able to cross a great river to a more gentle, yet powerful land and hopes. When crossing the bridge, let's join our voices and sing, and hold hands, and walk carefully and joyfully. When we come to the other side, the road ahead of us will be infinite. We can part our ways, and live our new lives, always keeping in contact (Anonymous 1989).

Also from the same class, another wrote:

> Three years ago when I was living in San Diego, California, I had a spiritual awakening. All my life I had searched for this Truth and at the age of 27 it was revealed to me. It came like a light illuminating my being with knowingness that I am a Spirit, that all of life is cyclic yet moving like a spiral toward enlightenment. I knew this Earth to be my Mother and my Father the Creator of all things (Anonymous 1989).

It is encouraging to see young minds and souls grasping the relatedness within the universe along with the experiences and insights of such authors as Thomas Berry, Matthew Fox, Susan

Griffin, Jonathan Schell and Teilhard de Chardin. If there is a
common thread throughout all these expressions, it is that of a
spiritual intention within the cosmos, and this intention moves
with purpose and order from simplicity to greater and greater
differentiation. Thus to be cognizant of the unique integrity of
each created being or thing within the pattern-of-things honors
the Creation.

Perhaps it is the negation of this relatedness that many
Indians perceive in an inclusive term such as Shamanism. They
intuit, within its generalized use, the potential dilution of unique
identity for a specific place. Apparently the term shaman was
first used in 1698 to describe the relationship of a family shaman
or spiritual helper for the Tungus group in Central Siberia. Later
European writers continued to use the word to describe these
Siberian aboriginal religious personalities; however, today the
Shamanistic movement has coopted this term and the "shaman" has
generally been portrayed as an individual who spontaneously
develops a relationship with a personal spirit helper that can be
demonstrated by dramatic dancing, rhythmic drumming, and
repetitive chanting without reference to group consensus and
spatial relatedness.

This is not to imply that all present shamanistic endeavors
are meaningless. There are many that have at least, as Vine
Deloria recently satirized, taught "people to cool themselves out,
have some confidence in themselves, and create a fantasy world
that supports them. It may be the kindest, most constructive thing
in the world." However, "the New Age" movement's most glaring
inequity seems to be its inability to attach to place or to root itself
in every aspect to the energy of a specific land. It does not seem
to act with authenticity to the forces and energy vibrating from
the unique entities enfolded in time and place. Invariably eons of
observation, discourse and experimentation are required before
agreement, felicity and healing may occur and song and dance
empower the people. These are the factors that seem to be
woefully missing from most "New Age Shamanistic" endeavors.

In Northwestern California the carriers of spiritual
responsibility are the Ridge Walkers. To call them Shamans would
tend to sever them from the unique topography and cosmology of
Northern California, as well as demean their roles within a vital
and specific community. The Hupas, for example, live along the
last six miles of the Trinity River before it joins the lower
Klamath River. At this confluence the Hupa meet the Yurok,
another riverine tribe inhabiting a similar environment but having
differing cosmological and linguistic features. The Hupas have
occupied a beautiful and abundant valley for thousands of years
and have effectively developed an epistemology and supporting

rituals that may fulfill the needs of those who embrace its rhythms. Like most tribes of North America, the Hupa propose primordial or prototypical beings prior to the coming of the ancestral Hupa Indians. In this "before-time," these spiritual beings were sent to this earth by the Creator to fight against evil that had been preparing for warfare from time beyond time. As the protracted battle was waged, both sides sought advantages until humanoids began to take form and they became the vital entity in the outcome. Therefore, the spiritual training of special men and women who may walk between these forces of good and evil holds not only the health and felicity of the people, but also determines their continuance and very survival. Thus their specific spiritual experiences demonstrate to all that they are here, within the physical, within this battle ground, at Creator's desire. Individuals have purposes for their existence, but their final choices are their loyalties to either good or evil. Yet, they are not sent into this darkness unarmed. They are given three weapons by the Creator: the prayer pipe, the spiritual dance grounds and the spiritual places on the mountains. It is to these spiritual places that the paths along the ridge tops lead, but each individual determines whether he or she will step upon these paths and fulfill the Creator's desire.

Once the decision has been made to walk the spiritual paths, the trainee under the guidance of the Indian Doctor begins to isolate himself or herself from the community by ritualized sweating and walking in the forest. After ten to twenty days of solitude and at least ten days of fasting, they may begin the journey upon the Spiritual trails. There are rituals to be observed until they arrive at the Spiritual training grounds within the mountains. Here the Spiritual places are approached and the trainee stands within the radiance of the spiritual beings. These beings are the teachers, the guides that allow the trainee an opportunity to incorporate their lessons within Creator's plan.

It is the commitment and the preparational activities that open the individual to understand the experiences upon the spiritual places. The activities within this area are defined by the knowledge that is sought by the trainee, and the lessons of the spiritual being will be dependent upon the recipient's receptiveness and demonstration of commitment. When the procedures are complete, the trainee returns along the Spiritual Paths to places that are specifically set aside for the security of those who are in prayer. These spiritual places provide a resting and recuperating area where the trainee may begin to eat but must remain in total isolation. One account of this process related that:

The trainee observes the world around him,
carefully. Reverently noticing and watching, he
begins to see how plants and animals, insects and
trees, clouds and shadows, all interplay and form
a relationship where family ties bind and where
each with its interdependence and relatedness
forms the integrity and right of being for all
others. No species, no thing exists inherently
superior to others, in fact, one quickly begins to
perceive that only by being genuinely humble can
humans begin to approach this family of creation
which we are born into and have the right to
participate in, but somehow may be driven from
its loving embrace and sustainment. All these
microscopic events, these small observations of
universal patterns, respect the macrocosmic relationships, where danger and survival are demonstrated unforgettably. One may, for example,
come upon an open prairie with a small stream
flowing through its center. Intuitively, consciously,
one waits within the trees, surveying the surroundings, alertly listening and watching, to make sure
that no other humans are about. Then quietly,
quickly, perhaps like a deer, one walks out into the
open. The water is a necessity, therefore, while
bending down to drink or filling the canteen,
waves of vulnerability sweep the area and, for a
moment, one begins to know how animals, plants,
and fish may feel in the world of both the good
and the evil. And at night, while dreaming or
while relaxing between awakening and sleep, a
spiritual woman may come and say, "You have
done well, my son. There are many things to
learn." Or just as easily a whirling disk brings
yellow shapes before one's eyes and slowly a head
takes form and a soft, seductive voice says, "Come
with me! I will show you many things." But one
hesitates. The voice seems to be, perhaps, too
sweet, almost syrupy, and one hears one's self say,
"No, I will stay here," and the disk disappears. The
days and the nights pass quickly (Heinze 1989:314-
315).

It is during this time that the experience of the Spiritual
lessons may become a part of the individual so that it touches and
integrates the heart and mind. It effects the way in which the

individual will forever see the world. It changes the eyes so that the heart will lead them in life. After usually ten days of isolation the individual may return to the sweathouse and basically prepare for the contact with the community. If, for example, the intent of training had been to strengthen oneself as a Spiritual Dancer, then participation in the religious dances such as the Deer Skin Dance or Jump Dance would be in order. In this way the individual, the community and the universe become a communion of interrelated forces, and to walk the spiritual paths allows for all life to survive and continue.

A Hupa-Karuk Spiritual Doctor recently stated in part that:

> The receptability to the call of the spiritual place is part of the innate gift that the Creator gave us. The absence of the spiritual places, the dance grounds, the prayer pipe, and those lifeways that are associated with it would leave Creator's children in the darkness without weapons and they soon would be consumed by the darkness. We would die as a people. We would die as individuals and be lost to Creator. Without the spiritual places, we do not exist as a people or as Indians. We would simply become more off-colored white people, lost, as most of us are, in other religions and not living the way Creator desired; the way Creator intended for us to be--to respond to his needs.

> We are at war. We are here with purposes and those purposes and our achievement serves Creator in his war against darkness. Without our weapons we lose, and Creator loses. We may lose the battle for this battleground, this physical--this what they call earth and what the Indians call North and South America. This is Indian--belong to us-- Creator intended it that way. Interference and destruction of those of his intention betray Creator's desires. There's no higher importance than the following of the heart to the spiritual places and living the heart in how the Creator planned for our ease and our greater achieve-ment--continuance.

> Without the spiritual places we have no continuance; without the sacred dances and the dance grounds or the prayer pipe there is no continuance. The people, like I said, would be lost

in the other religions without achievement; and
when they cross they will cross within the Indian
ground. If they can cross and if they are not
consumed within achievement, because of the war,
they will be judged according to Creator's purity
and Creator's needs in war. If we were unuseful
and successfully crossed into spiritual, we may still
be destroyed for what we have become in the
physical. There's a total accountability. The deeds
of your life remain with you and define who you
are at the present and when you cross your judged
accordingly and when you cross you are honored
accordingly for time--real time (Anonymous
(Hupa-Karuk Spiritual Doctor) n.d.).

Thus the Ridge Walkers would include those people that
Kroeber and others refer to as healing Doctors, seers, tracers and
herbalists. In addition, there are spiritual dancers, dance leaders,
medicine people and those who trained for spirituality within
cultural processes, such as killing a White deer or acquiring
spiritual wealth. However, it was recognized by all, that the
highest purpose was to fulfill the Creator's desire. And that the
ultimate reality was that anything that disrupted or directed one
from the Spiritual Path was evil.

Thus, this life within time and place is a battleground
between the physical and the non-physical, between the good and
the evil. And each of us must make the decision to determine
which we will embrace.

AJUMAWI DOCTORING

CONFLICTS IN NEW AGE/TRADITIONAL SHAMANISM

Floyd Buckskin

I am not a ceremonial leader. I have assisted doctors at times. I'm not a spiritual leader, although I help people if I can. And something that I always say: I am that which I've always been.

Having some experience with various people from around the world of many races and many nations, I thought I'd share some ideas with you. Mysticism, past lives, psychic healing, astral projection and many more fields of pursuit are of great interest to many people today, so it is to be expected that people also would have a keen interest in shamanism. As a result of these various interests, many Indian people have noted new faith among the parade or crowd of knowledge seekers.

Tribal people, spiritual leaders, traditional doctors, and knowledgeable elders have been and continue to be sought by this new crowd of people, who come with crystals, drums, dreams, past and future lives. Many of them claim to have been Native American warriors, chiefs and medicine people. Many have worked out very elaborate ceremonies.

They come with the cry: "Teach us! Lead us!" Many Indian people see this as a fulfillment of old stories and prophecies. I'm sure many of you have heard of Vinson Brown's book *Warriors of the Rainbow* (1988). We see this and think of the old prophecies that mention these things and we say, "Sure, if we can help we will teach." But sometimes it gets a little out of hand.

Others feel it is a mockery when these people come with crystals. They ask: "How did they get those crystals? Did they go the mountains and pray? Did they go to the springs and pray and sing? Did they go to the falls and dive into the falls?" These are the only places you can get these kinds of objects. You can't go down town and buy them. You had to do this thing. It was hard

work. It was a dangerous thing--it could kill you if your mind
wasn't right.

The old people always say, "Keep your mind right." If you
were going for this type of power, you had to have your mind
right. Be in one with the spirit. You couldn't just go dive off the
falls any time you felt like it, because perhaps your spirit wasn't
right. If you jumped off that falls and the spirit in the falls saw
what kind of person you were, he could reject you--throw you out
among the rocks--kill you right there.

Some of the elders say that one time an Indian from
Oklahoma came among our people. He felt that he was a man of
power, so he went out and killed a rattlesnake and made a
beautiful belt of the rattlesnake, and he wore this belt. One of the
local doctors saw the belt and he asked: "How did you get that
belt?" The man said: "I have power. I can do anything that I want.
I can go anywhere I want."

So the doctor called the people together and he said, "We
will go up to the mountain and gather wood and build a fire.
Pretty soon this man will come." So they went to the mountain
and they sat inside a low rock wall circle. They sang and helped
the doctor sing, and pretty soon this man came. He didn't know
what was going on; he couldn't see the other people. He didn't
know where he was or what he was doing. He was restless and
uneasy.

The people kept singing and pretty soon the Spirit came,
the spirit of the rattlesnake, the *hootalai*. And he (the *hootalai*)
came in and he was a beautiful man. He had on a long white robe,
perhaps buckskin or something else; it's hard to say. He walked
up to this man who had the rattlesnake belt and he touched him.
The man fell over dead. Then the people got up and left. They
left that man lying there on the mountain. This happened not too
long ago, sometime in the 1920s up in the Alturas area. They left
him lying there, and they went home. They didn't look back
because that's what they were supposed to do. So not everyone
who claims to have power has power. Not everyone who has these
objects is able to control them.

The Ajumawi concept and history of Indian doctors
appears in the creation account. The First People had these
powers and this way; *Kwahn*, *Loweja*, *Aleump*, and *Jamul* (Silver-
gray Fox, Eagle, Frog Woman and Coyote). They had these
powers and they demonstrated them during the creation of the
Earth.

Kwahn could interpret dreams and he could talk directly
with the Creator, who told him how to make things. *Loweja*,
through flying above and (singing) the song, was able to bring the

moon and the sun out of the ocean. *Aleump*, the Frog Woman, had the power of the whirlwind. She could travel any way she wanted by riding this whirlwind. And she could appear any way she wanted, as a different woman in many different ways. And the Coyote, of course, wasn't too well thought of, because of what happened when he was first created.

When the son of the Creator was going through the world to make these people right, he would walk up to each one and blow on them and they would be of right mind. But when he came to the old Coyote, the Coyote was scared and he immediately ran off into the world. And so he came under wicked influence. But he still had power. He could do good for people sometimes, not always because he intended good, but because that's the way it worked out.

So we see that in this way power was in the world. And we can see that as the world went along, people began to get sick and experience things that they had never experienced before because of the evil in the world. Then the doctors became more necessary. There is an old story that in the beginning there were no doctors, and at the end there will be no doctors. We will get into that a little later.

When Wildcat became a cannibal because of certain things he had done, it was the Spotted Fawn Woman, whose power was the butterfly, who prescribed his cure. His sister had to come along and ask for the cure, for the assistance. The cure can't be done unless you ask or someone asks for you. Then they have to wait until you're ready, until you're tired of what you have.

And so she was able to prescribe a cure. The sister had to lure her brother--because he was a cannibal--into a large basket filled with raw meat and raw blood, because he had this blood lust. So he climbed into the basket and she sealed it up with a fish net and a deer hide. She strapped it down and tied it up and took it out into the lake in a canoe. Wildcat became angry and shook and rattled the basket because he could feel that he was on the water. And she would say, "No, it's only the wind blowing," or "It's only an earthquake." Finally she was able to get him out onto the lake, where she stacked rocks onto the basket. At that time the large horned serpent (*Pal-act-k-sum*) came out of the water and took the basket into his mouth.

Later on, as he lay at the bottom of the lake, the water purified Wildcat, and the horns that were on his head and the wild look that was in his eyes, and his fur matted with blood were all taken away. Then he came up to the top of the lake. When the people saw him coming back out of the lake, they were afraid because they thought perhaps he would still be that way. But he was cured; he was healed.

In that little story we see a ritual. They always had to take care of that evil power some way. When a doctor cured someone, they had to do something with that power, that poison, that sickness. They could take it for themselves or they could send it back out into the mountains. Sometimes they would put it into a basket and drown it. Or they could throw it into the fire. Or sometimes they would vomit it out. But they had to do something with that vomit; they couldn't just leave it lying there on the ground for someone to step on to affect someone else. They had to cover it over and bless it, sprinkle tobacco on it. So just in that little story we can see a story of shamanism, or doctor curing.

Doctors were divided into several categories. There were herbalists. Just about anyone could become an herbalist. And many people in the tribe practiced herbalism. It had a specialized way, but it could also be practiced by the common people. You didn't have to be a doctor to be a herbalist, but you could become an herbal doctor. Even that way there was a division within.

There were Dreamers, who could see the future events in dreams and interpret dreams for other people. There were healers by the laying on of hands. They would just go and touch a person and pray over them. Trance healers would go into a trance. They could dance in fire and walk on the water.

Spiritual leaders didn't always have the ability to heal individual people, but they were able to heal the tribe, the nation, by the things they said and by the teachings they gave to the children and one another.

Prophets. And there were several others. All these people had power. Some of them had all of these powers. There was a way that they would rank these powers, and if you weren't high up in the list of categories, then you didn't have the power of the one above you. If you were high up, then you had all of the powers of anyone below you, the herbalists, the dreamers, the healers.

Doctors were chosen by the elders of the tribe, by the spiritual leaders of the tribe, by the headmen of the tribe. They would do this by looking at the children to see what their inclination was, see how they dealt with spiritual matters. They would take these children and begin to train them in special ways. They would treat them nice so that they would have a happy disposition all the time, so they wouldn't feel miserable like some children feel sometimes when life doesn't seem to be going right. So they would treat these children well.

Later on, as they got older, spirits would begin to visit them to tempt them to see what type of power they would have. These spirits weren't always very nice. They would cause the children to go out and begin to kill animals. This was a bad thing because you weren't supposed to kill just for the fun of it. So these children had to be made aware of these things. If you began to feel that way, to be mean and cruel to an animal, then it was time to have prayers done for you.

So they would pray for these children. Sometimes, at that point, not all the children who were chosen or set apart would want to continue on with becoming a doctor. Maybe it was too hard, or maybe they were afraid. So the doctor could take the power from them. Send it away or take the power for himself. In later times a lot of that was done, more so than in earlier times.

Becoming a doctor isn't easy, not even for one who is a chosen person. You had to abide by strict laws. There was no shedding of blood when you were on the doctor road. No human blood. You had to give up hunting. You had to stay away from the shedding of blood, because these animals might become your power. So you couldn't be killing them. There were other instances when that could be overlooked: it had to be dealt with. Maybe you were an older person and had become a great hunter and were able to kill a lot of animals, and then you were called to be a doctor. There were exceptions to even that. But after that time you went on and gave up that hunting way, the way of being a hunter or warrior. No more shedding blood.

These people would have these powers and they would go through all this training and this very exacting way of life. But sometimes, in spite of all the training, there was something inside of them, some weakness, some negative aspect that caused the power to go astray. The power would lead them off and they would take the wrong power. My grandfather always said: "Don't always take the first power that comes to you, because there are two powers in the world, two powers in the universe, the good and the bad, the right and the wrong."

The first one will always come to you trying to look beautiful, trying to look glorious, trying to look like something you would really want. It's there to test you. If you have a weakness, you might fail that test and accept that one that isn't right and you will have a hard time in your doctoring way. At different points in you life it will test you. Maybe there is someone over here you don't like. Maybe they've got more money than you or maybe they have a nice looking woman. You might want to kill that person, get rid of him so you can take his things. You had to get rid of those feelings, the negative attitudes, your hatred. You had to work on them to control them. And even then maybe you went down to the spring, down to the falls to dive in just because you have that one little negative thing. Maybe you weren't always totally aware of it all the time, but it would creep in at different times; then you could obtain the wrong power.

In this way, the poisoning of people came about, because they didn't guard themselves. They didn't guard their mind and heart. They let these things in and so they began to poison people, especially from the 1890s until about the 1950s. A lot of the Pit River doctors were killing one another off, poisoning one another, killing other people, because they let these things overtake them.

Also, while this was going on we had the Christian Evangelical people coming in telling us how terrible these things were. And so the doctors were fighting against them, placing curses on them and Christians were placing curses on the doctors.

Ralph Mike was a great doctor among the people, but I'm told that he could do both good and bad. From the stories I hear, it sounds as though he did a lot of good and a lot, a lot of bad.

He had come across this preacher, who began to call down on him curses from God and tell him how terrible these things were. And so Ralph Mike told him that this church would never survive among the Indian people and that they would have only a small following and that the church, the building itself, would burn down twice. It did burn down in the 1930s, not long after that. Even now, some of the elders are waiting to see the second burning of this church.

Ralph Mike himself had a horrible death because he used his power on another doctor. He was in McArthur during a Fourth of July celebration, and this woman (doctor) was in Alturas. He sent his power--his poison--out against this women. She happened to notice it there lying on the ground and she took it and built a fire and cast his poison into the fire and sent it back on Ralph Mike. When it came back, the old people said that his head burst into flames and he died a horrible death. That was how he died because he misused that power.

It was dangerous to misuse power, whether you had good power or bad power. At some of these places, like the Pit River Falls, you could obtain both types of power. There are some places where you could obtain only good power and some places where you could obtain only bad power, but there are some places where you could obtain both if that's how you were inside, if that's what you really wanted.

A public demonstration had to take place before you could doctor. You had to go out and do all these things, as many of these other people spoke of, going to the mountain, going to the springs, having dreams, having been taught by elders. But before you could doctor you had to demonstrate your powers. And so they would have a public display and gather all the people around and the new doctor would begin to show his power, (show) what he was able to do.

Sometimes an older doctor or several older doctors would be there to challenge him. They would hurl poisons and objects-- obsidian needles--through the air at great distances. Sometimes they would kill one another. Then they would demonstrate how great their power was by bringing the other doctor back to life. My stepfather told me a story of some doctors he saw one time who cut off each other's heads and danced around and then placed their heads back on and were able to live. That sounds pretty dramatic. It really does. It's a lot of power. It sounds unbelievable.

So these people had to have that type of training. They had to demonstrate that. If they didn't demonstrate that and began to doctor kind of undercover, working on people, then they weren't accepted and they were always under suspicion of being up to no good. So they had to do this. If you were to become a doctor and you had done all the things that were required, then you had to publicly display it.

Power objects themselves are a source of doctor power without which a doctor would not be allowed to practice. Until they acquired at least one or two of these objects, they weren't allowed to practice. The easier objects to obtain were flicker feather headbands and the making of an eagle feather cape. They were easier to obtain.

The giant moth cocoon was harder to obtain. It symbolizes the world. It symbolizes the Heart of the World, *tikado hadachi*. I think I'll sing a song now.

(Claps once)
Weianho, weianho, weianho, weianho, weianho, weianho,
weianho, weianho, weianho, weianho, weianho, weianho,
Hewisi tikada hadachi anukiwi, weianho,
weianho, weianho, weianho.
(Claps four times)

That was a hard thing to obtain, that moth. You had to look very hard. It lived high up. This world we're living on is that giant moth. This is the cocoon that we stand on. The old people say that at the end of time, when the destruction of the world comes about, then from out of the cocoon will come this beautiful moth, and beauty will be all around and no more will there be evil.

So this was a very powerful object. It symbolizes the destruction of evil. So they would gather these things and inside they would place quartz crystals taken from an ant hill. These were very powerful things.

Another thing that would be very hard to obtain was a *baqua*. It would be like a bundle of feathers, eagle feathers, and would have a root that would reach to the center of the earth, to the heart of the world. This root would be just like a major artery. When you came upon this thing, you would have to pull it out of the ground. Sometimes it would scream, and sometimes it would groan. It would be better if it groaned, because the screaming could sometimes frighten the person off and cause them to leave it there, and then it would become even harder to obtain.

It didn't always appear in the same place. It could appear anywhere at any time. When it was pulled out, and the doctor or the apprentice would take it back, he had to keep it in a hollow tree and bind it up and feed it so that it didn't go away. He would feed it with his own blood, an offering of blood. It didn't have to be made all the time, but the first time it had to be fed with your own blood if you were a doctor.

It would continue to bleed where the root was broken off. It would continue to bleed. So when they had public demonstrations, if this was one of their power objects, they would show it, and the people could see the blood dripping from this power object. Once they had these power objects, then they were officially recognized as being full fledged doctors and they were able to practice.

As I spoke of earlier, crystals had to be obtained from (water)falls. And you couldn't get these from every fall or every spring. Burney Falls, that's in northern California just outside Burney, and Pit River Falls, just out of Fall River, they were the two major sources of these. You would go there, especially if you were into doctor training, and dive from the top of these falls. I think Burney Falls is somewhere around 126 feet. Pit River Falls is not too high, maybe 20-25 feet, but it's very treacherous, a very treacherous place.

In 1982, two young men attempted to dive into Burney Falls. Non-Indian. One young man dove off down into the falls and that was the end of him. It killed him. It took a couple of days before they could find his body. When the other young man saw what happened, he just sat down and couldn't do any more. His life was ruined after that. He ended up in prison after doing a lot of things he knew he shouldn't have done. He always realized and he came back to that point where they were attempting to dive off the falls, where he watched his friend die.

These are dangerous places. If you weren't the kind of person to be chosen or if you weren't right in your mind, then that spirit had the right to kill you. And it would kill you.

Once they were able to dive off into the pool, the spirit would appear as some sort of animal, maybe a mermaid or something. It would take them down to a tunnel in the rocks behind the falls, and once they were in there, they would be shown all the different types of power and they would be given permission to take a quartz crystal--the old people called it a diamond--take that diamond and pull it loose from the rocks. It had to come away easily and quickly. If you had to hammer at it, then your life as a doctor would be very hard. You would have a hard time controlling your powers. You always had to be on guard. But if it came away easily you would have a good way to go, a good path of being a doctor.

Shortcutting is totally out of the question. There is no shortcut to doctoring. You can't go down to a local seminar and get a certificate over the weekend. But this is something that is going on, this is a real thing that's going on. Some people think you can read Michael Harner's book and become a doctor. Or you can go down to a local seminar that's being held by a native doctor and maybe you'll learn a few things there and maybe go out and begin practice doctoring. That can't be done. Or maybe you can go downtown and buy a crystal. Go out over here and buy some eagle feathers and put yourself together a bundle. That's not real. Indian people usually view that as taking the road of witchcraft. That's how it's viewed, at least by Ajumawi people, that's the witchcraft way.

You can buy your power. The old people used to speak of that. People who wanted to become doctors but weren't chosen. They could go out and buy songs and buy power, but it wasn't always effective, because maybe they didn't have control over the spirit that went with that spot. So that's what would happen, it would begin to backfire on them.

People who misused power would begin to suffer, not directly, but they would see the ones they loved around them suffer from grave illnesses or violent death. They watched this. If they were cold-hearted and greedy in their ways, then they would allow that. My stepfather (Griffith Mike) used to tell me this. There were some that would do that and there were some who could control that.

Maybe they had enemies in other tribes and they would send that power over there, so it wouldn't get their loved ones. But sometimes that power would come back and be angry with them, so they would make an image that looked like them and hide themselves. They would cover the image with blood so that the spirits would go in there because they could smell the blood. That power and these spirits that were being misused became very bloodthirsty and began to kill off people in their families, kill off people in the tribe, and if there was no more that you could feed it, then it would kill you, and you would die a very horrible death, maybe something worse than your head bursting into flame. It is a very serious thing to be a doctor.

As I was speaking of earlier, there were doctor wars and the wars [with the] Christians. This dealt a very severe blow to doctoring among the Pit River people. So there were a few other doctors, maybe from other tribes, and there were a few old doctors left among the Pit River people, but most of the younger people were discouraged from becoming doctors. That wasn't a good way to go. Maybe they would tell you about these things and teach you a thing or . . ., but you weren't allowed to become one. It was discouraged because of the doctor wars when doctors were killing other people. The last Pit River doctor died in about 1984. That was Elsie Thompson. There are several other young people who have learned doctoring ways from Flora Jones and some of the other doctors from other tribes, but right now there are no Pit River doctors.

So we come back again to the old story: at the beginning there were no doctors and at the end there are no doctors, at least for our area there are no doctors. There are people who have learned a certain amount of the doctor way, but there is no one who has gone to the mountain, there is no one who has dived off the falls.

There are some that have dived into the springs, but that could be done for personal power. There are two different types of power. Anyone could have personal power. Not everyone could have *damaagome*. You could have the *dinahowi* type of power by going to the mountain. It's similar, but it's a different thing. Now we have the New Age people coming in with, as I mentioned, crystals. Some have very elaborate drums, ceremonial drums, they carry in badger and bear hide cases. Coming about with eagle feathers attempting to doctor. Whether they ask or not, it really gets out of hand. I have a lot of people coming to me, personally, handing me crystals, which I don't believe I can have unless I can get those things in the way I was taught to get them, to go down and dive off the falls.

So they bring me these crystals, which some of them buy in town. Some of them go to certain caves (to get them). I had some people who said they went to a cave in Kentucky and broke off huge, enormous crystals, something I couldn't even lift, and want to give these things to me. Sometimes I take these things and put them in the river, because I can't have anything to do with these things.

The old people tell me that these crystals were made from the semen of evil spirits who misused their power, the Creator's power, so their semen was turned into crystals as a testament against them for the misuse of their powers. And if you are not in your right mind or if you don't have the right attitude, the crystals will begin to affect you that way. So an ordinary person can go out of control and go out and begin to engage in acts of lewd conduct, sleeping with anyone. The old people say you shouldn't do that. And we see today the results of that type of life.

I can't have those things around that people keep bringing me. I have to get rid of them. I have to put them in the river or burn them. I'm not the only one. Some of the elders have been approached by these people who want us to teach them our ways. We'd like to do that because we realize that is the prophecy also.

The elders would say, at the end of time the children of white people will be coming to us and they would like to learn our ways. But we always have to keep in mind there is a false rainbow shining, and there is the real rainbow. We try to keep that in mind and stay away from the false rainbow, which shines in the darkness around the moon, but to live in the rainbow that shines in the day when everyone is awake, where everyone can see.

On Mount Shasta a couple of years ago, there was a large gathering of people, and one of the springs that Flora Jones uses was clogged with these large crystals. She was pretty angry. She didn't say anything, but Theodore Martinez, a cousin of mine who works with her, was really upset, and he let those people know. He took those crystals out and threw them down the hill. They became upset with him, and told him to take his hatred and get out of there, that he had no business being there. That really goes against the ways that we believe.

We'd like to teach people how to live with the animals, how to speak with the animals, how to be one with the animals, how to take of the earth, how to take care of these springs. We want to do that because we believe that is a responsibility. We can't avoid it. But it becomes really hard when we see these activities going on. Prayer springs are very important to our people. When a woman or man is in mourning, they should go to that place and wash their face, wash their tears away. And then to go there and find some type of ceremonial staff, prayer stones made by non-Indian people, it's like someone's trying to poison us, like we're threatened with death, because we know that this is a very powerful thing.

Doctors had their own springs, their own springs where they would go. None of the ordinary people would go to these places. One of the elders of the tribe who had studied to be a doctor and later on went down the Christian road, his wife went to a doctors' spring. She got into the spring and she began to swim around because it was hot. She had been told by the elders to stay away from there, but she thought that because she had the power of God and Jesus that nothing could harm her. She broke out into a horrible rash, which she had for a couple of months. It almost killed her.

Finally, this old doctor came along and told her what she had done and where she had gone. She said, "Yes, that's what I did. I don't believe in those doctor ways, but I'm so desperate now I'll try anything." So he cured her, he took away this horrible rash that was all over her body and causing such great suffering. So that goes to show, you know, that whether you believe it or not, it's there. Many people don't believe in these things, even among the Indian people. They say, "That's the old way, we've got a new way now, we're following the bright light, the way of the white man." But, still, it's there. I think that's about all I have to say on that. I'll close, but I can't sing the song once and leave it, because even now, the power's here, so I'll sing the song again:

(Claps once)
Weianho, weianho, weianho, weianho, weianho, weianho, weianho, weianho, weianho, weianho, weianho, weianho, Hewisi tikada hadachi anukiwi, weianho, weianho, weianho, weianho.
(Claps four times)

REFERENCES CITED

Aberle, David
1962   A Note on Relative Deprivation Theory as Applied to Millenarian and Other Cult Movements. *In* Millenial Dreams in Action. Sylvia L. Thrupp, ed. Comparative Studies in Society and History, Supplement II. The Hague: Mouton & Co. pp. 209-214.

Aginsky, Burt W.
1943   Culture Element Distributions XXIV: Central Sierra. University of California Archaeological Reports 8(4):393-468. Berkeley.

Alcorn, Wayne
1932   Dance of the Indians. Unpublished manuscript, Yosemite Field School of Natural History file. National Park Service Research Library, Yosemite National Park.

Anderson, Robert H.
1975   Fetal Phosphenes and Newborn Pattern Preference. Developmental Psychobiology 8(6):571-572.

Anonymous
1903   Indians Condemn a Medicine Woman. San Francisco Chronicle, September 20.

1965   History of Washington Township. Research Committee of the Country Club of Washington Township. 3rd Edition (first published in 1904).

1976   A Witch Doctor Visits the Rancheria. The Mother Lode
        Weekly; February 4. 3(5):1-2. Sonora, California.

1989   Unpublished paper 1989. Humboldt State University,
        Arcata California.

Anonymous (Hupa-Karuk Spiritual Doctor)
n.d.   Film. Nin-a-saan, Set Here for You. Six Rivers National
        Forest. Eureka Office, Eureka, CA 95501.

Anonymous (young woman)
1989   Unpublished paper 1989. Humboldt State University,
        Arcata California.

Bahn, Paul G.
1988   *Comment on* The Signs of All Times: Entoptic Phenomena
        in Upper Paleolithic Art. J. D. Lewis-Williams and T. A.
        Dowson. Current Anthropology 29(2):217-218.

Ballereau, Dominique, Hans Niemeyer F., and Eduardo Pizarro W.
1986   Les Gravures Rupestres de la Quebeada Las Pintadas de
        Marquesa (Norte Chico, Chili). "Cahier" No. 8. Paris:
        Editions Recherche sur les Civilisations.

Barber, Bernard
1941   Acculturation and Messianic Movements.   American
        Sociological Review 6:663-669.

Barnett, Homer G.
1957   Indian Shakers: A Messianic Cult of the Pacific Northwest.
        Carbondale: Southern Illinois University Press.

Barrett. S. A. and E. W. Gifford
1933   Miwok Material Culture.   Bulletin of the Milwaukee
        Public Museum 2(4):117-377. Milwaukee, Wisconsin.

Baumhoff, M. A., R. F. Heizer, and A. B. Elsasser
1958   The Lagomarsino Petroglyph Group (Site 26-St-1) Near
        Virginia City, Nevada.   Reports of the University of
        California (Berkeley) Archaeological Survey 43, Part II.

Bean, Lowell John
1972   Mukat's People: The Cahuilla Indians of Southern Califor-
        nia. Berkeley and Los Angeles: University of California
        Press.

1974a Social Organization in Native California. *In* ʔAntap: California Indian Political and Economic Organization. Lowell John Bean and Thomas King, eds. Ramona: Ballena Press.

1974b Warfare in Native California. Unpublished manuscript.

1975 Power and its Application in Native California. Journal of California Anthropology 2(1):25-33. See also pp. 21-32, this volume.

1976 California Indian Shamanism and Folk Curing. *In* American Folk Medicine: A Symposium. Wayland Hand, ed. Berkeley and Los Angeles: University of California Press.

Bean, John Lowell, and Thomas C. Blackburn, eds.
1976 Native Californians: A Theoretical Retrospective. Socorro, NM: Ballena Press.

Bean, Lowell John and Thomas F. King, eds.
1974 ʔAntap: California Indian Political and Economic Organization. Ballena Press Anthropological Papers 2. Ramona, CA: Ballena Press.

Bean, Lowell John and Harry Lawton
1973 Some Explanations for the Rise of Cultural Complexity in Native California with Comments on Proto-Agriculture and Agriculture. *In* Patterns of Indian Burning in California: Ecology and Ethno-history. Henry Lewis. Ramona: Ballena Press.

Bean, Lowell John, and Katherine Siva Saubel
1972 Temalpakh: Cahuilla Indian Knowledge and Usage of Plants. Banning CA: Malki Museum Press.

Bean, Lowell John, and Sylvia Brakke Vane
1978a Cults and their Transformations. *In* Handbook of North American Indians, vol. 8 (California). Robert F. Heizer, ed. Washington, D. C.: Smithsonian Institution. pp. 662-672. See also pp. 33-52, this volume.

1978b Shamanism: An Introduction. *In* Art of the Huichol Indians. Kathleen Berrin, ed. New York: Harry N. Abrams, Inc. pp. 118-128. See also pp. 7-20, this volume.

Bean, Lowell John and Corinne Wood
1969 The Crisis in Indian Health. Indian Historian, 2, 3 (Fall),
      29-33.

Bednarik, Robert G.
1986 Parietal Finger Markings in Europe and Australia. Rock
      Art Research 3(1):30-61.

Bell, Horace
1881 Reminiscences of a Ranger.

Berman, Howard
1982 Freeland's Central Sierra Miwok Myths. Survey of
      California and Other Indian Languages Report 3.

1982 A Supplement to Robins' Yurok-English Lexicon. Inter-
      national Journal of American Linguistics 48(2):197-222.

Bibby, Brian
1985 Personal communication.

Bibby, Brian and Glen Villa
n.d. Maidu and Miwuk Biographies.

Blackburn, Thomas C.
1974a Ceremonial Integration and Social Interaction in Aborigi-
      nal California. In ʔAntap: California Indian Political and
      Economic Organization. Lowell J. Bean and Thomas F.
      King, eds. Anthropological Papers 2. Ramona, CA:
      Ballena Press. pp. 93-110.

1974b Chumash Oral Traditions: A Cultural Analysis. Ph.D.
      Dissertation, University of California, Los Angeles.

1975 December's Child: A Book of Chumash Oral Narratives.
      Berkeley: University of California Press.

1977 Biopsychological Aspects of Chumash Rock Art. Journal
      of California Anthropology 4(1):88-94.

Blaver, Alma
1982 Personal communication.

Blodgett, Jean
1978 The Coming and Going of the Shaman: Eskimo Shaman-
      ism and Art. Winnipeg: The Winnipeg Art Gallery.

Boas, Franz
1966   Kwakiutl Ethnography. Edited and abridged by Helen Codere. Chicago: University of Chicago Press.

Boscana, Fr. Geronimo
1933   Chinigchinich. *In* Chinigchinich, a Revised and Annotated Version of Alfred Robinson's Translation of Father Geronimo Boscana's Historical Account of the Beliefs, Usages, Customs and Extravagancies of the Indians of the Mission of San Juan Capistrano called the Acagchemen Tribe. Edited by P. T. Hanna. Santa Ana: Fine Arts Press.

Boysen, Mrs. J. T. (Mabel)
1934   [Interview with Mrs. Boysen conducted by Ralph Anderson, December 5, 1934.] Unpublished manuscript, Research Library, National Park Service, Yosemite National Park.

Broadbent, Sylvia M.
1964   The Southern Sierra Miwok Language. University of California Publications in Linguistics 38. Berkeley.

1972   The Rumsen of Monterey: An Ethnography from Historical Sources. University of California Archaeological Research Facility Contributions 14. Berkeley. pp. 45-93.

Brodzky, Anne Trueblood, Rose Daneswich, and Nick Johnson, eds.
1977   Stones, Bones, and Skin: Ritual and Shamanic Art. Toronto: The Society for Art Publications. (Reprint of Artscanada Magazine 30(4-5), December 1973/January 1974.)

Buckley, Thomas
1980   Monsters and the Quest for Balance in Native Northwestern California. *In* Manlike Monsters on Trial: Early Records and Modern Evidence. Marjorie Halpin and Michael M. Ames, eds. Vancouver: University of British Columbia Press. pp. 152-71.

1984   Yurok Speech Registers and Ontology. Language in Society 13:467-488. Cambridge University Press.

1986   Lexical Transcription and Archaeological Interpretation: A Rock Feature Complex from Northwestern California. American Antiquity 51(3):617-18.

1987 Dialogue and Shared Authority: Informants as Critics. Central Issues in Anthropology 7(1):13-24.

1988a Menstruation and the Power of Yurok Women. *In* Blood Magic: The Anthropology of Menstruation. Thomas Buckley and Alma Gottlieb, eds. Berkeley and Los Angeles: University of California Press. pp. 187-209.

1988b World Renewal. Parabola 13(2):82-91.

1989a The Articulation of Gender Symmetry in Yuchi Culture. Semiotica 74(3-4):289-311.

1989b Kroeber's Theory of Culture Areas and the Ethnology of Northwestern California. Anthropological Quarterly 62(1):15-26.

Buckskin, Floyd
1990 Pit River Reaction to New Age Shamanism. Presentation at the California Indian Shamanism; A Scholar's Conference in Celebration of Continuity and Change. May 12, 1990, California State University, Hayward. See also pp. 237-248, this volume.

Bunnell, Lafayette H.
1911 The Discovery of the Yosemite and the Indian War of 1851 which led to that Event. 4th ed. Los Angeles: G. W. Gerlicher.

Callahan, Robert O.
1976 [Notes] in Jaime de Angulo, Shabegok. Berkeley: Turtle Island.

Carranco, Lynwood and Estle Beard
1981 Genocide and Vendetta: The Round Valley Wars of Northern California. Norman: University of Oklahoma Press.

Castaneda, Carlos
1969 The Teachings of Don Juan: A Yaqui Way of Knowledge. New York: Ballantine Books.

Chadwick, N. Kershaw
1942 Poetry and Prophecy. Cambridge University Press.

Chafe, Wallace L.
1973   Language and Memory. Language 49:261-81.

Chagnon, Napoleon A.
1970   Ecological and Adaptive Aspects of California Shell
       Money. Annual Reports of the University of California
       Archaeological Survey 12:1-25. Los Angeles.

Chartkoff, Joseph and Kerry Chartkoff
1983   Excavations at the Patrick Site (4-Butte-1). *In* The
       Archaeology of Two Northern California Sites. Institute
       of Archaeology Monograph 22:1-52. University of Califor-
       nia, Los Angeles.

Chisum, Gary Lee
1967   Ethnography of the Sierra Miwok: Preliminary Notes. The
       Quarterly of the Tuolumne County Historical Society
       6(4):201-206. Sonora.

Clark, Galen
1904   Indians of the Yosemite Valley and Vicinity: Their Histo-
       ry, Customs and Traditions. Yosemite Valley, California:
       Galen Clark.

Clifford, James, and George F. Marcus, eds.
1986   Writing Culture: The Poetics and Politics of Ethnography.
       Berkeley and Los Angeles: University of California Press.

Cole, J. E.
1935   [Unpublished File of information regarding Yosemite
       Indians].   Research Library, National Park Service,
       Yosemite National Park.

Cook, Sherburne F.
1957   The Aboriginal Population of Alameda and Contra Costa
       Counties, California. University of California Anthropo-
       logical Records 16(4):131-156. Berkeley.

Costo, Rupert and Jeannette Henry Costo, eds.
1987   The Missions of California: A Legacy of Genocide. San
       Francisco: The Indian Historian Press.

Cox, Mary
1972- Personal communication.
1976

Crooks, Eleanor
1980   Personal communication.

Cummins, Marjorie Whiting
1942   [A Visit with Chief Lemme, Yosemite, July 17, 1942].
       Unpublished manuscript, Research Library, National Park
       Service, Yosemite National Park.

Curtis, Edward S.
1924   The North American Indian, Vol. 13. New York: Johnson
       Reprint Corporation (1976).

Davidson, Judith
1985   Jivaro: Expressions of Cultural Survival. San Diego: San
       Diego Museum of Man.

Demetracopoulou [Lee], Dorothy and Cora Du Bois
1932   A Study of Wintu Mythology.   Journal of American
       Folklore 24:375-500.

Dixon, Roland B.
1903   Sierra Miwok Field Notes; Moquelumnan (Sonora).
       Unpublished Field Notebook; Bancroft Library, Universi-
       ty of California, Berkeley.

Drucker, Philip
1937   The Tolowa and their Southwest Oregon Kin. University
       of California Publications in American Archaeology and
       Ethnology 36(4):221-300.

1955   Indians of the Northwest Coast. New York: McGraw-
       Hill.

Du Bois, Constance (Goddard)
1908   The Religion of the Luiseño Indians of Southern Califor-
       nia. University of California Publications in American
       Archaeology and Ethnology 8(3):69-186. Berkeley and Los
       Angeles.

Du Bois, Cora
1935   Wintu Ethnography. University of California Publications
       in American Archaeology and Ethnology 36:1.

1939   The 1870 Ghost Dance. University of California Anthro-
       pological Records 3(1):1-152. Berkeley.

1940   Wintu Ethnography. University of California Publications in American Archaeology and Ethnology 36(1):1-148.

Eliade, Mircea
1964   Shamanism: Archaic Techniques of Ecstasy. Willard R. Trask, trans. Bollingen Series No. 76. Princeton, N. J.: Princeton University Press.

Elmendorf, William W.
1960   The Structure of Twana Culture, with Comparative Notes on the Structure of Yurok Culture by A. L. Kroeber. Monographic Supplement 2, Washington State University Research Studies 28(3).

Elmendorf, William W.
1981   Last Speakers and Language Change: Two California Cases. Anthropological Linguistics 23:36-49.

Emeneau, Murray B.
1964   Oral Poets of South India--The Todas. *In* Language in Culture and Society. Dell Hymes, ed. New York: Harper & Row. pp. 330-343.

Erikson, Erik H.
1943   Observations on the Yurok: Childhood and World Image. University of California Publications in American Archaeology and Ethnology 35(10):257-302. Berkeley.

Ewing, Donald
1985   Personal communication.

Forbes, Jack D.
1969   Native Americans of California and Nevada. Healdsburg, California: Naturegraph Publishers.

Fuller, Richard
1971   Personal communication.

Furst, Peter
1965   West Mexican Tomb Sculpture as Evidence for Shamanism in Prehispanic Mesoamerica. Antropologica 15:29-80.

1969   Myth in Art: A Huichol Depicts His Reality. Los Angeles County Museum of Natural History Quarterly 7(3):16-25. (Reprint, UCLA Latin American Center, Reprint No. 11.)

1977   The Roots and Continuities of Shamanism. *In* Stones, Bones, and Skin: Ritual and Shamanic Art. Anne Trueblood Brodzky, et al., eds. Toronto: The Society for Art Publications. pp. 1-28.

Galbraith, John S.
1982   Appeals to the Supernatural: African and New Zealand Comparisons with the Ghost Dance. Pacific Historical Review 51(2):115-133.

Galvan, Philip Michael
1968   The Ohlone Story. The Indian Historian 1(2):9-13. San Francisco: American Indian Historical Society.

Gardner, Ruth A. and Connie S. Madsen
1976   Miwok Use of the Stanislaus River. *In* An Ethnographic Study of the New Melones Lake Project, Part II: Native Americans in and Around the Project Area. Compiled by Dorothea J Theodoratus, Ph.D., New Melones Ethnographic Research Project Calaveras and Tuolumne Counties, California. pp. 485-500.

Gayton, Anna H.
1930   The Ghost Dance of 1870 in South-Central California. University of California Publications in American Archaeology and Ethnology 28(3):57-82. Berkeley.

Geertz, Clifford
1976   "From the Native Point of View": On the Nature of Anthropological Understanding. *In* Meaning in Anthropology. Keith H. Basso and Henry A. Selby, eds. Albuquerque: University of New Mexico Press. pp. 221-238.

Gifford, Edward W.
n.d.a   Central Miwok Shamans. Unpublished manuscript, Bancroft Library, University of California, Berkeley.

n.d.b   Southern Miwok Ceremonies. Unpublished manuscript, Bancroft Library, University of California, Berkeley.

1926   Miwok Cults. University of California Publications in American Archaeology and Ethnology 18(3):391-408. Berkeley: University of California Press.

1927   Southern Maidu Religious Ceremonies. American Anthropologist 29(3):214-257.

1955   Central Miwok Ceremonies. University of California Anthropological Records 14(4):261-318. Berkeley.

1958   Karok Confessions. Miscellanea Paul Rivet Octogenario Dictata, Vol I. Mexico City: Universidad National Autonoma de Mexico. pp. 245-55.

Goldschmidt, Walter R.
1951   Ethics and the Structure of Society: An Ethnological Contribution to the Sociology of Knowledge. American Anthropologist 53(4):506-524.

Gould, Richard A.
1966   The Wealth Quest among the Tolowa Indians of Northwestern California. Proceedings of the American Philosophical Society 110(1):67-89. Philadelphia.

Grant, Campbell
1965   The Rock Paintings of the Chumash: A Study of California Indian Culture. Berkeley and Los Angeles: University of California Press.

Grant, Campbell, James W. Baird, and J. Kenneth Pringle
1968   Rock Drawings of the Coso Range, Inyo County, California. Maturango Museum Publication 4. China Lake, California: Maturango Press.

Halpern, A. M.
1955   A Dualism in Pomo Cosmology. Kroeber Anthropological Society Papers, Nos. 9 and 9, pp. 151-9.

Handelman, Don
1972   Aspects of the Moral Compact of a Washo Shaman. Anthropological Quarterly 45(2):84-101.

Harner, Michael, ed.
1973   Hallucinogens and Shamans. London: Oxford University Press.

Harrington, John P.
1932   Tobacco among the Karuk Indians of California. Bulletin of the Bureau of American Ethnology 94.

1934 A New Original Version of Boscana's Historical Account of the San Juan Capistrano Indians of Southern California. Smithsonian Miscellaneous Collections 92(4):1-62. Smithsonian Institution, Washington, D. C.

1942 Culture Element Distributions, XIX: Central California Coast. University of California Anthropological Records 7(1):1-46. Berkeley.

Hedges, Ken
1970 An Analysis of Diegueño Pictographs. Master's Thesis, San Diego State University.

1975 Kumeyaay Rock Paintings in Southern California. *In* American Indian Rock Art: Papers Presented at the 1974 Rock Art Symposium. Shari T. Grove, ed. Farmington, New Mexico: San Juan County Museum Association. pp. 111-125.

1976 Southern California Rock Art as Shamanic Art. *In* American Indian Rock Art, Volume 2: Papers Presented at the Second Annual Rock Art Symposium. Kay Sutherland, ed. El Paso: El Paso Archaeological Society. pp. 126-138.

1982 Phosphenes in the Context of Native American Rock Art. *In* American Indian Rock Art, Volumes 7 and 8. Frank G. Bock, ed. El Toro, California: American Rock Art Research Association. pp. 1-10.

1983 The Shamanic Origins of Rock Art. *In* Ancient Images on Stone. Jo Anne Van Tilburg, ed. Los Angeles: UCLA Institute of Archaeology, Rock Art Archive. pp. 46-61.

1986 The Sunwatcher of La Rumorosa. *In* Rock Art Papers, Volume 4. Ken Hedges, ed. San Diego Museum Papers 21. pp. 17-32.

1987 Patterned Body Anthropomorphs and the Concept of Phosphenes in Rock Art. *In* Rock Art Papers, Volume 5. Ken Hedges, ed. San Diego Museum Papers 23. pp. 17-24.

Heinze, Ruth-Inez, ed.
1989 Proceedings of the Fifth International Conference on the Study of Shamanism and Alternative Modes of Healing. Independent Schools of Asia.

Heizer, Robert F.
1964 The Western Coast of North America. *In* Prehistoric Man in the New World. J. D. Jennings, and E. Norbeck, eds. Chicago: University of Chicago Press. pp. 117-148.

Heizer, Robert F., ed.
1974a They Were Only Diggers: A Collection of Articles from California Newspapers, 1851-1866, on Indian and White Relations. Ballena Press Publications in Archaeology, Ethnology, and History No. 1. Ramona, California: Ballena Press.

1974b The Destruction of California Indians. Santa Barbara: Peregrine Smith, Inc.

Heizer, Robert F. and Alan F. Almquist
1971 The Other Californians. Berkeley: University of California Press.

Heizer, Robert F., and Martin A. Baumhoff
1962 Prehistoric Rock Art of Nevada and Eastern California. Berkeley: University of California Press.

Hern, Della
1985 Personal communication.

Hill, W. W.
1944 The Navaho Indians and the Ghost Dance of 1890. American Anthropologist 46(4):523-527.

Hinton, Leanne
1977 Havasupai Songs: A Linguistic Perspective. University of California, San Diego, Ph.D. dissertation.

Hittman, Michael
1973 The 1870 Ghost Dance at the Walker River Reservation: A Reconstruction. Ethnohistory 20(3):247-278. Tucson.

Hudson, John W.
1901 [Field Notebook for 1901.] Manuscript on file, The Sun House Archive Collection, Ukiah, California.

Hurtado, Albert L.
1988   Indian Survival on the California Frontier. New Haven:
       Yale University Press.

Hutchings, J. M.
1888   In the Heart of the Sierras: The Yo Semite Valley. Yosem-
       ite Valley and Oakland: The Old Cabin and Pacific Press
       Publishing House.

Johnson, Jay
1974   Personal communication.

Johnston, Bernice E.
1962   California's Gabrielino Indians. (Frederick Webb Hodge
       Anniversary Publication Fund 8). Los Angeles: Southwest
       Museum.

Katz, R.
1982   Boiling Energy: Community Healing Among the Kalahari
       !Kung. Cambridge: Harvard University Press.

Keeling, Richard
1980   The Secularization of the Modern Brush Dance: Cultural
       Devastation on Northwestern California. American Indian
       Culture and Research Journal 4(4):55-83.

Kellogg, Rhonda, M. Knoll, and J. Kugler
1965   Form-Similarity Between Phosphenes of Adults and Pre-
       School Children's Scribblings. Nature 208(5015):1129-
       1130.

Kelly, John
1968   Personal communication.

King, Chester D.
1971   Chumash Inter-village Economic Exchange. The Indian
       Historian 4(1):30-43.

Kirkland, Forreset, and W. W. Newcomb, Jr.
1967   The Rock Art of Texas Indians. Austin: University of
       Texas Press.

Klüver, Heinrich
1966   Mescal and Mechanisms of Hallucinations. Chicago:
       University of Chicago Press.

Knoll, M., J. Kugler, O. Hofer, and S. D. Lawder
1963   Effects of Chemical Stimulation of Electrically-Induced Phosphenes on their Bandwidth, Shape, Number and Intensity. Confina Neurologica 23(3):201-226.

Kroeber, Alfred L.
1907   The Religion of the Indians of California. University of California Publications in American Archaeology and Ethnology 4(6):320-356. Berkeley.

1908   A Mission Record of the California Indians. University of California Publications in American Archaeology and Ethnology 8:1-27. Berkeley.

1925   Handbook of the Indians of California. Bureau of American Ethnology Bulletin 78. Smithsonian Institution, Washington, D. C.

1932   The Patwin and their Neighbors. University of California Publications in American Archaeology and Ethnology 29(4):253-423. Berkeley.

1939   Cultural and Natural Areas of Native North America. University of California Publications in American Archaeology and Ethnology 38:i-xii, 1-242.

1971a Elements of Culture in Native California. *In* The California Indians: A Source Book. Robert F. Heizer and M. A. Whipple, eds. Berkeley and Los Angeles: University of California Press. pp. 3-65.

1971b The History of Native Culture in California. *In* The California Indians: A Source Book. Robert F. Heizer and M. A. Whipple, eds. Berkeley and Los Angeles: University of California Press. pp. 112-128.

1976   Yurok Myths. Berkeley and Los Angeles: University of California Press.

Kroeber, Alfred L., and Edward W. Gifford
1949   World Renewal: A Cult System of Native Northwest California. University of California Anthropological Records 13(1):1-156. Berkeley.

Kunkel, Peter H.
1962 Yokuts and Pomo Political Institutions: A Comparative Study. Unpublished Ph.D. Dissertation in Anthropology, University of California, Los Angeles.

LaPena, Frank
1987 The World is a Gift. San Francisco: Limestone Press.

Latta, Frank F.
1936 California Indian Folklore. Shafter: Shafter Press.

1949 Handbook of the Yokuts Indians. Oildale, California: Bear State Books.

Lee, D. Demetracopoulou
1941 Some Indian Texts dealing with the Supernatural. The Review of Religion 5:403-11.

Lee, Georgia
1979 The San Emigdio Rock Art Site. Journal of California and Great Basin Anthropology 1(2):295-305.

Lessa, William A. and Evon Z. Vogt, eds.
1979 Reader in Comparative Religion: An Anthropological Perspective. New York: Harper & Row, Publishers.

Lévi-Strauss, Claude
1964 The Raw and the Cooked: Introduction to a Science of Mythology, I. John Weightman and Doreen Weightman, trans. New York and Evanston: Harper and Row.

Lewis, Dio
1881 Gypsies, or Why We Went Gypsying in the Sierras. Boston: Eastern Book Co.

Lewis-Williams, J. David
1982 The Economic and Social Context of Southern San Rock Art, with CA comment and reply. Current Anthropology 23(4):429-449.

1985 The San Artistic Achievement. African Arts 18(3):54-59, 100.

1986 Cognitive and Optical Illusions in San Rock Art Research. Current Anthropology 27(2):171-178.

Lewis-Williams, J. David, and T. A. Dowson
1988   The Signs of All Times: Entoptic Phenomena in Upper Paleolithic Art, with CA comment and reply. Current Anthropology 29(2):201-245.

Levy, Richard S.
1978a Eastern Miwok. *In* Handbook of North American Indians, Vol. 8 (California). Robert F. Heizer, ed. Washington, D.C.: Smithsonian Institution. pp. 398-413.

1978b Costanoan. *In* Handbook of North American Indians, vol. 8 (California). Robert F. Heizer, ed. Washington, D. C.: Smithsonian Institution. pp. 485-495.

Linton, Ralph
1943   Nativistic Movements. American Anthropologist 45:230-240.

Lionel, Julia (Powell)
1985   [Letter to Ferdinand Castillo.] National Park Service Research Library, Yosemite National Park.

Loeb, Edwin M.
1932   The Western Kuksu Cult. University of California Publications in American Archaeology and Ethnology 33(1):1-137. Berkeley.

1933   The Eastern Kuksu Cult. University of California Publications in American Archaeology and Ethnology 33(2):139-232. Berkeley.

Lommel, Andreas
1967   Shamanism: The Beginnings of Art. Michael Bullock, trans. New York: McGraw Hill.

Madsen, Connie S.
1976   Spiritual Life, Illness and Life Cycle. *In* An Ethnographic Study of the New Melones Lake Project, Part II: Native Americans in and Around the Project Area. Compiled by Dorothea J Theodoratus, Ph.D., New Melones Ethnographic Research Project Calaveras and Tuolumne Counties, California. pp. 443-484.

Maniery, James Gary and Dwight Dutschke
1989 Northern Miwok at Big Bar: A Glimpse into the Lives of
      Pedro and Lily O'Connor. American Indian Quarterly,
      Fall:481-495.

Meighan, Clement W., and Francis A. Riddell
1972 The Maru Cult of the Pomo Indians: A California Ghost
      Dance Survival. Southwest Museum Papers 23. Los
      Angeles: Southwest Museum.

Merriam, C. Hart
1910 Dawn of the World: Weird Tales of the Mewan Indians of
      California. Cleveland: Arthur H. Clark.

1955 Studies of California Indians. Berkeley and Los Angeles:
      University of California Press.

Miller. Virginia P.
1976 The 1870 Ghost Dance and the Methodists: An Unexpect-
      ed Turn of Events in Round Valley. The Journal of
      California Anthropology 3(2):66-74. Banning, CA: Malki
      Museum, Inc., Morongo Indian Reservation.

Momaday, N. Scott
1969 The Way to Rainy Mountain. University of New Mexico
      Press.

Mooney, James
1896 The Ghost Dance Religion and the Sioux Outbreak of
      1890. *In* 14th Annual Report of the Bureau of American
      Ethnology for the Years 1892-1893. Part 2. Washington.
      pp. 641-1136.

Myerhoff, Barbara
1966 The Doctor as Culture Hero: The Shaman of Rincon.
      Anthropology Quarterly, 39, 2, 60-72.

1974 Peyote Hunt: The Religious Pilgrimage of the Huichol
      Indians. Ithaca, N. Y.: Cornell University Press.

Nabokov, Peter
1981 Land As Symbol. Speech given at Ames, Iowa. (National
      Public Radio Tape)

1986 Unto These Mountains: Toward the Study of Sacred Geography. *In* Voices of the First America: Text and Context in the New World. Gorden Brotherston, ed. Special Issue of New Scholar 10, 1-2, pp. 479-489.

Nash, Philleo
1955 The Place of Religious Revivalism in the Formation of the Intercultural Community on Klamath Reservation. *In* Social Anthropology of North American Tribes, Fred Eggan, ed. Chicago: The University of Chicago Press. pp. 377-442.

Noll, Richard
1985 Mental Imagery Cultivation as a Cultural Phenomenon: The Role of Visions in Shamanism, with CA comment and reply. Current Anthropology 26(4):443-461.

Norton, Jack
1979 Genocide in Northwestern California. San Francisco: The Indian Historian Press.

Ortiz, Bev
1989 Mount Diablo as Myth and Reality: An Indian History Convoluted. American Indian Quarterly 13(4):457-470. Berkeley.

Oster, Gerald
1970 Phosphenes. Scientific American 222(2):82-87.

Palmquist, Peter E.
1985 California Indian Portraits from the North Coast. The Californians 3(6):21-27.

Park, Willard Z.
1938 Shamanism in Western North America: A Study in Cultural Relationships. Northwestern University Studies in the Social Sciences, No. 2.

Parker, Julia
1974 Personal communication.

Pawley, Andrew and Frances Syder
1976 Sentence Formulation in Spontaneous Speech: The One-clause-at-a-time Hypothesis. Ms. Read at 1st Annual Congress of the Linguistic Society of New Zealand.

Pilling, Arnold R.
1978 Yurok. *In* Handbook of North American Indians, Vol. 8. Robert F. Heizer, ed. Washington: The Smithsonian Institution. pp. 137-54.

Pitkin, Harvey
1984 Wintu Grammar. University of California Publications in Linguistics, Volume 94.

Powers, Stephen
1877 Tribes of California. Contributions to North American Ethnology 3. Washington: U. S. Geographical and Geological Survey of the Rocky Mountain Region.

Pruitt, Alice C.
1973- Personal communication.
1980

Reichel-Dolmatoff, Gerardo
1978 Beyond the Milky Way: Hallucinatory Imagery of the Tukano Indians. Los Angeles: UCLA Latin American Center.

Richards, Whitman
1971 The Fortification Illusions of Migraines. Scientific American 224(5):88-96.

Ritter, Dale W., and Eric W. Ritter
1977 The Influence of the Religious Formulator in Rock Art of North America. *In* American Indian Rock Art, Volume 3. A. J. Bock, Frank Bock, and John Cawley, eds. El Toro, CA: American Rock Art Research Association. pp. 63-79.

Robins, R. H.
1958 The Yurok Language: Grammar, Texts, Lexicon. University of California Publications in Linguistics 15:i-xiv, 1-300.

Rudkin, Charles, trans. and ed.
1956 Observations on California 1772-1790 by Father Luis Sales O. P. Los Angeles: Dawson's Book Shop.

Rust, Jim
1981 Personal communication

Samarin, William J.
1969 Glossolalia as Learned Behavior. Canadian Journal of Theology 15:60.

1972 Variation and Variables in Religious Glossolalia. Language in Society 1:121-130.

1973 Glossolalia as Regressive Speech. Language and Speech 16:77-89.

Schubnell, Matthias
1985 N. Scott Momaday. University of Oklahoma Press. p. 149.

Schultes, Richard Evans
1972 An Overview of Hallucinogens in the Western Hemisphere. *In* Flesh of the Gods. Furst, ed.

Schultes, Richard Evans, and Albert Hoffman
1979 Plants of the Gods: Origins of Hallucinogenic Use. New York: McGraw-Hill Book Company.

Shafer, Harry J.
1986 Ancient Texans: Rock Art and Lifeways Along the Lower Pecos. Austin: Texas Monthly Press, Inc.

Shepherd, Alice
1989 Wintu Texts. University of California Publications in Linguistics, Volume 117.

Shipek, Florence C.
1977 A Strategy for Change: The Luiseño of Southern California. Dissertation, University of Hawaii; Honolulu.

1982 Kumeyaay Socio-Political Structure. In Journal of California and Great Basin Anthropology 4(2):296-303.

1989 An Example of Intensive Plant Husbandry: the Kumeyaay of Southern California. *In* Foraging and Farming: The Evolution of Plant Exploitation. David R. Harris and Gordon C. Hillman, eds. Unwin and Hyman: London. pp. 159-170.

Siegel, Ronald K.
1977 Hallucinations. Scientific American 237(4):132-140.

Siegel, Ronald K., and Murray E. Jarvik
1975 Drug-Induced Hallucinations in Animals and Man. *In* Hallucinations: Behavior, Experience, and Theory. Ronald K. Siegel and Louis Jolyon West, eds. New York: John Wiley & Sons. pp. 81-161.

Slocum, W. A.
1882 History of Contra Costa County, California. San Francisco: W. A. Slocum & Co., Publishers.

Slotkin, J. S.
1972 The Peyote Way. *In* Reader in Comparative Religion: An Anthropological Perspective. William A. Lessa and Evon Z. Vogt, eds. New York: Harper & Row, Publishers. pp. 519-522.

Sparkman, Philip Stedman
1908 The Culture of the Luiseño Indians. University of California Publications in American Archaeology and Ethnology 8(4):187-234. Berkeley and Los Angeles.

Spier, Leslie
1935 The Prophet Dance of the Northwest and its Derivatives: The Source of the Ghost Dance. General Series in Anthropology, No. 1. Menasha, Wisconsin: George Banta Publishing Company.

Spott, Robert, and Alfred L. Kroeber
1942 Yurok Narratives. University of California Publications in American Archaeology and Ethnology 35(9):143-256. Berkeley.

Stanley, Dorothy A.
1972- Personal communication.
1990

Steinbach, Marion
1963 [Notes from interview of Mrs. Gloria Matson (Mrs. Earl) of Lafayette with her aunt and uncle]. Published ms. in possession of author.

1965 [The story of a true experience Mrs. Phoebe Hogan of Yosemite had with bad and good "Doctors" as told to me in September 1965 at her home in Yosemite Valley.] Unpublished ms. in the possession of the author.

Steward, Julian H.
1961   Alfred Louis Kroeber 1876-1960. American Anthropolo-
       gist 63(5, Part 1):1038-59.

1963   *Review of* Prehistoric Rock Art of Nevada and Eastern
       California. Robert F. Heizer and Martin A. Baumhoff.
       American Anthropologist 65(4):975.

Stewart, Omer C.
1944   Washoe-Northern Paiute Peyotism: A Study in Accultura-
       tion. University of California Publications in American
       Archaeology and Ethnology 40(3).

1972   The Peyote Religion and the Ghost Dance. The Indian
       Historian 5(4):27-30. San Francisco: American Indian
       Historical Society.

Strong, William D.
1929   Aboriginal Society in Southern California. University of
       California Publications in American Archaeology and
       Ethnology 26(1):1-358. Berkeley.

Swezey, S. L.
1975   The Energetics of Subsistence-Assurance Ritual in Native
       California. University of California Archaeological
       Research Facility Contributions 23:1-46. Berkeley.

Tadd, Brown
1984   Personal communication.

Tauhindauli
1979   Sunusa Stopped the Rain. Carmichael, CA: Chalatien
       Press.

Taylor, Mrs. H. J.
1932   The Last Survivor. San Francisco: Johnck & Seeger.

Theodoratus, Dorothea J
1981   Native American Cultural Overview, Shasta-Trinity
       National Forest. Report on file, U. S. Department of
       Agriculture, Forest Service, Shasta-Trinity National
       Forest, Redding, California. Prepared by Theodoratus
       Cultural Research, Fair Oaks, CA.

1984   Ethnographic Inventory for Public Law 95-341, North Central California. Report on file, U. S. Department of Agriculture, Forest Service, Shasta-Trinity National Forest and Mendocino National Forest (Corning and Stonyford Ranger Districts) in Cooperation with U. S. Department of Interior, Bureau of Land Management, Redding Resource Area, Redding, CA. Prepared by Theodoratus Cultural Research, Fair Oaks, CA.

Thompson, Lucy
1916   To the American Indian. Eureka, CA: Cummins Print Shop. (Reissued by Heydey Books, Berkeley, 1991.)

Tofflemier, Gertrude and Katherine Luomala
1936   Dreams and Dream Interpretation of the Diegueño Indians of Southern California. *In* The Psychoanalytic Quarterly 5(2):195-225.

Turner, Frederick Jackson
1963   The Significance of the Frontier in American History. New York: Frederick Ungar Publishing Co.

Tyler, Christopher W.
1978   Some New Entoptic Phenomena. Vision Research 18:1633-1639.

Valory, Dale Keith
1966   The Focus of Indian Shaker Healing. Kroeber Anthropological Society Papers 35:67-111.

1970   Yurok Doctors and Devils: A Study in Identity, Anxiety, and Deviance. Ph.D. dissertation, Department of Anthropology, University of California, Berkeley. Ann Arbor, MI: University Microfilms.

Vastokas, Joan M.
1977   The Shamanic Tree of Life. *In* Stones, Bones and Skin: Ritual and Shamanic Art. Anne Trueblood Brodzky, Rose Daneswich, and Nick Johnson, eds. Toronto: The Society for Art Publications. pp. 93-117.

Vastokas, Joan M., and Romas K. Vastokas
1973   Sacred Art of the Algonkians: A Study of the Peterborough Petroglyphs. Peterborough, Ontario: Mansard Press.

Vogel, Virgil J.
1970 American Indian Medicine. Norman: University of Oklahoma Press.

Walker, Jearl
1981 About Phosphenes: Luminous Patters That Appear When the Eyes are Closed. The Amateur Scientist [column]. Scientific American 244(5):174-184.

Wallace, Anthony F. C.
1956 Revitalization Movements. American Anthropologist 68:264-281.

Waterman, T. T.
1910 The Religious Practices of the Diegueño Indians. University of California Publications in American Archaeology and Ethnology 8(6):271-358. Berkeley and Los Angeles: University of California.

1920 Yurok Geography. University of California Publications in American Archaeology and Ethnology 16(5):174-314.

Weiss, Gerald
1973 Shamanism and Priesthood in Light of the Campa Ayahuasco Ceremony. In Hallucinogens and Shamanism. Harner, ed.

Wellmann, Klaus P.
1978 North American Indian Rock Art and Hallucinogenic Drugs. Journal of the American Medical Association 239:1524-1527.

1979 A Survey of North American Indian Rock Art. Graz, Austria: Akademische Druck-u. Verlagsanstalt.

Wessell, Viola F.
1970 Personal communication.

White, Raymond C.
1957 The Luiseño Theory of Knowledge. American Anthropologist 59:1-19.

1963 Luiseño Social Organization. University of California Publications in American Archaeology and Ethnology 48(2):1-194. Berkeley: University of California Press.

Willoya, William and Vinson Brown
  1988   Warriors of the Rainbow: Strange and Prophetic Visions
          of the Indian Peoples.   Healdsburg, CA: Naturegraph
          Publishers.

Winkelman, Michael
  1986   Trance States: A Theoretical Model and Cross-Cultural
          Analysis. Ethos 14(2):174-203.

OTHER BALLENA TITLES (Prices subject to change)

Bean, Lowell John, ed. SEASONS OF THE KACHINA: PROCEEDINGS OF THE CALIFORNIA STATE UNIVERSITY, HAYWARD CONFERENCES ON THE WESTERN PUEBLOS 1987-1988. 1989. ISBN 0-87919-115-5, clothbound, $32.95; ISBN 0-87919-114-7, $21.95.

Bean, Lowell John, and Thomas C. Blackburn, eds. NATIVE CALIFORNIANS: A THEORETICAL RETROSPECTIVE. 1976. ISBN 0-87919-055-8, $17.95.

Bean, Lowell John, Sylvia Brakke Vane, and Jackson Young. THE CAHUILLA LANDSCAPE: THE SANTA ROSA AND SAN JACINTO MOUNTAINS. 1991. BP-AP No. 37. ISBN 0-87919-120-1, paperbound, $14.95; ISBN 0-87919-121-X, clothbound, $19.95.

Blackburn, Thomas C., and Travis Hudson. TIME'S FLOTSAM: OVERSEAS COLLECTIONS OF CALIFORNIA INDIAN MATERIAL CULTURE. 1990. BP-AP No. 35. ISBN 0-87919-116-3, paperbound, $24.95; ISBN 0-87919-117-1, clothbound, $34.95.

Chamberlain, Von Del. WHEN STARS CAME DOWN TO EARTH: COSMOLOGY OF THE SKIDEE PAWNEE INDIANS OF NORTH AMERICA. 1982. ISBN 0-87919-098-1, $17.95.

Ericson, Jonathon E., R. E. Taylor, and Rainer Berger. PEOPLING OF THE NEW WORLD. 1982. ISBN 0-87919-095-7, $19.95

Great Basin Foundation. WOMAN, POET, SCIENTIST: ESSAYS IN NEW WORLD ANTHROPOLOGY HONORING DR. EMMA LOUISE DAVIS. BP-AP No. 29. 1985. ISBN 0-87919-106-6, $30.00.

Heizer, Robert F., ed. FEDERAL CONCERN ABOUT CONDITIONS OF CALIFORNIA INDIANS, 1853-1913. 1979. ISBN 0-87919-084-1, $9.95.

*Hudson, Travis, and Thomas C. Blackburn. MATERIAL CULTURE OF THE CHUMASH INTERACTION SPHERE. 5 Volumes, 1982 -1987. Paperbound, ISBN 0-87919-100-7, $120.00. Clothbound, ISBN 0-87919-101-5, $190.00. Prices of individual volumes on request.

*Hudson, Travis, and Ernest Underhay. **CRYSTALS IN THE SKY: AN INTELLECTUAL ODYSSEY INVOLVING CHUMASH ASTRONOMY, COSMOLOGY AND ROCK ART.** 1978. ISBN 0-87919-074-4, $18.95.

Jewell, Donald P. **INDIANS OF THE FEATHER RIVER: TALES AND LEGENDS OF THE CONCOW MAIDU OF CALIFORNIA.** 1987. ISBN 0-87919-111-2, $12.95.

Miller, Jay. **SHAMANIC ODYSSEY: THE LUSHOOTSEED SALISH JOURNEY TO THE LAND OF THE DEAD.** 1988. Paperbound, ISBN 0-87919-112-0, $28.95. Clothbound, ISBN 0-87919-113-9, $39.95.

Shipek, Florence Connolly. **DELFINA CUERO: HER AUTOBIOGRAPHY, AN ACCOUNT OF HER LAST YEARS AND HER ETHNOBOTANIC CONTRIBUTIONS.** 1991. Paperbound, ISBN 0-87919-122-8, $27.50. Clothbound, ISBN 0-87919-123-6, $33.00.

Stewart, Irene. **A VOICE IN HER TRIBE: A NAVAJO WOMAN'S OWN STORY.** 1980. ISBN 0-87919-088-4, $8.95.

Stickel, Gary E., ed. **NEW USES OF SYSTEMS THEORY IN ARCHAEOLOGY.** 1982. ISBN 0-87919-096-5, $9.95.

Sutton, Mark Q. **INSECTS AS FOOD: ABORIGINAL ENTOMOPHAGY IN THE GREAT BASIN.** 1988. ISBN 0-87919-114-7, $17.95.

Vane, Sylvia Brakke and Lowell John Bean. **CALIFORNIA INDIANS: PRIMARY RESOURCES, A GUIDE TO MANUSCRIPTS, ARTIFACTS, DOCUMENTS, SERIALS, MUSIC AND ILLUSTRATIONS.** 1990. BP-AP No. 36. ISBN 0-87919-118-X, paperbound, $33.00; ISBN 0-87919-119-8, clothbound, $45.00.

Wilke, Philip J., ed. **BACKGROUND TO PREHISTORY OF THE YUHA DESERT REGION.** BP-AP No. 5. ISBN 0-87919-058-2, $7.95.

*Cooperatively published with the Santa Barbara Museum of Natural History.

Orders to:
Ballena Press, Publishers' Services
P.O. Box 2510, Novato, CA 94948